The Disney Way

REVISED AND FULLY UPDATED

The Disney Way

Harnessing the Management Secrets of Disney in Your Company

Bill Capodagli and Lynn Jackson

Foreword by John Christensen,
coauthor of the best-selling book *FISH!*

McGraw-Hill

New York   Chicago   San Francisco   Lisbon   London
Madrid   Mexico City   Milan   New Delhi
San Juan   Seoul   Singapore
Sydney   Toronto

1 2 3 4 5 6 7 8 9 0   FGR/FGR   0 9 8 7 6

ISBN-13: 978-0-07-147815-1
ISBN-10: 0-07-147815-9

This publication is designed to provide accurate and authoritative information in regard to the subject matter covered. It is sold with the understanding that the publisher is not engaged in rendering legal, accounting, or other professional service. If legal advice or other expert assistance is required, the services of a competent professional person should be sought.
> —*From a declaration of principles jointly adopted by a committee of the American Bar Association and a committee of publishers.*

McGraw-Hill books are available at special quantity discounts to use as premiums and sales promotions, or for use in corporate training programs. For more information, please write to the Director of Special Sales, Professional Publishing, McGraw-Hill, Two Penn Plaza, New York, NY 10121-2298. Or contact your local bookstore.

To those who continue Dreaming, Believing, Daring, and Doing despite continual economic change and a nation at war—we salute you.

Contents

PUTTING IT TOGETHER:
FEATURED ORGANIZATIONS

Foreword

I can still remember the feeling of excitement that came over me every Sunday evening—the great anticipation of getting my grilled cheese sandwich and tomato soup on a TV tray and awaiting the start of my favorite show.

Then, on the screen it would begin. The beautiful castle would appear, Tinker Bell would wave her wand and the "pixie dust" would drop, and the "Wonderful World of Disney" would begin. Wow! All those feelings come back like it was just last night. For me, that was over 40 years ago, but that feeling still excites me every time I have a Disney experience.

What is the *magic*? Part of me wants to know, while the other part of me just wants to keep on experiencing it, like wanting and not wanting to know how a magic trick is performed. Bill and Lynn have cracked open the curtain so we can all have access to some of the insights into the Wonderful World of Disney.

It was the Disney standard of imagination and engagement that inspired me so many years ago, and with that "pixie dust" in my heart I discovered the FISH! Philosophy, a group of daily practices that reflects the ideals Walt Disney shared with the world. Now, Bill and Lynn bring these ideals and practices into practical use, with something for any dreamer to use.

We have all heard of the Disney secrets: customers are called "guests"; theme parks are called the "show"; and behind the scenes is called "backstage." But the real magic that Bill and Lynn share with us is Walt's underlying philosophy of "I dream, I test my dreams against my beliefs, I dare to take risks, and I execute my vision to make those dreams come true: Dream, Believe, Dare, Do."

The Walt Disney Company has seen many changes over the years and is going through change now, but what keeps on guiding this great big Dream are Walt's values and beliefs. Few people have had the chance to see the true magic behind the curtain, but learning about these guiding principles opens the magic for so many of us.

In this book, Bill and Lynn give you practical applications of how these principles Dream, Believe, Dare, Do are lived, not only in Disney's worldwide locations, but also in organizations as wonderful as The Cheesecake Factory, Men's Wearhouse, and the incredible experiences of Four Seasons Hotels & Resorts.

Walt gave the world so many gifts—the gifts of dreaming big, believing in your dreams, daring to take risks, and doing it (executing it)—and you can share in those dreams too.

Make your dreams come true.

John Christensen
Playground Director, coauthor of *FISH!*
Charthouse Learning—Home of the FISH! Philosophy

Preface

Peter Drucker once said, "When you see a successful business, someone once made a courageous decision." Those who have prospered despite a pathway of obstacles have done so with an inner compass that steers their course: deeply held values that have crystallized and led them to achieve tangible results. Walt Disney, the great storyteller and innovator, had such a compass that defined his enviable empire. His four steps were simple:

1. Dream beyond the boundaries of today.
2. Believe in sound values.
3. Dare to make a difference.
4. And then just go out and do it: Dream, Believe, Dare, Do.

For the past 10 years, Capodagli and Jackson have inspired and led thousands of leaders, employees, and conference attendees to adopt these four principles, the success formula that worked for Walt. *The Disney Way: Harnessing the Management Secrets of Disney in Your Company* was anointed by *Fortune* magazine as a "1999 Best Business Book" and "so useful, you may whistle while you work." Translated into eight languages, the magic is working in the lives of countless individuals, teams, and organizations.

The Disney Way is still a popular choice among readers, evidenced by the *Los Angeles Times*: "There is still magic in Disney's words."

For the past five years, Capodagli and Jackson have been unveiling a collection of unique organizational stories of triumph. You will get to know how these seven featured organizations have uniquely applied Walt Disney's Dream, Believe, Dare, Do principles. Some of the players are widely recognizable; others are known only to those to whose lives they have brought meaning. One is a quiet visionary named David Overton, CEO of The Cheesecake Factory. David is the classic embodiment of perfectionism, having launched the now legendary mega-menu, themed restaurants characterized by seemingly endless lines of people anticipating a divine culinary experience. Another is Patrick Charmel, the so-called "community savior" of Griffin Hospital, who transformed this ill-reputed facility rapidly approaching bankruptcy to a cutting-edge profitable provider of healthcare, now the envy of its esteemed southern neighbor, Yale Medical Center. Rounding out the list of the featured organizations are Downtown School of Des Moines, Ernst & Young, Four Seasons Hotels & Resorts, John Robert's Spa (Cleveland area), and Men's Wearhouse.

The revised edition of *The Disney Way* will captivate readers by these real-world stories of Dream, Believe, Dare, Do passion that testify to the importance of holding dear a set of self-evident and unwavering values. These four simple principles have been practiced by great leaders for decades, standing against the proliferation of fads and so-called new economy success principles that quickly fade from view. The industry and community leaders in these inspiring tales are dedicated to the long term, building their futures one step at a time.

At the end of each chapter is a riveting example of how one of the featured organizations has put into action the lessons of the chapter. Adherence to *The Disney Way* principles of Dream, Believe, Dare, Do has sparked these leaders and their teams to achieve great things together. How each of these seven leaders applied Walt's four principles is the subject of Chapter 13.

At the time of the original writing of *The Disney Way*, the Disney organization was the envy of every CEO. Disney had it all: a decade of stock increases beating the S&P average tenfold; growing theme-park attendance; animation blockbusters that ruled the box office, rivaling Walt's earlier classics; and a culture of innovation, mutual respect, and trust.

With the 2000 recession, the horrific acts of 9/11, and stock prices plummeting, suddenly everyone had it in for the Mouse. In 2004, Roy Disney (Walt's nephew) rallied stockholders to oust Eisner: Pixar severed its ties with the company; and Wall Street demanded loftier results. The stage was set for the death of Disney's image as "the happiest place on earth."

In 1984, when Michael Eisner and Frank Wells were respectively named CEO and president, they demonstrated the leadership to launch the Disney organization from status quo to the iconic international organization it arguably remains today. For a multitude of reasons (one being the tragic death of Wells in 1994), by the late 1990s Michael had lost the "pixie dust" that had created one of the most recognizable brands in the world. It was high time for the new chairman, Bob Iger, to reawaken this sleeping princess of a company using Walt's legacy as a compass. Chapter 12, "Re-Creating the Magic," provides our recommendations for restoring the magic relished under Walt.

Nothing was ever really easy for Walt Disney. From the early days of teetering on the edge of bankruptcy after dumping his entire savings into his "dream," to being viewed as small time by Hollywood insiders who refused to view cartoons as candidates for Academy Awards, Walt lived his credo: an unwavering commitment to Dream, Believe, Dare, Do. These four sound principles are essential to reaching desirable outcomes in personal and business endeavors alike. Yet, there is never any real "pixie dust" for making things happen. It's simply about stepping up to the plate and being willing to swing the bat. The great nineteenth-century Swiss writer, Henri-Frederic Amiel, said, "The man who insists upon seeing with perfect clearness before he decides, never decides."

Every business has two choices:

1. Wait to see if competing on price alone will generate a profit, or
2. Exercise the passion required to produce truly "magical moments" that keep guests coming back for more.

Thriving in the new economy will never happen without strong values that are embraced by all employees. With these values as an internal compass, employees will provide their customers with a unique experience that is not easily duplicated by others in the marketplace. Similarly, every individual has two choices:

1. Wait and hope that something or someone will provide the motivation needed to act, or
2. Take control of your own dream and work to see it through.

This book tells the inside story of just how Disney's success was achieved— not by epiphanic flashes of creative insight that produced a Pinocchio or a Dumbo, but by the force of a much considered, carefully wrought process of managing innovation and creativity by the adherence to a firmly held system of beliefs. The succeeding chapters will bring to life how passion for people, product, and service translated into immeasurable success for Walt Disney and other great role models. Their stories come to life through examples of real drive, courage, humanity, and a compelling thirst to make a difference. Their values allow them to make decisions that are best for their people and their businesses—in that order. These leaders possess a charismatic quality that naturally inspires others to challenge themselves. In the same vein, they rely on the power of everyone on their teams to journey together and unlock the future possibilities that they believe are endless.

At the conclusion of each chapter, "Questions to Ask" and "Actions to Take" will provide readers with a roadmap to living the Dream, Believe, Dare, Do principles and sustaining outstanding rewards in doing so. Readers will also be enlightened as to how a diverse array of leaders and teams chose a course to prosperity by exercising Walt's credo, and, in turn, created "magic" for their customers.

The inspirational stories in the revised edition of *The Disney Way* will challenge the original readers to examine their Dream, Believe, Dare, Do results and provide new readers with a framework to soar beyond the limits of traditional management through these four powerful principles. From entry-level recruits to CEOs, from private companies to public agencies, the Disney principles are redefining the nature of business in our age and revolutionizing the art of management.

Acknowledgments

After *The Disney Way* was released in 1998, we met many business leaders from nonentertainment companies who wondered if they could really apply Walt's original success credo to any great end. Their doubts were soon put to rest as countless organizations, from healthcare to hospitality, have since demonstrated to capture the "magic" through a focused and unwavering dedication to implementing Dream, Believe, Dare, Do over the long term. We wish to thank the many companies, associations, and chambers of commerce that have invited us to bring the Dream, Believe, Dare, Do principles to their employees and audiences through "Dream Retreats," seminars, and keynote presentations. We would also like to thank the many clients who helped make the first edition of *The Disney Way* so successful. A special thanks to John Dunn of Dunn Hospitality Group, United States Senator Richard Lugar of Indiana, and Jeff Merhige of Camp Kern YMCA for their input.

We want to thank our wonderful executive editor, Mary Glenn, who provided a perfect opportunity to showcase some of the "best of the best" organizations that have so graciously opened their doors and gave of themselves to make this book possible. We are thrilled to present such Disney-ized business icons as Ernst & Young, Men's Wearhouse, and, once again, Four Seasons Hotels & Resorts. For the past five years, we have studied their business practices at length and tracked their phenomenal results. We wish to thank personally each of the leaders for their time and for providing such great examples from which others can learn: David Overton of The Cheesecake Factory; Jan Drees of Downtown School; Jim Turley of Ernst & Young; Isadore Sharp of the Four Seasons Hotels & Resorts; Patrick Charmel of Griffin Hospital;

John and Stacy DiJulious of John Robert's Spa; and George "I Guarantee It" Zimmer of Men's Wearhouse.

We thank John Christensen, our friend and *FISH!* guru, for his heartfelt and well-penned foreword. We appreciate our years of friendship with John!

After September 11, countless U.S. organizations faced some degree of financial hardship and were either contemplating or instituting cost-cutting measures such as reducing staff hours and positions. Many of the leaders of our seven featured organizations, however, made a different choice: they put their people first. These were among the few who were steadfast in their conviction that their employees were the primary reason for their corporate strength, and these same employees would be the ones to achieve great things for their companies in the future. Thankfully, there are still leaders like these who will not compromise what they believe—that employees should be cherished, no matter what.

A special thanks to Joan Hoffman and Bill R. Capodagli, Bill's son, for their help: to Joan, who worked tirelessly in the editing of the manuscript, and to Bill, who assisted with statistical research and graphics support.

Bill Capodagli

Lynn Jackson

The
Disney
Way

Chapter 1

Walt's Way

*My only hope is that we never lose sight of one thing . . . that it all
started with a mouse.*

Walt Disney, 1954

When a young Midwestern artist was struggling to get his first film-making business off the ground in 1923, he borrowed $500 from an uncle. The uncle insisted on repayment in cash rather than taking an ownership interest in the venture. That young artist, Walter Elias Disney, went on to advance the demanding art of animation to new heights and founded a company based on such sound business principles that it has survived for over three-quarters of a century and has influenced virtually every aspect of American culture.

Hindsight, of course, has a well-deserved reputation for startling clarity, and we don't know if the uncle lived long enough to feel a full measure of regret. But had he opted for stock in The Walt Disney Company instead of a cash repayment, the return on his $500 would have amounted to almost a billion dollars from 1923 to the present.

How did a boy born into rather modest circumstances in turn-of-the-century Chicago accomplish so much? Legend has it that Walt Disney explained his success this way:

I dream, I test my dreams against my beliefs, I dare to take risks, and
I execute my vision to make those dreams come true.

1

Dream, Believe, Dare, Do: These words reverberate across the decades of Disney achievement. Everything Walt did—every choice he made, every strategy he pursued—evolved from these four principles. And as the bedrock upon which his life and work rested, they naturally informed the basic values that dictated how he ran his company. Thus, the ways in which The Walt Disney Company trained and empowered its employees, managed creativity and innovation, and provided service to its customers were all influenced by this four-pillared philosophy.

Why Disney?

The more we learn about this legendary figure and his achievements, both as an artist and as a creative business leader, the more certain it becomes that the Disney story embodies valuable lessons for every company. But most of us were originally drawn to Walt Disney and the company he founded the same way one is drawn to a favorite uncle.

Like nearly everyone else alive today, we, the authors, grew up being almost as familiar with the Disney name as we were with our own. Many childhood hours were spent sitting on the floor before the TV set watching "The Wonderful World of Disney" and being transported to the Magic Kingdom.

Neither one of us has forgotten the thrill of seeing *Peter Pan* for the first time. As a young father introducing my own children to the film, I [Bill] marveled at its ability to rekindle the emotions I had initially felt as a six-year-old. Disneyland, too, had much the same effect the first time I visited some 35 years ago. Not surprisingly, my then three-year-old son didn't want to leave and, I might add, I felt a little bit that way myself.

In this instance, though, I was captivated by much more than the fabulous attractions. Viewing the park through the eyes of an industrial engineer, I was thoroughly intrigued by the processes. How did the Disney people manage all those crowds? How did they train their employees? How did they run their customer service? What was the secret of the success of their complex technology? I came away from that first visit deeply impressed by the organization—and with a lot of questions.

As for me [Lynn], "The Wonderful World of Disney" was one of the best things about being a child. Later, when I became heavily involved in the field of training and development, I realized the true magic of Disney's philosophy. For me, the seed for benchmarking Disney was planted when I took a copy of *Service America* with me on a trip to Florida in the mid-1980s. I knew it would help prepare me to conduct an upcoming seminar for a group of salespeople from all over the country. Reading Albrecht and Zemke's book, I had one of those experiences when a light goes on in your head: Walt Disney insisted that every employee **is** the company in the mind of the customer. From that point on, my goal in training salespeople was to inspire them to begin living that mindset. Then, on my next trip to Walt Disney World, I closely observed the best of the best in action doing just that.

Years later, when we started looking around for companies that could serve as examples in our consulting business, we found ourselves coming back again and again to Disney. A great deal of scrutinizing, analyzing, and researching of various companies led us to conclude that none compared to Disney in every aspect of running an organization. Whereas one company might excel in customer relations or another might work well with its suppliers, Disney's consistency in direction and overall strategy, its unrivaled customer service, its employee training and relatively low turnover, its product creativity, and its spectacular profitability combined, in our view, to make it the perfect business model.

Having studied the Disney phenomenon for several decades, we are convinced that the management techniques we call "Walt's way" are as valid today as they were in 1937, when the classic *Snow White and the Seven Dwarfs,* the very first animated feature film, captured the hearts of moviegoers. Skeptics need only look to the spectacular successes The Walt Disney Company continues to achieve year after year, decade after decade, for affirmation of Walt's way.

And if you're wondering whether the Disney magic has legs, we can answer with a resounding yes! Over the years, we have encouraged clients in many different industries to use Walt's fundamental credo to improve their customer service, productivity, and internal operations, while at the same time creating an atmosphere of fun. The company that Disney founded has, in effect, served as a laboratory for us and, in turn, our clients.

This chapter introduces the 10 concepts at the heart of the Disney legend. Subsequent chapters then take up these principles in detail and show how they are still being lived at the company today and how some of our clients have adapted them to fit their specific circumstances, enabling them to create winning solutions. Their success stories attest to the continuing power of Walt's way.

Benchmarking a Legend

Like many other young men of his time and place, Walt Disney held a succession of jobs punctuated by stints of formal education. His skill as an artist and his interest in cartoons took him to California in 1923, and only four years later he formed Walt Disney Productions. Disney's first big success came the following year, in 1928, when he introduced the character of Mickey Mouse in the synchronized sound cartoon *Steamboat Willie*. The cartoon and the mouse were an instant hit.

By the 1930s, this endearing little scamp had captured the hearts of audiences worldwide. Known as *Michael Maus* in Germany, *Miki Kuchi* in Japan, and *Miguel Ratonocito* in Spain, he even had a car named after him! When Fiat, the Italian automobile company, produced its first small car shortly after World War II, it was christened *Topolino*, Mickey's Italian nickname. Even though Mickey became a senior citizen a few years back, his ageless persona continues to be recognized and loved by young and old on every continent.

Mickey may have led the parade, but Disney was not a one-mouse band by a long shot. No other company in the notoriously chancy entertainment business has ever achieved the stability, phenomenal growth, and multidirectional expansion of Disney.

In spite of its ever-increasing reach, however, The Walt Disney Company has consistently kept to the central course described by its founder at the outset: to provide the finest in family entertainment. Firmly grounded in Walt's innate sense of principle and his Midwestern values, this mission has, over the years, become clearly associated with the Disney brand. Audiences expect it, and they are seldom disappointed.

Whatever form the entertainment might take—a theme park ride, a Broadway musical, an Ice Capades production—it has to be a good show in every regard. When Walt talked about delivering "the good show," he didn't mean simply a glittering spectacle relying on superficial bells and whistles. He meant an entirely original, perfectly executed production with substance—one created to delight a wide audience. He believed that this was what customers wanted and expected from him, and he was fanatical about providing it.

What's more, the concept of a good show encompasses far more than the on-stage action in a single production. Because Disney insisted that customers be treated like guests, great customer service has become a standard feature of the total package The Walt Disney Company offers. And wrapped up in that package is a gift of creativity—in product, service, and process—that makes even jaded adults smile with childlike delight.

Accomplishing such magic obviously requires the contributions and assistance of a talented, dedicated, and loyal staff as well as an army of suppliers and other partners. Extensive training, constant reinforcement of the Disney culture and its values, and recognition of the valuable contributions that employees and partners make combine to keep people turning out one fantastic show after another as they strive to meet the exacting standards Walt established.

It is this consistency of direction, obsession with customer service, commitment to people, and creative excellence that make The Walt Disney Company a standard by which others might be judged and an exemplary enterprise from which others can learn.

A Consummate Dreamer

Walt Disney was so successful as a businessman that people are often startled to learn that he was a lifelong dreamer who started out as a commercial artist. But it was precisely his unfettered imagination, coupled with a bent for experimentation that propelled him to the pinnacle of success. Far from being a hindrance, dreaming was the wellspring of Disney's creativity.

The story is told that, as a schoolboy in art class, Walt was assigned to draw flowers. In what might now be seen as a quintessential touch, and, indeed, the precursor to many of Disney's animated characters, young Walt embellished his work by sketching a face in the center of each flower. His teacher was less than impressed by the boy's deviation from the norm, and, lacking a mirror like the one the wicked queen had in *Snow White,* failed to recognize the creative genius whose dream world would make him one of the most famous artists in history.

Perhaps because he himself was the greatest of dreamers, Walt encouraged both his artisans and his hundreds of other employees to unleash their imaginations too. He knew that a reservoir of creative power often languishes within a company's ranks simply because no one ever bothers to tap it. Rather than hire someone for one specific purpose and forever pigeonhole that person—as is the norm at too many companies—Disney not only welcomed ideas from all of his employees, he actively sought to turn them into reality.

From dreams spring ideas, and from ideas comes innovation, the lifeblood of any company. Walt Disney instinctively knew, however, that an unshakable belief—in one's principles, in one's associates and employees, and in customers—is necessary before ideas can successfully evolve into innovation.

No matter how ingenious an idea was, no matter what kind of financial interests were at stake, Disney demanded that the company adhere to his belief in and commitment to honesty, reliability, loyalty, and respect for people as individuals. Whether he was producing a cartoon or building an amusement park, he refused to palm off a shoddy product on his audience.

When *Pinocchio* was released in February 1940, the *New York Times* hailed it as "the best cartoon ever made." But *Pinocchio* had a difficult birth. The story of the puppet-maker Geppetto and his "son" Pinocchio, the all-but-human puppet he created, was six months into production, and the team of animation artists was almost halfway through its meticulous, time-consuming drawings for the full-length feature when Walt Disney called a halt. Pinocchio was altogether *too* wooden, he said, and the character proposed for Jiminy Cricket made him look too much like, well, a cricket. Never mind that $500,000 had already been spent, Disney was not deterred. Previous efforts were tossed aside, and Disney called Ward Kimball, one of his talented young animators, into his office.

Kimball, who was upset because his labors on *Snow White* had ended up on the cutting-room floor, was planning to use the occasion to resign when Disney summoned him. But the animator never had a chance. He got so excited listening to Disney talk about his dreams for the film and his ideas about Jiminy Cricket that Kimball entirely forgot his own intentions of resigning. Instead, he stayed at the company and went on to create a cricket that was more human than insect, one that embodied the spirit of hope that children of all ages possess but which sometimes needs reinforcing.

The decision to halt the production of *Pinocchio* was made because the movie was failing to live up to one of Walt Disney's principles, his insistence on excellence. At the time, Disney already had won worldwide acclaim. He probably could have let the film go as it was without doing any serious damage to his company or his reputation—and with substantial savings. But Disney recognized the difference between adequate and excellent, and he would not compromise.

That's not to say that Disney was a spendthrift. Quite the contrary: He was always acutely aware of the bottom line; he simply refused to let it dictate every decision he made. "Why should we let a few dollars jeopardize our chances?" Walt once wrote to his brother Roy[1]. Before it was finished, *Pinocchio* cost $3 million, more than any other animated picture up to that point. Although high-priced for its day, this film classic long ago paid for itself in the degree of sophisticated animation, craft, and artwork it achieves.

Disney's strength as an imaginative and principled creative force grew from his willingness to take risks, to experiment, and to invest his resources and his time in new ventures. From the beginning, he searched for innovative ways to give his audiences the best of all possible entertainment fare. He pioneered a new art form in making *Snow White,* and he did it in the face of nearly unanimous ridicule.

"No one will sit through a 90-minute cartoon," people told him. But Disney ignored the naysayers and clung tenaciously to his dream, confident that he could produce a film that would appeal to both adults and children. His willingness to buck accepted wisdom and take a risk paid handsome dividends: *Snow White and the Seven Dwarfs,* which was released in 1937, grossed $8 million, an astonishing amount when you consider that at the time movie tickets cost only pennies. It received a special Academy Award, and some consider it to be one of the greatest films ever made. *Snow White* has been equally popular in reissue, with a box office take that places it in the top 50 all-time highest-grossing films.

In just a dozen years, roughly 1930 to 1942, Walt Disney managed to transform animation from a marginal segment of the entertainment industry to a new art form. He used technical innovations to create a seamless mixture of story, color, and sound. Knowing that great visions require great, but calculated, risks, Disney dared to follow his instincts.

Turning Dreams into Reality

Walt Disney's stellar accomplishments might suggest that he had no difficulty in taking whatever action was needed to bring his dreams to fulfillment. It was not always easy, however, particularly when a lot of skeptics stood in the way. But Disney knew that dreams are sterile things unless the dreamer can do what it takes to make them come true.

When his fertile mind produced an idea, he set about transforming that idea into a concrete product, service, or process. If his methods of executing his vision were sometimes unconventional or broke the accepted rules, so be it. The point was to put on the good show.

For example, when Disneyland was being built in the early 1950s, Walt himself was often on site checking every detail. He spent countless hours with the creative and knowledgeable staff he had hired, putting his personal stamp on everything from landscape design to attractions to music.

But then he did something rather unusual: He asked everyone who was working on Disneyland, from electricians to executives, to test each ride as it was completed. There was nothing new about Disney's reaching for perfection, but the park was on a tight schedule with opening day near at hand, and this idea clearly seemed to be a waste of time and money. Imagine asking your janitors, elevator operators, or other low-level employees for critical input about a new product or service just before you're ready to launch it. Disney's request was a bit farfetched. Or was it?

Although a great deal of what Disney did sounds strange to many managers, this was Walt's way of doing whatever needed to be done to achieve his vision. It was another way of making absolutely sure that everything was the best that it could be and that nothing was missing.

As it turned out, something *was* missing from a swashbuckling Disneyland attraction called The Pirates of the Caribbean. A construction worker, or "cast member" in Disney's language, who happened to hail from Louisiana bayou country, approached the boss after taking the ride and told him, "Something's missing, but I can't figure out what it is."

"Ride it again and keep on riding until you've figured it out," Walt told him.

Finally, after repeated trips through Disney's Caribbean, the cast member realized what was wrong: in tropical climates, the night should be alive with fireflies, but there were none on this attraction. In short order, Walt Disney saw to it that his version of a Caribbean fantasy had fireflies blinking in the dark.

Whether it was fireflies in a theme park attraction, the portrayal of a wise and lovable cricket, the treatment of a Disney "guest," or the removal of a candy wrapper threatening to litter Disneyland's landscape, Walt was a perfectionist down to the last detail. As for those candy wrappers, it isn't only the staff of street cleaners that is charged with litter removal at Disney parks. *Any* employee who spots a bit of trash sweeps it up practically before it flutters to the ground. That is part of the Disney culture that is ingrained in everyone from the beginning. Employees of The Walt Disney Company are trained extensively, and the Disney mindset is constantly reinforced because Walt considered such an approach essential to executing his vision.

He also knew that execution was impossible without a framework within which ideas could be effectively implemented while controlling costs. To that end, the company follows a rigorous process of project management. And to solve problems that arrive in planning and communicating project ideas, it has adapted the storyboarding technique originally used to keep track of the thousands of drawings needed for animation of cartoon features.

Execution of ideas is never left to chance in the Disney universe. It is a well planned process.

Embracing the Disney Spirit

Dream. Believe. Dare. Do. Just as Walt Disney never wavered from his four-pillared philosophy, history is replete with examples of great accomplishments derived from the same commitment. We are reminded, for example, of President John F. Kennedy's challenge to America in 1961 to put the first person on the moon in the ensuing decade. Kennedy had a dream that he firmly believed could become a reality because he saw that it fit perfectly with the can-do spirit that has driven the United States from its outset. To make such a commitment and to embark on this monumental space project was daring, to be sure. But in the doing, America not only saw a man set foot on the moon's surface, it reaped scientific benefits of far-reaching significance for the entire world. (See Figure 1-1.)

So, too, have the principles that Walt Disney espoused led to unimagined glories as the empire he established continues to grow and thrive. Back

Figure 1-1. President John F. Kennedy's challenge to America in 1961 to put the first man on the moon.

in 1923, it's doubtful that even Walt himself could have foreseen that the Disney interests would one day extend to movies, television, Broadway theater, amusement parks, and a vacation club (not to mention the nation's largest laundry facility at Walt Disney World).

Disneyland, which recently marked its fiftieth anniversary in the year 2005, draws ever more guests from the far reaches of the world, and Walt's way has made such an impression on guests at Walt Disney World that over 70 percent of them are repeat visitors!

Disney's financial record is equally impressive. It continually proves to be a solid investment. One thousand dollars invested in Disney stock in 1984, for example, would be worth nearly $25,000 today, representing an 18 percent compound annual growth rate. By comparison, a similar investment in the S&P Index of 500 stocks would be worth a little over $8,000, representing a 12 percent compound annual growth rate.

Such is the power of Walt's way: Dream. Believe. Dare. Do. You too can incorporate those words into your business vocabulary by following the 10 concepts that are at the heart of the Disney methodology:

1. Give every member of your organization a chance to dream, and tap into the creativity those dreams embody.
2. Stand firm on your beliefs and principles.
3. Treat your customers like guests.
4. Support, empower, and reward employees.
5. Build long-term relationships with key suppliers and partners.
6. Dare to take calculated risks in order to bring innovative ideas to fruition.
7. Train extensively and constantly reinforce the company's culture.
8. Align long-term vision with short-term execution.
9. Use the storyboarding technique to solve planning and communication problems.
10. Pay close attention to detail.

For Terry Dischinger of Dischinger Orthodontics in Portland, Oregon, Walt's principles are at the core of his success:

I've used the Dream, Believe, Dare, Do motto in orthodontics for years. We are innovators. I dream what I would like to do, I believe that it can happen, I dare and then I find a way to do it. That has allowed us to develop products and treatments that were not available in the orthodontic industry prior to our dreams. I can't imagine life without dreams to make life better, and the same holds true with our business and our practice.

In the chapters that follow, you will see how the Dream, Believe, Dare, Do principles are being put into action on a daily basis by organizations from healthcare to manufacturing. We will share our insights as to how even Disney stumbled along the way, especially over the last decade of Michael Eisner's regime, and we will present our recommendations for re-creating the magic.

We will follow the Whirlpool Global No-Frost team in a series of sidebars as they experience and test the limits of each of the highlighted guidelines. Last, we will feature seven dynamic organizations that share an inner compass that steers their course: deeply held values that have crystallized and led them to achieve tangible results. The leaders in these inspiring tales are dedicated to the long term, building their futures one step at a time. Most of all, they continue to prosper in both personal and financial measures. These illustrations in practice, combined with a list of questions to ask and actions to take, will help you to make Walt's way your way.

We, however, are not suggesting that managers merely imitate Disney. Obviously, each company's and each individual's situation is different, and the wholesale adoption of another's methods is neither wise nor practical. But more importantly, Disney itself has won continued success by constantly reinventing its products to maintain superb quality. To imitate another and adopt a particular method lock, stock, and barrel implies a contentment with the status quo that flies in the face of everything Walt stood for.

Rather, we believe that gaining an understanding of the hows and whys of The Walt Disney Company's growth and excellence, and embracing the spirit of Walt's four-pillared philosophy will enable businesspeople everywhere to innovate, make changes, and find their own unique pathways to continued success.

A Groundbreaking Project

In the mid-1990s, we became consultants to the Whirlpool Company during a restructuring that the Evansville Technology Center was preparing to undertake. In the process, one of our challenges was to set up teams for a variety of different projects. Among these, there was one team whose mission it was to design a radically new refrigerator for the company's global markets, which stretch from Latin America to Europe and Asia.

(Continued)

This story begins when the company decided that the refrigerator it sold abroad had to have a different design and be smaller than the refrigerator sold in the United States. In other words, this was, technologically, a completely new product, which needed to be built from a different set of blueprints.

The project was a groundbreaker from the beginning. Not only was the refrigerator a departure from previous products, but the approach to the implementation of its engineering, its design, and its marketing was a departure from accepted procedures. And the team we helped to establish to carry through these plans, from the first step to the last, was as much of a groundbreaker as the product itself.

We developed a close relationship with Jerry McColgin, who had been appointed leader of the team. An engineer by training who also had marketing experience, Jerry had led a team before. It had been a disappointing experience, but he had come away from it with a vision of how this global team should be created and how it would function. Later, when we reviewed the progress and the final success of the team, we concluded that here was a group of people, diverse in profession and in nationality, who exemplified everything that Walt Disney meant when he talked about his dreams, his beliefs, and his willingness to take risks in the execution of his vision. It is for this reason that we have decided to tell the story of this team, from its inception to its final celebration of success.

Our Featured Organization: Men's Wearhouse

I GUARANTEE IT!

George Zimmer, founder and CEO of Men's Wearhouse, is a leader in the Walt Disney mold of dreaming, daring, and following gut instincts. Having crafted one of the largest men's business attire retail organizations in the United States on a simple slogan, George is the antithesis of a traditional CEO. Seated behind his modest desk cloaked in a dark sweater and sporting an unlit cigar in the corner of his mouth, he seems as relaxed as a party host who is totally prepared for the guests to arrive. He is as charming as he seems delivering his now famous trademark line, "You're going to like the way you look. I guarantee it." He seems an unlikely candidate for the TV commercial spot, and when asked why he chose to be the spokesperson, he replied "I have more credibility than a hired actor."[2] He truly believes that his average-guy persona translates to comfortable shoppers.

In early 1973, young George could be seen driving through the South in an old Buick Electra, selling for his father's coat-manufacturing business. Even then, George was dreaming about setting his own standards and defying his father's "no return policy." He had more than a hunch that customer returns had a direct relationship to building and maintaining customer loyalty.

"Although all four of Walt's principles are important, it begins with the Dream. Because, ultimately, what makes businesses successful is their ability to do something that in effect has not been done before," George told us. After making a number of what he terms serious mistakes over the years, Men's Wearhouse basically wore down the competition and became number one in its industry.

Dream

Chapter 2

Make Everyone's
Dreams Come True

A dream is a wish your heart makes.

Jiminy Cricket

I t is no easy matter to convey a dream. Dreams are, by nature, deeply
personal experiences. But true to his imaginative genius, Walt Disney
was able to transform his dreams into stories that effectively articulated
his vision to others. More importantly, the stories served to draw others into
his fantasies, thereby marshaling the power of their collective creativity for
the benefit of his dream.

In the early days, when The Walt Disney Company was small, Walt
used to call his five or six animators into his office to discuss an idea for a
new film project. With dramatic effect, he would embark on a story—not a
literal narrative account of his idea, but an ancient myth, perhaps, or some
other related tale that conveyed the feelings and emotions behind his dream
and his hope for the project's success. In short order, the master would
capture the imaginations of his "cast members" ("employees" in the usual
corporate parlance) and in the process stimulate the kind of excitement and
commitment of minds and hearts that he well knew was necessary to turn
Disney-size dreams into reality. For example, he insisted that the castle at
Disneyland be built first—before anything else—so that this visual structure
could help shape the vision and rally everyone around the dream he was trying to create. (See Figure 2-1.)

Figure 2-1. Bill Capodagli at the castle that helped shape Walt Disney's dream of the Sleeping Beauty Castle in Disneyland—"Mad" King Ludwig's Neuschwanstein Castle in Bavaria.

He was such a vivid and persuasive storyteller that his listeners usually found themselves swept up—like Ward Kimball on the *Pinocchio* project—in a passionate endorsement of Walt's vision. Long before concrete plans were in place for the next movie or cartoon, before any budgets were prepared or administrative and engineering problems ironed out, Walt had established a team atmosphere around the forthcoming venture. Thus, he began nearly every new project with eager and enthusiastic participants, an enormous advantage in a process that often involved long hours of work seven days a week.

Storytelling can be a powerful tool for focusing an organization on a particular problem or project and for unleashing employees' creativity by giving them the power to dream. We have helped clients in a variety of industries tailor the technique to fit their particular situations. As you come to understand how this age-old art and other methods are used today by The Walt Disney Company and by many of our clients, you will begin to see how dreams can drive desired change.

Dream Retreats Inspire Creativity

The use of storytelling to rally all project members around a vision is still an important element of the Disney approach, thanks to Walt's formation in the early 1950s of a creative group called "Imagineering." Organized during the building of Disneyland, the group's purpose is to carry on the Disney tradition by dreaming up new creative venues, such as the theme park attractions.

Today, there are approximately 2,000 Imagineers at the five Disney theme parks. They are the inspiration for an event that we call a "Dream Retreat." As we tell our clients when we explain the Dream Retreat methodology, "If you can Dream it, you can Do it." Having employed this technique for many years, we know from experience that even seemingly frivolous, blue-sky notions can lead to realistic, yet innovative, outcomes.

When The Walt Disney Company set out to build an additional water park at Walt Disney World, for example, a small team met in the office of the team leader, a senior vice president, to get the project under way. The office was decorated with all manner of personal memorabilia, including those little glass snow domes that, when shaken, produce a flurry of swirling snowflakes.

Picking up a dome and shaking it, the vice president commented, "Too bad we can't make a park out of one of these." After a general pause, a team member asked, "Why not?" From that simple question, the team took off on the apparently impossible notion of building a ski resort in the sunshine of central Florida.

One artist sketched a picture of an alligator wearing earmuffs and careening down a slope on skis. Another drew a fanciful rendition of a winter resort enclosed in a snow dome. Not suitable for Florida, everyone agreed, but loath to discard the idea, they turned instead to the well established Disney storytelling method and devised a tale based on a blizzard.

Here's how it developed: A capricious winter storm brought a heavy load of snow to Florida. An entrepreneur came along and built a ski resort. He did well until the weather returned to normal, melting the snow and turning the ski runs into rushing waterfalls. But the waterfalls were then turned into . . . what else? water rides for adventurous athletes.

Using this fantasy story as their inspiration, Disney engineers and architects built the new water park and gave it the name Blizzard Beach.

Another example of this tried-and-true approach was when the Imagineers actually constructed a story to enhance the romance of Pleasure Island. To set the stage for the envisioned experience, they wove an entirely fictitious tale about the history of the location, to wit: The land originally belonged to a seafaring adventurer, Merryweather Pleasure, who settled there to build a successful canvas and sail-making company. Pleasure built a thriving industrial complex. As the years passed and Merryweather Pleasure listened to the stories told by visiting seagoing types and other adventurers, his nostalgia for his past proved too strong to resist. He sailed away from Pleasure Island forever, leaving his company in the hands of two sons. They were lazy and indifferent to their father's legacy, however, and gradually the warehouses fell into disrepair.

Imagineers refurbished the island, turning its rundown warehouses into exciting restaurants and nightclubs designed to reflect the regional themes of Pleasure's functional buildings. Once again the district bustles with the activity of world travelers who come together in the spirit of fun and adventure, a tradition established here a century ago.

But the real importance of both the Pleasure Island and the Blizzard Beach examples is that they united team members around whimsical notions that piqued their creative playfulness and drew them completely into the visions for the projects. Repeating and embellishing the fantastical stories engaged team members in a way that discussion of budgets and staffing problems could never have done. A team linked by a central idea, even one built on whimsy, is better able to tackle the mundane matters that must be dealt with in order to bring a project to completion. It's the primary reason that Walt Disney wanted the castle at Disneyland to be the first building constructed.

> Today, everybody is referring to corporate this and corporate that and a change is taking place. They want more production and they want it cheaper. But no matter what happens, the creative idea will only be perpetuated by somebody who comes up with a vision. I don't care if there are three CEOs, it takes one guy with an idea. And Walt (Disney) was the perfect example of that.
>
> JOE GRANT, DISNEY ANIMATOR, WRITER

We often ask our Dream Retreat participants to write an imaginary newspaper story reporting their company's triumphant turnaround. The chroniclers are asked to describe the winning ways embraced by their company and how they were implemented.

The purpose of this exercise is to force the group to think about how forthcoming cultural changes should be developed, how they would affect their company, and how these employees personally would execute them. A number of different scenarios typically emerge. Some are nuts-and-bolts pieces; others have a streak of fantasy about them; but all evidence an understanding of the company's goals. "The Dream principle has been crucial for the telecommunications industry as it grapples with disruptive technological changes. Telecom executives need to have the vision and confidence to transform their business models while keeping employees and customers happy at the same time," comments Scott Stevenson, Telecommunications Association of Michigan president.[3]

Dream Retreats Foster Participation

Walt Disney instinctively knew that participation by cast members in the development of a new "show" gave them a sense of commitment, both to the project in question and to the company itself. Judging from the extremely low turnover rates at his namesake company, we can say that Walt's instincts were, as always, right on target. Whereas a 100 percent turnover rate is the norm at most theme parks, rank-and-file turnover at Disney is less than 30 percent. And within the company's management ranks, turnover is less than 6 percent.

What's more, everything we have learned in working with companies worldwide lends support to the validity of Walt's inclusive approach. Employees everywhere, whether in China or India or Italy, basically agree on what is important and what is offensive in a corporate culture. They dislike arrogance on the part of management, and they desperately want real two-way communication that includes them in planning and resolving critical issues.

The employees of CMA Canada are of this mindset. CMA Canada represents 37,000 certified management accountants (CMAs) and 10,000 students and candidates in Canada and around the world.

Since 2003, they have been involved in a journey to change the culture of their organization. One of the exciting developments came out of a full-staff Dream Retreat last summer on The Disney Way of customer service. At that session, they were determined to dream how they could encourage an atmosphere of mutual respect and trust. The result of this session was the creation of a Mutual Respect and Trust (MRT) Committee—a cross-functional task force with folks from the internal areas of accreditation, corporate services, and IT.

Dream Retreat participants felt that there was a need to take the ideas and thoughts expressed and to work toward resolving some of the issues identified. The MRT Committee decided to focus on communication and came up with four initial recommendations: establish a company newsletter, create a virtual calendar of events, build an intranet site, and hold regular interdepartmental meetings.

Last December, the newsletter, *Bridges*, was introduced to CMA Canada employees in all provinces and territories across Canada. The first issue focused mainly on introductions and explained some of the roles and new initiatives taking place at the national office. As Richard Benn, vice president of program development explained, "We were very pleased that the newsletter met with such a favorable response. Later this year we will be encouraging submissions from our provincial partners about the exciting things that are happening with them so as to further 'bridge' our interconnectivity."[4]

The CMA Canada intranet was designed and built to provide seamless access to a host of internal information from CMA Canada's current Strategic Plan and its Mission, Vision, and Values to a library of documentation for all key projects and activities. CMA Canada also instituted a virtual calendar of events that provides online access to events and projects planned and happenings in and outside of its regional offices. There is also an ongoing effort to hold regular interdepartmental meetings to help realize common goals.

Results of a staff survey show that these efforts have not been in vain. Although there is still more work to be done, CMA's leadership is encouraged by the data, and the staff continues to work together toward a culture of excellence.

Never is employee participation more important than when a company decides to embark on a program of change. Perhaps customer service is suffering, or employee turnover is reaching unacceptable levels, or the product offering is tired and stale. Whatever it is that provides the eventual impetus, one thing will be clear: the old way is no longer working, and a new framework of operation is needed. When that happens, companies invite disaster if they don't involve front-line employees in the process. As we have seen so many times in working with our clients, such involvement is a key part of communicating with people during times of change.

A Dream Retreat has proved to be an ideal way of helping companies initiate needed change. Besides involving employees in strategy and facilitating their understanding of the vision and direction the company is pursuing, a Dream Retreat environment propels participants into a world of new ideas that often spark innovative solutions to the problems at hand.

The retreats, which can last anywhere from one to five days, are conducted away from the company premises. We have found that off-site gatherings are a great way to break down barriers and begin the planning process for the kind of change that ultimately revolutionizes a culture. When people are removed from daily routines and placed in an atmosphere that encourages free expression of their dreams, amazing ideas begin to emerge and flourish. Dreaming in this context is not a solitary occupation; participants bat around project ideas, argue, laugh, and brainstorm solutions as a group.

Storytelling is always encouraged at the Dream Retreats, but occasionally a new client will balk at learning and practicing the technique. Such reluctance is understandable. After all, we are proposing a radical departure from the customary business procedure. In the traditional environment, employees are informed of a new project when most of the preliminary details are in place. They are told who will work on a project, what the budget is, and what the deadlines are. To suggest that management invite employees into the strategy and planning process through storytelling is at odds with received wisdom.

Most of our clients, however, are open-minded and willing to experiment once they understand that communicating their vision is pivotal to innovation and project success. We tell them that if they want employees to get behind a corporate vision, they have to let those employees know what that vision is. We often think of a former client that literally kept its strategic plan under lock and key. Employees cannot possibly help advance specific goals if they aren't privy to the overall plan.

New clients sometimes have difficulty in understanding the basic value of Dream Retreats. "What will my company gain from such an idea?" we are asked. "It sounds like some kind of a vacation to me. Everyone will probably just want to play golf."

But a Dream Retreat is only a vacation from operating in the old, less-than-optimal style. In reality, a Dream Retreat involves a lot of hard work and grappling with tough decisions. Employees are removed from the administrative details that hamper their creativity at the office so that they can focus on strategy and planning in a fresh, innovative way.

The Dream Retreat in Action

While disabusing our clients of the notion that a Dream Retreat is a break from work, we want them to understand the excitement that such an experience generates. The power of the collective intelligence and the power of teaming amid a spirit of fun create a unique atmosphere that is rich with inventive possibilities.

One of our favorite examples is Whirlpool's Global No-Frost team (featured in the sidebars at the end of each chapter). In 1994, this team was formed to create a new international product that would require building a plant in India. The team was composed of members from India, China, Brazil, Italy,

Canada, and the United States. Under the old way of doing business, leaders from the six areas involved would have gotten together to devise a plan, then taken pieces of that plan back to their respective countries and started working separately.

This time, though, things were to be different. Instead of following marching orders issued from the top, an empowered team was charged with examining the options and coming up with an agenda. Team leader Jerry McColgin wasted no time in setting the tone for how he wanted his group to tackle the work ahead. His first order of business was to insist on a new layout for the team's office space at its Indiana facility. Out went the walls, the cubicles, the compartmentalized look to create a space that resembled an old-fashioned newsroom: open, convivial, and barrier-free.

The project officially got underway with a five-day Dream Retreat for 40 people from all over the world. There, in the dead of an Indiana winter, the Global No-Frost team assembled its collective talent.

The retreat began with people talking about their personal dreams and their sense of the team's mission. The individual interests of each sector were weighed against the overall goals of the company as the team strove to achieve a realistic balance for the project. As the five days unfolded, however, something exciting and gratifying began to happen: the barriers between the various functional areas started to crumble. Technicians accepted responsibility for engineering tasks; engineers listened attentively to marketing concerns; marketers assumed the critical business role of evaluating suppliers. Even the usually standoffish finance people willingly jumped into the trenches with purchasing and marketing folks. The flow of ideas became a flood. By the end of the retreat, everyone was working together for the common good of the team.

The Dream Retreat was an essential first step on a project that ended up surpassing everyone's initial expectations. Never before had new Whirlpool products arrived on the market so quickly. That's because the Global No-Frost team met every deadline and achieved every goal. When, in the middle of the project, team members found that they needed to lower costs further than originally planned in order to increase competitive position, they rallied to the cause and did it without cutting quality. And here's the icing on the cake: the entire project came in *under* budget. It's not unusual for our clients to credit a Dream Retreat for keeping costs in check.

As Brian Hartke, manager of project engineering at the Bristol-Myers Squibb Company's Mead Johnson Nutritional division, aptly points out: "If you change something in the planning stage, it costs you a dollar. If you change something in the design phase, it costs you 10 dollars. If you change something after the plant is built, it costs you a hundred dollars." A Dream Retreat increases the opportunities for figuring out what's needed early in the process, before you spend a lot of change for the change.

In 1993, before Mead Johnson Nutritional division began constructing the world's largest production facility for infant-formula powder in Zeeland, Michigan, Hartke brought his diverse construction team together for a Dream Retreat at a hotel in Holland, Michigan. The team members, both workers and suppliers, "really got to know one another there," Hartke says. "They put together plans through formal and informal conversations." And because of that initial interaction, the team continued face-to-face meetings throughout the project. End result: the plant was completed on time and on budget.

Another example of the value of a Dream Retreat occurred when we worked with British Petroleum Ltd. in 1990. But far more than just a single project was at stake in this instance. As the worldwide oil company bluntly admitted, "Nothing short of a complete overhaul . . . was needed." The company was too autocratic. It was strangling in red tape. Turf consciousness was impeding efficiency, and the company was hierarchical to the point of paralysis. Not surprisingly, employee morale was also frighteningly low.

"The business climate is challenging," a company report concluded, "and only the best oil companies will survive into the 21st century." At the rate the octogenarian BP was going (the company was founded in 1909), that it would live to see the next millennium was far from certain. Old oil fields were declining, and because of fiercely competitive conditions, new ones were tougher to find. Costs were escalating. And skilled technicians were becoming scarcer.

To remedy the situation, the company had an ambitious organization-wide innovation initiative. In fact, it envisioned an entirely new corporate culture, one where a more participatory environment would give employees the freedom and responsibility, within certain limits, to make decisions. A far cry from the rigid command-and-control policies of the past, such an initiative would be quite a change if the company could pull it off.

Bill launched a Dream Retreat that produced a major turnaround in day-to-day office procedures. Managers became visible and present for their employees, not deskbound behind closed doors. No longer were meetings run from on high, with orders handed down and questions distinctly unwelcome. Teams replaced the previous hierarchy throughout the company. Training and coaching of employees was the order of the day. To bring the message of this new company vision to all employees, BP held town-hall meetings.

Something of what this change-management initiative has meant to British Petroleum can be discerned from one small incident. Prior to the overhaul, a team of high-powered geologists and engineers at the company's U.S. exploration headquarters in Anchorage, Alaska, produced a monthly report for the president that analyzed seismic data and estimated potential oil reserves at the Prudhoe Bay field. It was a complex, time-consuming task that took energy away from other vital duties.

As part of the new atmosphere of empowerment, the scientists and engineers scrutinized the process, evaluated its costs, and discovered that an inordinate number of worker-hours were being devoted to it. Then they asked why. Was the monthly process really vital to the interests of the company? Or was it being done just in case the president happened to ask for an estimate of the latest oil reserves? They made their case to the president, who agreed that since the report was, at best, an estimate, an assessment every three months was entirely sufficient. The savings in time and money were considerable.

Although the revitalized BP is still evolving, old habits have been eliminated, and the refrain "we have always done it this way" is rarely, if ever, heard these days. In June 1998 *Industry Week* reported that British Petroleum expects 20 percent more oil from its oil-production operations in Alaska. Officials reported that reduced costs and technological advances have made expansion on the North Slope feasible. Moreover, as the Prudhoe Bay example illustrates, management is upholding its end of the bargain by supporting empowered employees who make smart, solid recommendations. And as for the bottom line, John Browne, BP's group chief executive, speaking to the financial community recently, recounted sustained improvement in cost reduction and volume increases in the five years from 1992 through 1996. During that period, Browne said, profits grew by more than $3 billion.

Tracking Good Ideas

Dream Retreats offer the fastest and most productive way to achieve flexibility and openness within a company's ranks. But once people become accustomed to acknowledging their own creative powers, you must implement a system outside the retreat setting that encourages them to bring their ideas to management.

Mike Cryan, president of Windsor Capital Group, clearly understands the value of harnessing the ideas of his management team. Windsor Capital

Group, Inc. is a Santa Monica–based hotel company that owns and manages nationwide properties, largely Embassy Suites and Marriott Hotels. In 2002, Mike championed a two-day Dream Retreat for his management team in the Arizona desert, where they turned their organizational "Dream" into concrete objectives: track customer perceptions through feedback; contain costs; and grow the business. "The process helped us work on our goals, corporate team arm in arm with the hotel staff members, through the creation and visualization of the storyboard. This really simplified our ability to communicate these goals to the department heads and line-level employees when we returned to our properties. After the Dream Retreat, our president provided a platform at subsequent operations meetings for us to discuss how we were achieving these goals," commented Regina Samy, vice president.[5] Today, WCG is one of the leading companies in the hospitality management business with a results-oriented approach that produces bottom-line operating numbers that are among the best in the industry.

When Walt Disney was at the helm of the company, everyone was invited to voice his or her opinions and to make suggestions—in fact, not just invited but required. The corporate hierarchy dissolved when it came to offering ideas for improving a movie script, a theme park ride, or an animated sequence. Anyone could bring suggestions for cartoons and features to Walt himself. Basically, the same holds true today, but the size of the company makes a casual approach impractical. The company does provide regular opportunities to harvest good ideas from all corners of the organization, however.

In the early days at the helm of The Walt Disney Company, Michael Eisner instituted a thrice-yearly event known as the Gong Show, named after a television program popular in the 1970s and 1980s. Animators, secretaries, and anyone else who thought he or she had a good idea could formally make a pitch to a panel of top brass that included then CEO Michael Eisner; vice chairman of the board, Roy Disney; executive vice president of animation, Tom Schumacher; and president of the animation division (now president of the film division), Peter Schneider.

On average, 40 ideas were presented as succinctly as possible. It was a tough milieu because the listeners at the table provided immediate and honest reactions. "You must have immediate communication and not worry about people's egos and feelings," Schneider says. "If you do that enough and people do not get fired or demoted, they begin to understand that no matter how good, bad, or indifferent the idea, it can be expressed, accepted, and considered."[6]

The "Gong Show" was a valuable learning experience for many employees, helping them to see why one idea works and another doesn't. It was also an experience that enhanced the atmosphere of freedom—freedom both to dream and to share those dreams with the company's highest authorities. And by creating an environment in which people felt safe to express their creativity, the The Walt Disney Company opened itself up to literally thousands of good ideas—ideas so good that they have sewn the seeds for many of Disney's animated features. *Hercules,* for example, grew from an animator's idea that a man is judged by his inner strength and not his outer strength. Though the story line ended up changing, the basic premise stood and the movie went on to be a commercial success.

Not long ago, we were showing an executive from British Petroleum around Disney World. "What a pity that Walt Disney did not live to see this place," he remarked. "But he did see it," we said. "That's why it's here."

Obviously, The Walt Disney Company is involved in an industry that is equal parts art and commerce. But there is no industry, no matter how basic, that couldn't benefit from injecting a dollop of Walt's unfettered visionary spirit into too-often sclerotic corporate veins. Many of the greatest figures in American business—from Thomas Edison to Bill Gates—have been dreamers, and it's no accident that Steven Spielberg, an American icon approaching Disney status, has named his new company DreamWorks SKG. Companies *must* give themselves permission to dream. Whether or not they come up with an equivalent of Walt Disney World in which to showcase their fantasies, the simple act of letting imaginations run free will increase creativity and innovation.

Any kind of cultural change comes slowly, and the powerful transformation to be fueled by adoption of the Dream principle is no exception. If your company is large and if old attitudes and methods are firmly entrenched, it may take three to five years for the new culture to take permanent root. However, we have worked with organizations that began realizing improvements in service and productivity within a few months.

In spite of visible short-term gains, however, some companies will still voice concern over the slowness of the overall transformation process, at which point we relate the story of the hundredth monkey.

In the 1950s, on the Japanese island of Koshima, scientists studying macaque monkeys dropped sweet potatoes in the sand. The monkeys liked the taste of the potatoes, but they found the sand to be unpleasant. One innovative monkey discovered that washing the potatoes in seawater eliminated the grit and made the potatoes taste better. She quickly taught this to her mother and several of her playmates.

As one would expect, other young monkeys in the troop were soon imitating this monkey's intelligent behavior. Then, after several years had passed, the last lines of resistance were finally eroded after one particular incident. Legend states that one morning, a certain number of monkeys were washing their potatoes. The exact number is not known, but for the sake of the story, we'll say that it was 99. Later that morning, one more monkey learned to wash his potato. As the day progressed, each of the remaining dirty-potato-eating monkeys began washing his or her potato until, by evening, every monkey in the troop had developed a taste for clean potatoes!

A similar transference of learned behavior also occurs in organizations that are undergoing change. Although the exact number may vary, a point is reached where, if only one more person adopts a new set of values, the synergy is so great that nearly everyone else will internalize the behavior too.

Whether or not this story is legend or fact, there are several lessons that we can learn from the hundredth monkey story.

- First, total transformation takes time. In the case of the Koshima monkeys, it took several years.
- Second, the benefits of transformation must be real. Just as the monkeys enjoyed the benefits of eating clean potatoes, employees must be able to experience real gains as they adopt cultural change.
- Third, management must consistently model the desired behavior. The innovative monkeys continued to exhibit the potato-washing method before other members of the troop. Be persistent.
- Fourth, there must be top management commitment at the outset. When the first monkey learned to wash her food, she taught the skill to her mother and to a handful of adults. The adult converts provided positive feedback by embracing and using the newly learned skill. Without their early commitment, it's unlikely that the entire troop transformation would ever have taken place.

Time, persistence, and commitment are the keys to long-term benefits. And remember, as we always say, "The first 99 are the hardest!"

The Dream concept is first and foremost a visionary undertaking, but both management and employees must keep the overall organizational values firmly in mind as they plan new strategies and set about implementing cultural change. In other words, if innovation is to be successful over the long term, it's imperative that a company remain true to itself. In the chapter that follows, we explore what Walt Disney did to ensure that his dreams and those of his company remained firmly grounded in a set of basic core beliefs. And we examine how a Disney-like adherence to a values-based approach is helping other companies to achieve bottom-line success.

Questions to Ask

- Does top management acknowledge that the process of "dreaming" inspires creativity?
- Does top management understand that adopting new paradigms takes time and commitment? Is it willing to see the transformation through to its fruition?
- Do your teams participate in off-site retreats where they engage in strategy and planning?
- Do you utilize the storytelling technique in planning projects?

Actions to Take

- Hold annual, off-site Dream Retreats for top management and all departmental teams.
- Unleash creativity by encouraging all employees to participate in structured dreaming to solve problems and develop solutions.
- Engage employees in developing the story of what the organization could be like in five years. From these stories, develop a vision of what the company will look like five years from now.
- Determine the values the organization must embrace to achieve its vision.
- Communicate the organizational vision and values to your coworkers, customers, suppliers, managers, directors, and stockholders.
- Display the organizational vision and values in prominent places throughout the company.

■ Use the storytelling technique as a method to assist teams in launching projects.

A Shared Vision

When Jerry McColgin agreed to take on the job as leader of the Whirlpool team, he drew on past experience. He had headed up a team whose structure and way of operating were entirely company-mandated. "We did not have full-time dedicated resources," Jerry explained, "the engineers on whom I was dependent actually reported to the engineering department in their respective locations." Furthermore, he had been asked to work with a lot of part-time people. The people on the project had lacked cohesion and a unity of purpose. If Jerry came to them and explained what should be done, they would agree, but when they discussed it with their department heads, the answer was, "That's all very good and fine, but here's how we're really going to do it." It had been an international project with no contribution from the targeted markets. As a result, the project failed.

McColgin was determined that there would not be another failure. When the company tried to tell him how the project was to be run, he dug in his heels. He believed that he now knew how to create a successful team. This time, he brought together an international group of people and announced that there would be no part-time participation and no divided loyalties. From the outset, the team would be unified in a shared vision.

The company was also building a new plant in Pune, India, to manufacture the product. Among its many goals, the team was to design the equipment, figure out costs, and plan the marketing, all for a number of different countries. All these countries needed representation on the team, whose numbers included engineers, designers, and finance experts speaking different languages and coming from dissimilar cultures. Style differences between the members were apparent at the beginning of the project. Yet people from Brazil, China, Italy, and India would all be sitting next to one another every day and working together. Their main goal was to develop the model for a common refrigerator that could be built around the world. As a selling point, it was also to be manufactured with a frost-free freezing compartment—hence the name of the team, the Global No-Frost Team.

Our Featured Organization: Griffin Hospital

WHERE IS THE HOSPITAL?

It was early in the morning when we arrived at Griffin Hospital. Visitors and day-shift hospital staff were still at home having breakfast. We parked our car in the lot several hundred yards from the entrance. As we started walking toward the building, a strange feeling came over us and we wondered, is this really a hospital? For starters, the pavement was impeccably clean and there was tranquil music wafting from concealed speakers along the walkway. Did we get on the wrong flight? Were we really at Walt Disney World? We checked our tickets and, indeed, we were in Derby, Connecticut. This Disneyesque experience continued as we wandered into the softly lit lobby adorned with beautiful art work, a grand piano, and a reception desk that looked like it belonged in the Four Seasons Hotel of New York. We were nearly an hour early for our appointment with Patrick Charmel, Griffin's president and CEO, so we decided to experience the cafeteria. We found that the Disney similarities were not merely limited to the physical elements of brass and glass. Of the six or seven employees we encountered on our way to the cafeteria, each, without exception, either said "Good Morning," or stopped to ask if they could be of assistance to us.

But things were not always this "magical" at Griffin Hospital. In 1980 the community perception of Griffin was less than stellar; in fact, 30 percent surveyed said they would avoid Griffin Hospital at all costs. Of the eight local hospitals surveyed, Griffin was the lowest on the list. Patrick Charmel told us, "On top of this bad rating, the hospital was struggling financially, so there was a serious question about our future viability. We knew we couldn't compete, based on the clinical prowess of other area hospitals that are much larger and have greater capabilities, so we decided to become extremely consumer-focused and responsive. This was a pretty radical concept for healthcare 20 years ago."[7]

The transformation began in 1987 with an innovative renovation of the Childbirth Center and continued into the 1990s with hospital-wide improvements. But the road to becoming the hospital of choice in the area involved more than brick, mortar, and ingenious architecture. Employee pride became the roadmap to patient satisfaction. Rallying around a common vision consistent with the personal values of the employees, looking at patient care from the patient's perspective, and eliminating fear were goals

Patrick and his team set out to accomplish. To achieve the desired results, Griffin implemented a mandatory two-day employee orientation program that had to be completed before beginning patient care. Within the first six months, employees must also attend an additional two-day retreat where they share rooms and really absorb the experience of being patients. During this retreat, employees participate in exercises to increase handicap awareness, such as leading one another around blindfolded, walking with crutches, and feeding one another. "It makes you think twice when you're doing things with patients…about what they must be going through," says nurse Cathy Higgins. "You understand what it's like to lose control of your life."[8]

During most of this transformation, Charmel was COO and had responsibility for the day-to-day operations of the entire hospital. His popularity seemed to increase proportionate with the hospital's escalating employee engagement. Then, in 1997, Patrick and the former CEO of Griffin began to differ on the hospital's future goals and direction. The two men's dreams for achieving a world-class culture collided and forever altered the state of affairs at Griffin Hospital. In Patrick's words, "He was de-emphasizing the acute-care side of the hospital and trying to develop our HMO. We were spending a lot on this and depriving the hospital of the resources it needed." The former CEO decided it was time for Patrick to go and represented this decision to the troops as "mutual." No wonder people didn't trust him! It was Thanksgiving of 1997 when the announcement was made: Patrick would be leaving at year's end. The news not only shocked hospital and medical staff, it also stunned many in the community. After all, Patrick had been the architect of Griffin's metamorphosis. Griffin Hospital was the largest employer in the community and, if it failed, the community would be devastated.

As the New Year dawned, Patrick was gone but not forgotten. There was a rumbling in the hospital halls; a series of maneuvers were underway to bring Patrick back. The employees cried out in protest and penned an underground newspaper, *Griffin Uncensored*; hospital physicians voted "no confidence" in the current administration; and the community started a yellow-ribbon campaign in and around the town of Derby. Local newspaper headlines: "We Want Pat Back" . . . "Employees & Docs, United We Stand" . . . and "Unforgettable Thursday" spoke volumes. "Unforgettable Thursday" referred to January 8, 1998, when as *Griffin Uncensored* reported, "We made history when we stormed the boardroom and stood proud and principled for our hospital and our community. This show of unity finally

(Continued)

awakened the few who had yet to believe how much we are willing to sacrifice to get Griffin back."

In early February, Patrick was asked to return to the hospital and informed that the former CEO would be leaving. Charmel returned as Griffin's deserving leader on February 23, 1998. "There was an emotional reception with hundreds of employees," Patrick recalled. "When I came in 'Tie a Yellow Ribbon 'round the Old Oak Tree' was playing. There were banners, balloons, and speeches." What was really striking was Patrick's humility through all of this pomp and circumstance on his behalf.

As CEO, Patrick began a thorough investigation of the hospital's finances and discovered that things were worse than he thought. "The HMO never grew to become a significant player in the market. It was losing money and using depleting hospital funds. We had to get out of the HMO business and cut our losses."

Can one even imagine how Patrick must have felt coming back to a hero's welcome, and then weeks later having to lay off some of the same employees who had stormed the boardroom on his behalf? Patrick told us, "I had to make this type of decision about people who supported me so strongly. That was extremely painful. We cried together." Several laid-off employees we interviewed told us they were later rehired when the hospital's financial situation improved. Though none relished having been fired, they all said that they understood what would have happened if Patrick had not reduced expenses. Newspaper headlines might have read, "Griffin Hospital forced to close its doors." Better to have 100 people lose their jobs than 1,000.

Was all of this worth the effort? Today, 18 years after "Unforgettable Thursday," Griffin Hospital enjoys in-patient satisfaction rates of over 95 percent, and it captured the fourth highest ranking on *Fortune* magazine's 2006 "100 Best Companies to Work For." Not only is this the highest ranking ever achieved by a hospital, but Griffin is the only hospital in the United States to be named to the prestigious list seven times.

A leader's job is to create an environment of mutual respect and trust. We have yet to see any other place where the level of respect and trust is so great that employees will put their jobs on the line and storm the boardroom in support of their leader. That type of culture does not happen overnight. It takes hard work to create and to maintain, but Patrick and his team have kept the focus, and the results are exceptional.

Believe

Chapter 3

You Better Believe It

When you believe a thing, believe it implicitly and unquestionably.[9]
Walt Disney

When Walt Disney was still an infant, his family moved from Chicago to a farm in Marceline, Missouri, about 100 miles east of Kansas City. Farm life is hard and demanding, and a growing boy, then as now, always has chores to do. But after the barn was mucked out or the apples picked, young Walt would lie in the grass and gaze up at the Missouri sky or watch insects and butterflies flit overhead. These were memories that he treasured all his life.

From those early years growing up in a rural environment, Disney formed beliefs and values that stuck with him throughout his life from which he never deviated. His love of nature, handsomely depicted in numerous animated and live action films, surely can be traced to those experiences, as can the basic foursquare family values that still guide The Walt Disney Company today.

Perfectly complementing Walt's firmly held beliefs was the philosophy expressed by his brother, Roy: "When values are clear, decisions are easy."[10] Together, these precepts formed what is, in effect, The Walt Disney Company's mantra: "Live your beliefs"—or what we simply call *Believe*.

Carrying that theme a step further, we might add that if "seeing is believing," then the unparalleled success of The Walt Disney Company is convincing proof of the power inherent in the Believe principle. But as our clients know, before success can be achieved, a personal set of core values must be formalized, communicated to the company at large, and actually lived day to day. Disney has shown the way.

Built on Beliefs

Early on, Walt infused his work with the personal core values that also came to define his company. In his initial Mickey Mouse cartoons, for example, the character of Mickey was overly rambunctious and even a bit crude at times. But Walt quickly recognized that such behavior would never do if Mickey was to be embraced by audiences young and old. The mouse would have to reflect the solid values held by his viewers. Thus, Walt saw to it that honesty, reliability, loyalty, and respect for people as individuals—the same principles he would espouse within the company—formed the essence of Mickey's character.

In more recent times, the "Gong Show" idea that grew into the 1997 movie *Hercules* was approved precisely because it fit so perfectly with the Disney Company's core values. Inspired by the tale of the mythical Greek hero, the film idea was based on the premise that a person should be judged not only on his or her outer strength but by inner moral strength as well.

"The core value puts process into creativity," says Peter Schneider, president of the film division. That's the way The Walt Disney Company sees it. Thus, the first step in any project, moviemaking or otherwise, is to determine what core value is being promoted. When it came to the making of *The Hunchback of Notre Dame*, for example, the creative team decided, after much discussion and soul-searching, that the core value of the story was self-value. They had to agree on this premise before they could go forward.

We are convinced that a refusal to compromise values is necessary if an organization is to scale the heights. What's important is not necessarily the content of a company's core ideology, but rather how consistently that ideology is expressed and lived. In Chapter 2, the story of Patrick Charmel of Griffin Hospital illustrates how one great leader was unwilling to allow outside influences to alter his beliefs and decisions.

The Levi Strauss Company, for example, has shown an extraordinary commitment to core values in its everyday operations. The original maker of the quintessentially American blue jeans has long enjoyed a reputation as a good place to work, and it is known for its commitment to empowering workers and compensating them generously. In addition, it has formalized its beliefs in its mission and aspiration statements, and in 1991 became the first multinational company to set down guidelines governing business partners abroad. Its aim is to ensure that workplace standards and business practices in foreign operations are in line with company policies.

When tough competition in the mid-1990s forced the company to close 11 of its 37 factories and lay off more than 6,000 employees—its first major cutback in more than 140 years of operation—the experience was an understandably painful one for management. In characteristic fashion, the company set about making careful preparations to ease the trauma of the layoffs. Each affected employee was given eight months' notice, and $31,000 per laid-off employee was put aside to help facilitate job searches. The company worked with unions and with local governments to get retraining programs off the ground quickly. Every step taken by Levi Strauss was an expression of its core values and its basic respect for each individual in its workforce.

"Our people will know," CEO Robert Haas said, "that if bad things happen, they will be treated much better than they would be elsewhere."[11] In the midst of extremely difficult times, both financially and culturally, the company held firm to its values while also making sure that its product continued to be the best it could be.

Offering your customers the best product or service means not only establishing certain values, as Walt Disney did, but also having the good sense to recognize when the situation dictates that one value takes precedence over another. Walt insisted on safety, courtesy, the good show, and efficiency, but he also expected common sense to prevail. First and foremost, it was never permissible to jeopardize a guest's safety in any way, at any time, no matter what the attraction or performance. That meant that if a child was in danger of falling out of a Jungle Cruise Boat, for example, courtesy, show, and efficiency temporarily fell by the wayside until the situation was corrected. Or if someone was having difficulty understanding directions, courtesy to that guest won out over show and efficiency.

By the same token, the concept of the good show carried more weight than did a desire for efficient operations. Excellence at every level was, and is, the watchword at Disney, because Walt believed that only by giving audiences the best of entertainment could he live up to his core values of honesty and reliability. He refused to take short cuts merely to inflate the bottom line.

Dick Nunis, retired chairman of Walt Disney Attractions, started his career selling popcorn at Disneyland. One of the jobs Dick had on his way up the corporate ladder was managing the Jungle Cruise Boat attraction at Disneyland. Shortly after being promoted to manager, Dick devised a way to save money whenever the wait times become too long. Scheduling more boats meant more cast members, which resulted in a larger payroll. Instead of adding more boats, Dick simply increased the speed, told his cast members to talk a little faster, and perhaps leave out a joke or two. In those days, Walt would frequently walk around the park to observe the reaction of the guests. He would even ride many of the attractions. One day, Walt decided to take a Jungle Cruise and experienced the "super charged" speed. Needless to say, he was not happy. When he got out of the boat, he called Dick aside and read him the riot act. He told Dick that guests expect a consistent show. Walt also reminded Dick of his responsibility for ensuring the quality of the show, and that if that meant bringing on additional crew to deliver the "good show," then so be it. Walt said, "Frontline equals bottom line." Deliver unforgettable front-line customer service and the bottom line dollars will follow.

Just as Walt refused to accept a substandard *Pinocchio*, even though reworking the characters significantly bumped up the cost, so too are certain extravagances countenanced on a regular basis today because they greatly enhance the show. The exquisite topiaries in the theme parks are one example. Because it takes 3 to 10 years to grow and shape the trees to look like Dumbo, Mickey, and other characters, it would obviously be more efficient and less costly to install plastic statues instead. But the topiaries add natural beauty that imparts a greater level of excellence to the entire show. Plus, they are enjoyed and photographed by thousands of guests.

In the end, of course, Disney's adherence to basic beliefs and the company's willingness to spend time and money to deliver the excellence it values have been amply rewarded by the huge success of its films, theme parks, and other ventures.

Formalizing the Beliefs

To ensure that employees at all levels would be guided by his beliefs and his visionary sense of purpose, Walt Disney fostered what amounted to an almost cultlike atmosphere. His passionate belief in the need to instill a company culture led him to set up a formal training program that has come to be known as Disney University.

The program, which stresses the uniqueness of the company and the importance of adhering to its values, came into being as a result of a situation Walt encountered when Disneyland opened in 1955. Initially, he hired an outside security firm and leased out the parking concession. "I soon realized my mistake," he said, explaining that with "outside help" he couldn't effectively convey his idea of hospitality.[12] That's when the company began recruiting and training every one of its employees.

Walt wanted each and every cast member to embrace the basic Disney belief of courtesy to customers, of treating them like guests in their own homes. "I tell the security officers," he once said, "that they are never to consider themselves cops. They are here to help people."[13] Setting up a security force and training the officers in the company's values and beliefs was no doubt more expensive than outsourcing the job, but monetary considerations took a backseat to ensuring that everyone exhibited courtesy.

Every new cast member must spend several days in Traditions training before starting the job. During this orientation period, the Disney culture is communicated through powerful storytelling. The value of the program was proven several years ago when cost-cutting corporate types decided to reduce the training period by just one day. Complaints from supervisors throughout the parks began to pour in. "The quality of guest service is not the quality we had last season," they said. "Have you changed the hiring policy?"[14]

Top management took a close look at the process and found out that only one thing had changed. The missing day of Traditions training was added back in and the complaints stopped. Instilling the culture takes time, but anyone who has visited a Disney theme park is well aware of what the training program brings to the show: Questions are answered courteously, crowd control is unobtrusive, and cast members at every turn willingly go the extra mile to make each guest's dreams come true.

On the face of it, our advice to strictly adhere to a formalized set of beliefs and values may sound naïve and unsophisticated, if not downright impractical. It may come across as the kind of do-good counsel you read about in an inspirational pamphlet. But this is not theoretical; it is practical and proven in the stories of companies that have adopted the Believe principle.

One company that displays a strict adherence to its own values is Lensing Wholesale. A long-standing, family-owned business in Evansville, Indiana, which distributes building products, Lensing's strong family values are transparent to all who enter its doors. While the company provides outstanding service to all its customers, we were especially impressed to witness the determination of Lensing's president, Joe Theby, to formalize the company's values and mission in written statements at our recommendation. Many family businesses ignore this important step, believing that employees are already clear about company values, since they have been in place since the company's formation.

In formalizing Lensing values, Joe's first priority was to define the word *value*. At Lensing, a value is "a desirable standard of personal conduct or action; a worthy trait." Joe and his team decided on 11 core values, ranging from quality to customer relations.

At one company meeting that we attended, Joe gave a heartfelt speech to his employees about the value of customers and great service. During the meeting, he said that anybody could put up a warehouse and stock it with wholesale building products, but few could gain a reputation for truly understanding their customers and being there when the customers needed them. Illustrating the importance Lensing places on its ability to do just this, the company's customer relations value incorporates the following aspects: to deal well with customers; display honesty, integrity, and a sincere concern for their needs; remember names and faces; and maintain poise, integrity, and confidence during all interactions. A firm belief in this value and a strict adherence to its concept is what comes through loud and clear when speaking to any Lensing employee.

The Long-Term Mentality

Again and again, we have witnessed how companies are strengthened when they impart a clear understanding of their basic beliefs and core values. For one thing, a set of bedrock values gives a sense of security to all stakeholders and serves as a touchstone for company leaders. Although Walt Disney often teetered on the edge of bankruptcy, he was able to stay focused on his goals for the future because he believed so strongly in what he was trying to do and how he was trying to do it.

We call that the *long-term mentality*, but unfortunately, many companies manifest just the opposite. Their satisfaction with present achievements evidences a short-term view of the world and causes them to rest on their laurels—often with disastrous results. The Xerox Corporation, for example, squandered its lead in the copying-machine market to the Japanese and found itself left with only a 7 percent market share before it began a turnaround in the 1980s. So, too, with the Raytheon Company, which invented the microwave oven in 1947. Raytheon now has an insignificant share of the microwave market. The point is that even companies with innovative product ideas can be paralyzed by a short-term mentality that causes them to end up on the losing side.

It is a measure of Walt Disney's certain belief in his product that he was also able early on to envision a continuing demand for his cartoons and movies.

With brilliant foresight, Disney decided on a re-release policy that would bring his movies to a new generation of viewers at 5- and 10-year intervals. But again, Walt's prescience was dependent on his adherence to core values. He intended his movies to last—and last they did, because he insisted on excellence.

Disney's cartoons and animated films look as fresh today as when Walt's animators created them. That's because he paid attention to even the smallest detail of production and combined the most skillful drawings with the best available technology. At a time when many animators were using 6 to 8 drawings per second, for instance, Disney insisted on 24 drawings. (All animation went to 24 frames per second with the advent of sound, but the superiority of the Disney technique can be better understood by comparing it to today's average Saturday morning cartoon. Even though these cartoons run 24 frames per second, they use only 6 to 8 *drawings* per second, which means the same drawing is repeated three to four times. Disney animation provides 24 unique drawings per second.)

Equally important to Walt's long-term planning was the fact that he never lost sight of his market and the family values that endure. Re-released Disney films have made as much, if not more, money on their second release than they did on the first.

Today, The Walt Disney Company applies the same policy to the DVD market. When a Disney movie is released on DVD, it stays on the store shelf for six months and is then withdrawn for a specified period. People who don't buy it during the Disney-designated time frame simply have to wait until the next time it's back on the shelf. Tightly controlling distribution allows Disney to market its product over and over to succeeding generations of viewers. Since 1992, according to *Video Store Magazine,* six of the eight top-selling videos were Disney videos, with *Snow White and the Seven Dwarfs* and *The Lion King* tied for number 1.

The long-term mentality is apparent throughout the Disney empire—in its real estate transactions, for example. Although Walt was never interested in real estate as a personal investment, he took a wholly different approach when it came to his theme parks. And his experience with Disneyland only served to harden an already instinctual tendency to take the long view.

In 1954, when Walt bought the 160-acre Anaheim, California, parcel for Disneyland, he was constrained from acquiring additional land by limited financial resources, the already heavy debt he was incurring, and estimates of what it would cost to build his park. But Walt never ceased to regret not buying more land, especially as his extraordinarily successful park became hemmed in by tawdry fast-food outlets and motels. He vowed that he would not make the same mistake twice.

When it came time to plan for Walt Disney World, Walt was not hampered by such monetary constraints. He bought 29,500 acres of Florida real estate for an average price of $200 an acre. Less than half of that acreage is being used today, while the remainder has risen in value to more than $1 million an acre. Selling off the undeveloped land would bring more than $10 billion into corporate coffers.

Why doesn't the company sell the Florida acreage? Because such a sale would be at odds with the Disney long-term mentality. Still adhering to Walt's beliefs, the company is looking ahead to expansion that will further upgrade the show. The theme-park business, after all, is driven by a need to constantly offer new attractions that will entice both first-time and repeat guests.

Michael Eisner made it clear that short-term gains are not what Disney is about when he said at an industry conference in 1997: "I'm not looking for some outrageous, ridiculous multiple that blows in the wind or gets battered by changes in the economy. I hope people like the company, but I don't want to promise them Nirvana."

Leadership for the Long Term

In today's business world, where technology is driving an accelerated pace of change, a long-term mentality is a must for survival. But not everyone recognizes this imperative, as evidenced by some of our consulting experiences. The one-man roadblock we encountered when we began working with a large Fortune 500 manufacturer is a case in point.

We had asked a top management team to formalize the plans and specifications for an initiative intended to take their division into the future. The team worked for three months on the plan, meeting one full day a week to establish their values, decide on the organizational structure, and determine how best to communicate the vision underlying the plan.

The plans were great, but the boss failed to act on them. Sure, he *talked* about what he was going to do, but he never, as the saying goes, *walked the talk*. No changes were made until the boss was transferred and a young engineer named Steve was installed in his place.

Suddenly, plans turned into actions. Working together with his planning team, Steve established four subteams charged with developing new technologies, providing back-up systems and facilities support to engineers, improving processes, and empowering teams and individuals. Another group set about redesigning the workspace to facilitate better communication.

It is worth noting that none of these changes were part of any kind of overall directive from corporate headquarters. In fact, about the only thing in the way of change that emanated from headquarters was an annual gesture amounting to little more than calling in a consultant who prepared brochures and produced videos touting the value of some "new" culture.

Later, headquarters had issued another new cultural initiative. This time it included a management kickoff meeting at which a "talking-head" video was shown to communicate the importance of getting everyone on board with the high-performance principles. Steve's division was apathetic about the whole thing—and understandably so.

"It's almost an insult," some said, "when we've already been practicing these principles for years." These team members knew that Steve embodied the vision, and under his leadership they had achieved what the rest of the company was still contemplating. They had been living the vision.

The key element in this situation was the presence of a well-respected leader with a clear, long-term mentality. He had, in effect, become a pioneer in the company. What a contrast between Steve and his predecessor, who not only lacked vision himself but couldn't even muster the energy to implement the ideas generated by his staff.

Our experience working with Abbey Press further confirmed that leaders who uphold their strongly held values, even in times of economic downturns, are a key to solid achievement. Abbey Press, which publishes inspirational books and sells religious merchandise, is run by Benedictine monks with the support of a secular staff. As Gerald Wilhite, general manager of Abbey Press, told us, "Father Carl believed in his dream of a transformed workforce, which one monk said was 'very Benedictine.' He perceived that our success had waned a bit, and worked to rebuild the culture, and that brought big paybacks."[15]

We organized a Dream Retreat for Father Carl and his staff. At the end of our three-day retreat, John Wilson, Father Carl's boss, who had been invited at Carl's request, jumped to his feet to declare somewhat sheepishly that he had been reluctant to attend the meeting. Three times in the days before the retreat, Wilson had been ready to pick up the phone and say that he and his staff would not be able to participate after all. Only his respect for Father Carl, who had voiced great excitement about the teamwork a new culture would bring, stopped Wilson from backing out.

Now Wilson was admitting how close he had come to making "a big mistake." After experiencing the Dream Retreat, he, too, was pleased and excited about the initiative and, in fact, wanted to bring the process to "the Hill," the term used to describe the various administrative functions that support the monastery.

One step had led to another in the unfolding of events. Father Carl's pre-retreat enthusiasm and his strong belief in the value of the change process had captured John Wilson's attention. After listening carefully and participating in the retreat, Wilson came to share Father Carl's enthusiasm. Through the leadership of these two, the plan for cultural change was communicated to the entire staff and to the board of directors and has now taken root throughout the organization. "We benefited greatly from the changed culture," said Gerald. "Many of our people have remained with us for years, and are contributing to our new dreams to do things differently in keeping with our new kind of customer. Through all the rebuilding…our values, what the product stands for, and how we want to do business remain unchanged."

Believing in Innovation

For Walt Disney, innovation was second nature, which is one of the reasons he was such a strong leader. Our definition of leadership, in fact, revolves around the ability to create and manage an environment for innovation. But as we've discovered over the years, too many managers find the idea of innovation downright scary; some even react as if we are suggesting a revolution without a cause. Another common reaction is that of the CEO or vice president who, while looking completely self-satisfied when we mention innovation, remarks, "We have one of the best R&D divisions of any company in the country. It's their job to come up with new products."

Our response to this statement is that R&D product innovations rarely change the whole culture of a company. Innovation is a three-legged animal that must encompass product, service, *and* process. In terms of product, innovation not only means making something entirely new, but perhaps rethinking how the old works or how it is used. Process innovation leads to improvements in the way the product is produced, and service innovation changes the way the product is integrated into the entire organization.

As we remind our clients, the goal of every organization should be to encourage innovation at all levels and in all functional areas, not just R&D. But in order for everyone in the company to become an innovator, the leadership has to be committed to creating an atmosphere in which people and teams are motivated to achieve team goals while still maintaining respect for one another's personal values.

And what exactly does an innovative environment look like? For one thing, there is no such thing as "crazy." Radical departure from the old ways is often precisely what's needed if you are going to come up with solutions to customer problems. In 1937, Walt Disney sent Jake Day to the woods of Maine to take hundreds of photos and make numerous drawings in preparation for the production of *Bambi,* which would be released in 1942. *Crazy* is probably one of the kindest words that many of Walt's contemporaries in the animated film business used to describe such a radical and innovative approach to capturing the magic of the forest. But Disney let his beliefs guide his actions regardless of what the naysayers thought.

The message is: Go the extra mile yourself and encourage your people to do the same. Let them know that it's okay to take risks, to let their off-the-wall ideas take flight. Above all, encourage everyone to have fun!

In our research into companies that are considered to be particularly innovative, we found that certain core values repeatedly jumped out at us. One of the most common of these was respecting individuality and encouraging individual initiative. From service organizations such as Ernst & Young to manufacturing organizations such as the Whirlpool Corporation, top companies in a variety of industries all make it a point to clearly state their faith in their employees. They encourage everyone to contribute, or as Walt would say, they encourage everyone to dream. And from those vast stores of knowledge and creativity flow the innovative ideas that consistently keep them at the pinnacle of business success.

Other oft-stated core values are honesty, integrity, and an insistence on superior quality. Our featured organizations—Downtown School (Des Moines), Ernst & Young, Four Seasons Hotels & Resorts, Griffin Hospital, John Robert's Spa (Cleveland), Men's Wearhouse, and The Cheesecake Factory—all espouse these upright notions, and all are among the greatest of American business success stories. It's fair to assume that an adherence to these basic beliefs has helped foster an atmosphere in which innovation can flourish.

And so it goes. Service to customers, hard work, continuous self-improvement, responsibility to society: These, too, are values that frequently carry great weight at many of the top companies. But don't mistake this as a laundry list from which you should choose your core values. While any or all of these may be relevant to your personal situation, the point to be made is that successful, innovative companies define what is important to them and then communicate those values to their employees. By encouraging everyone to live those values day to day, a secure, familiar atmosphere arises in which employees at every level feel comfortable breaking down traditional barriers and participating in a worthwhile way.

Innovation in terms of service is much of what defines Disney; indeed, stories of the company's employees going to great lengths to provide extraordinary service are common. One such story concerns a family that visited Walt Disney World and stayed at a Disney hotel. The family included three little girls still young enough to take their teddy bears with them.

At the end of the first day, the family returned to their hotel room. There, seated around the table, were the three bears with cookies and milk placed before them. The little girls were delighted, of course, and the following evening they urged their parents to hurry back to the hotel. This time, the three bears were placed sitting up in bed "reading" Mickey Mouse books. One can imagine the joy this scene evoked in the youngsters. The third evening, the girls found their bears again at the table, but this time they were arranged as though playing cards!

The hotel cast member had truly taken to heart Walt's pronouncement that "visitors are our guests" and had come up with an innovative way to please the children and, by extension, their parents. At some shortsighted companies, management might have objected to spending extra money on cookies and milk. But at Disney, this welcoming gesture was a natural outgrowth of the company's unshakable commitment to customer service.

At Disney, providing innovative service extends into the business process arena as well. Some years ago, as we were walking through one of the parks, we noticed a kiosk for the Disney Vacation Club time-share condominiums. The first surprise came when we approached the kiosk operator; the lack of pressure was the complete opposite of our previous such experience at Lake Tahoe. There, after a high-pressure, two-hour sales pitch at a resort on the top of a mountain, we decided to forget the whole idea.

The Disney approach, we later learned, came about because Michael Eisner firmly vetoed any high-pressure sales tactics when he permitted the selling of time-share condominiums. So at Disney, we were told the purchase price right up front and were asked if we wanted to see the units. When we declined, the Disney cast member gave us what proved to be an informative and fun video that allowed us to tour the units at our leisure when we returned home. After our video tour, we were hooked.

Despite our excitement over buying a Disney product, we still dreaded the thought of closing, particularly a closing conducted by long distance. We both had memories of incomprehensible papers to read and sign, not to mention the mind-numbing and time-wasting interval spent sitting through the formalities. When we spoke to a Vacation Club cast member about our desire to buy and our fear of closing, he assured us that Disney had taken the pain out of the process. What an understatement! Within a few days, we were sent an accordion file with color-coded and tabbed sections, all clearly marked and explained in understandable, nonlegalese. Even the place for signatures was designated by its own color. Plus, there was another video. This one walked us through each step of the closing process. It was so simple, so attractive, and so enjoyable that we were almost tempted to buy a second unit just to repeat the experience!

In coming up with a successful process innovation, Disney basically reinvented the entire sales and closing procedure that has been standard in the real estate industry since time immemorial. The result for us and for every other Disney time-share condo buyer is fabulous service. Our experiences with The Walt Disney Company reinforce the point that innovative companies begin to achieve real success by clearly stating their values and communicating them effectively to their staffs. An inspiring, well-written vision statement is imperative in achieving full employee participation. However, writing such statements is not a simple task. Michael Snyder, former vice president of public relations at Caldwell VanRiper (now MARC USA), relayed to us his experience in this area:

> During Caldwell VanRiper's conversion to client-centered teams, we began the task of preparing a new vision statement of what the agency would reflect in the year 2002. The first two versions I prepared were rejected; they contained the content of an executive retreat we conducted in 1997 but did not reflect the spirit. After the second version was rejected, I had the opportunity to hear your presentation of "Dream, Believe, Dare, Do." Following this, I rewrote the statement as I really believed it ought to be. When the statement was later presented for the discussion, there was total silence. One of the first comments from a CVR executive was, "I want to work for this agency!"

Surging energy, great people, and a near-fanatical obsession with excellence will drive Caldwell VanRiper into national prominence. Top clients and superb talent will choose CVR because of its hot, progressive environment, where people don't care about what you look like or where you come from. At CVR, mediocrity is condemned. Superlative work sets the bar. Caldwell employees will celebrate life, achieving a positive balance between their professional and personal lives, fostered by the environment at CVR.

Client marketing problems are not just resolved at CVR, they are attacked and consumed by staffers, culminating in a reputation that transcends the definition of traditional communications. Experts and editors nationwide will eagerly seek out CVR staffers to tap into its communication mindset, which is akin to a band of well-trained, highly armed guerillas storming a stronghold. Winning awards and achieving 30 percent growth annually are considered by staffers to be a by-product of CVR's savage and unyielding commitment to brilliant solutions.

Aligning the Mission

The Walt Disney Company is part of an industry that draws its strength from artistic talent, an intangible asset. At the same time, however, it must keep an eye on the very tangible bottom line. This is the kind of balancing act that concerns many businesses, not just those involved in providing entertainment. We help our clients to understand that missions clearly aligned with the overall values and beliefs of an organization produce hard-core business success. A visionary spirit can indeed rejuvenate a slumbering company. We have seen it happen often.

On one such occasion, we had the privilege of working with Jake Egan, former manager of the product-testing lab at the Whirlpool Refrigeration Technology Center. Jake was managing two pilot teams, the "testers" and the "technicians," in the organization's new cultural initiative. We asked both teams to individually contemplate their missions and draft statements that embodied their decisions.

The technician team's resulting statement seemed like motherhood and apple pie. Their generic sentences could easily have been pulled from any textbook or corporate mission statement poster. In a group meeting, we weighed the value of the statements against the following criteria: Does the mission address a means as well as an end? In other words, does it address how the mission should be accomplished as well as its desired result? Does it meet stakeholder needs, and is there buy-in from the critical stakeholders? Will the mission be used as the constitution?

In the case of the technicians, the team members were unable to explore the depths of their true purpose and decide what values were important to them. We challenged them to go back and rethink their original draft, which they begrudgingly agreed to do.

After a few weeks, we reconvened. The leader of the technician team stood up and said, "When you asked us to go back and rethink our mission, we thought, "What's the point? It's only a bunch of words.' But then we began discussing our values and listening to everyone's opinions on how we served our business partners."

The result was that when the team seriously answered the mission questions we posed in the earlier meeting, their values became crystallized and were evidenced by the inspired words in their new statement.

The important point to this story is that this team of hourly technicians had the motivation and conviction to reexamine critical aspects of how they do business without any supervision from management. This was a team that had fared poorly on all of the team categories, from goal-setting to conflict, by which they were benchmarked during their initial year of teaming. However, largely as a result of a visionary mission statement clearly aligned with company values, they made incredible advances within the next two years, perhaps more than any other team in the entire organization, while at the same time increasing the productivity of the entire department.

That's not to say that aligning team missions with the organizational vision is an easy task. It isn't. But with a little effort, you can come up with a system that allows you to integrate short-term activities with your longer-term vision. In tackling what we refer to as Vision Align, you will realize a number of benefits, such as:

- Creating an established process for executing strategy
- Increasing departmental cooperation
- Giving your leadership a mechanism by which to understand key problem areas
- Enabling quicker, more accurate feedback

The concept of Vision Align involves setting up a structure that will allow your organization's overall objectives to cascade down through the various staff levels to the natural work group. We worked with a manufacturing team that used Vision Align to illustrate the process. (Figure 3-1 illustrates the Vision Align process for a client manufacturing team.)

Legend:
- ✓ Obvious Fit
- ? Potential Fit
- ! Area of Concern

Vision/Mission Key Points	Core Strengths				Values					Objectives				Stakeholders				
	Customer focus lab	Global engineering expertise	Rigorous design methodology	Name recognition	Teamwork	Innovation	Continuous learning	Customer focus	Respect	10x quality improvement	2% net material cost reduction	10% increase in team self-observation scores	Foster coworker development planning	End-product consumer	Internal process partners	Coworkers	Community	Company
Better quality	✓	✓	✓		✓	✓	?	✓		✓	!	?		✓		?	?	✓
Faster cycle times			✓		✓	✓	!			?	!	✓	!	?				✓
Lower costs	?	?	?		?	✓		!		✓	✓		!	✓				✓
Preferred consumer product	✓		✓	✓	✓			✓			!			✓		?		✓
Fun place to work						✓	?	✓					✓		✓	✓		?

Figure 3-1. Vision Align process for a client manufacturing process.

The organization's core strengths, values, objectives, and stakeholders are recorded on one axis. This represents a set of criteria by which the organization is measured. On the other axis, the key points of the mission or vision are recorded. The use of check marks (✓), question marks (?), and exclamation points (!) designates how well the mission or vision is aligned with the measurement criteria. In this example, the preferred consumer product vision is not supported by any of the objectives. One objective, the 2 percent net material cost reduction, could even be in conflict with the mission if the cost reductions compromise customer needs. The general manager of this organization said, "The value of Vision Align is not in the final output document; it is in the process that my staff and I went through to develop the document."

No company outdoes Disney in concern for its guests. But even Disney has occasionally made mistakes by failing to align short-term missions with overall beliefs and values. In the end, the company had to change its approach.

When its Pleasure Island attraction at Walt Disney World opened with a jazz club, restaurants, and nightclubs, it was intended as a place for guests to go after other attractions had closed. The entertainment was still geared for the family, though, and even the nightclub atmosphere was relatively sedate. But in a reversal of Disney's usual policy, Pleasure Island was not gated; anyone could just walk right in. Problems arose almost immediately at this new entertainment complex. In the words of the company, "The fact that it was an 'ungated' attraction led to a number of security and guest-service issues."

Some guests were disturbed by the entertainment offered at the nightclubs, the company discovered, claiming it was too close to adult entertainment and not appropriate for their teenage children. It didn't take long for Disney to respond to the complaints. Within a year, new leadership entered the scene and used a similar matrix (see Figure 3-2) to highlight where the misalignment to the Disney measurement criteria had taken place. Once the misalignment was identified, a new vision of Pleasure Island was created to conform to the overall measurement criteria of the Disney theme park. The attraction was gated to control the entrances and promote safety; the entrance policy was changed to bar teenagers, with or without parents; nightclub entertainment was aimed at audiences between the ages of 22 and 45.

In this case, The Walt Disney Company briefly lost sight of the vision that had guided it for so many years, but in typical Disney fashion, it wasn't long before the mistake was rectified. Management's swift reaction saved the attraction from failure and turned it into a success.

You may not share all of Walt Disney's beliefs. He insisted, for example, that every production celebrate, nurture, and promote "wholesome American values." Cynicism was verboten at all levels. He could not and would not countenance a cynical attitude in his films, among his employees, or even from potential partner companies. Whatever your particular beliefs and values are, however, they should serve as a filter through which all decisions pass in order to test their validity and worthiness. The German writer Goethe observed that "when values are clear, laws are unnecessary. When values are not clear, laws are unenforceable."

Nor do we expect that most organizations will want to establish their own universities to train employees. Nevertheless, they can devise a process that will effectively communicate beliefs and values to employees, partners,

Original Vision

Legend:
- ✓ Obvious Fit
- ? Potential Fit
- ! Area of Concern

Vision/Mission Key Points	Core Strengths				Values					Objectives				Stakeholders				
	Live entertainment	Variety of entertainment	Themed experience	Guest service	Risk-taking	Diversity	Originality	Creative imagination	Finest family entertainment	20% annual earnings/20% ROE	World's premiere entertainment company	Protect Disney name & franchise	Foster quality, imagination, & guest service	Family guest	Adult guests	Cast	Community	Company
Entertainment for families	✓ / !		✓	✓					✓ / !	?	✓ / !	✓	✓ / !	✓ / !	✓			
Provide experiences to keep guest on property	✓	✓		✓				✓	✓ / ?	?	✓	✓	✓	✓	✓	✓		✓
Provide nightclub atmosphere in the "Disney" way	✓	✓	✓	✓	✓	✓	✓	✓ / !	✓ / !		✓	✓ / !	✓	✓	✓		✓	
Non-gated to invite people to walk in		✓	✓ / !	✓ / !	✓ / !			? / !				!	✓		✓	!	? / !	✓ / !

New Vision

Vision/Mission Key Points	Live entertainment	Variety of entertainment	Themed experience	Guest service	Risk-taking	Diversity	Originality	Creative imagination	Finest family entertainment	20% annual earnings/20% ROE	World's premiere entertainment company	Protect Disney name & franchise	Foster quality, imagination, & guest service	Family guest	Adult guests	Cast	Community	Company
A party for adults	✓	✓	✓	✓	✓	✓	✓	✓	!	?	✓	!	✓	?	✓	?	?	?
Provide experiences to keep guest on property	✓	✓		✓				✓	?	?	✓	✓	✓	?	✓	✓		✓
Provide nightclub atmosphere for the 22- to 45-year-olds	?		?	✓	✓	!			!	?		?	✓		✓			
Gated to promote safety and entrance controls				✓											✓	✓	✓	✓

Figure 3-2. Vision Align process for realignment of Pleasure Island to the Disney criteria.

Source: Disney University

and customers. In short, we are not suggesting that you embrace Disney's beliefs, values, and actions wholesale.

What we are urging is that you consider Disney's four principles—Dream, Believe, Dare, Do—and come to understand how devotion to your *own* core ideology can strengthen your organization. Having done that, you will be ready to enjoy the power that flows when everyone is engaged in living the same set of values and beliefs.

In the next two chapters, you will see how Disney extended the Believe principle to encompass both customers and suppliers.

Questions to Ask

- What are the values your company lives by?
- Who established those values?
  Customers?
  Employees?
  Managers?
  Directors?
  Stockholders?
  Founders?
- Are your personal values in conflict with those of the organization?
- What products and services does the organization provide?
- What methods does the organization apply to provide these products and services?
- For whom does the organization provide the products and services?
- Why does the organization exist?
- Are the actions and behaviors of your leaders consistent with the company's values?
- What mechanisms do you use to communicate your values to new employees?
- Does every department/team have a mission?
- Does the mission statement take advantage of the organization's core strengths?
- Does the mission create value for these stakeholders?
- Is each mission aligned with the overall company vision, values, and objectives?
- Do all departmental or work group goals, objectives, and tactics support the organization's vision and values?

- Do you refer to your mission when making decisions about products, services, customers, or coworkers?
- Do you share the mission statement with potential new hires?
- Can everyone, including the company janitor, articulate the organization's mission and values?
- What do your product development policies say about your values?
- Are all employees encouraged to be innovative in product, process, and service?
- Do your recent business decisions confirm your company's values?

Actions to Take

- Formalize your mission and values in a written statement to be used as the constitution.
- Encourage each department to prepare a Vision Align exercise that aligns their mission with the organization's vision, values, core strengths, objectives, and stakeholder needs.
- Communicate all missions throughout the organization.
- Exhibit commitment to the organization's values through everyday actions.
- Evaluate all business decisions in light of the values.
- Conduct regular companywide meetings to reinforce the organizational vision and values.
- Hold a semiannual crazy-invention contest where *everyone* can submit off-the-wall product and service ideas. Reward winners and prototype their ideas.

A Shared Vision

It isn't enough to corral a bunch of people and then expect them to function like a team. It needs much more than that. Every member's personal view of the project must be linked to the team's ultimate purpose so that a shared vision propels everyone's commitment.

"The way I saw my role," Whirlpool team leader Jerry McColgin remembers, "was one of bringing this group together, of making sure I was utilizing the talent that was there. I had an incredibly high level of competency within this group and my task was to harness this competency and to guide and direct the team."

One of the first steps Jerry undertook was to determine the personal values, the expectations, and the dreams of his group. As we facilitated this discussion during the team's Dream Retreat, spotting the similarities and striving to reinforce them was extremely rewarding. Jerry wanted to understand how the members saw the long-term value of their work and how strongly they believed in what they were doing. He attempted to paint a picture of what the team's work would involve. He pointed out that most major projects like theirs were given three to four years to bring to completion. Management expected the team to finish in a little over two years. In addition, the budget had been cut by a third.

McColgin, in consultation with us, decided that the best start would be to take the team off-site for a five-day retreat, a kick-off session. There, removed from outside distractions, this disparate group of people could begin to develop a true team spirit. We had created other teams for the company, but they were more traditional groups. As Jerry likes to say, he had "a whacko group of people from around the world who clearly weren't going to fit into a conventional business mold." Then, too, he had specific ends in mind: He wanted to establish a culture; he wanted the team to understand what his expectations were; and, most of all, he was determined to create a 100 percent commitment from each team member.

Our Featured Organization: Four Seasons Hotels & Resorts

THE GOLDEN RULE IS ALIVE AND WELL

Walt Disney set the standard for animation and theme parks as we know them today. Isadore Sharp, chairman, CEO, and founder of Four Seasons Hotels & Resorts, has set the standard for luxury hotels. Both The Walt Disney Company and Four Seasons have become legendary for offering experiences of exceptional quality. And, like Walt Disney before him, Isadore (known to his loyal staff as "Issy") has built his Canadian-based company on the premise that mediocrity is not an option.

In the mind of Isadore Sharp, being innovative and delivering an unsurpassable level of service are the only options. After a decade of building hotels in the 1960s, Isadore came to understand that what business travelers want

(Continued)

most is personalized, round-the clock service. He was determined to grow his business through delivering fabulous personalized service and distinguishing Four Seasons from the competition. But how does one go about becoming the best service provider in the hotel industry? Rather than just talk about giving good service, would it be possible to differentiate ourselves from the competition by simply treating the customer as a true guest? Could service really be a competitive advantage? Could a workforce become so dedicated and loyal that they would become our greatest asset? Could we create a culture and work environment that would allow our people to develop to their maximum potential?

These were some of the questions Isadore mulled over in the late 1970s before his company became the international icon it is today. He set out by testing the strategy of having a dedicated workforce live by The Golden Rule of "treating others as we would wish to be treated." Ever the consummate, unassuming gentleman, Isadore told us, "There was no list of rules. It was just that we trust you to use your common sense, and we trust you in terms of how you do your job. I think that if people know you are trusting them, they will rise to levels beyond their own expectations of themselves."[16]

The night before our first meeting with Isadore in 2001, we arrived at the flagship location, Four Seasons Toronto, and asked a bellman what was so special about the Four Seasons. To the best of our knowledge, this 22-year veteran employee had no idea who we were, and without hesitation, he recited the company's heartfelt credo, The Golden Rule. The next day when we shared with Isadore the story of the bellman encounter, he was not the least bit surprised. We think he would have been very surprised had the bellman failed to recite The Golden Rule.

Selling The Golden Rule as an acceptable and appropriate business strategy to his senior management team was no easy feat for Isadore. When he made the presentation at a formal board meeting, they nearly laughed him out of the room. They asked, "Are you joking? This is like motherhood and apple pie, and you're going to put this out as a business strategy?" Isadore replied, "Maybe you're right, but you know what? We are going to do it." Before he announced The Golden Rule mandate, Isadore had discussed the idea with his team members and listened to their reactions. What he discovered was that they believed in The Golden Rule but didn't feel particularly comfortable talking about it openly. Isadore encouraged and challenged each and every one of them to consider what

The Golden Rule meant to them personally. After much contemplation, all but one team member was ready to move forward and adopt the strategy. "We had to ask the most senior person in the company to leave," confessed Isadore, "because if you don't have the senior people prepared to abide by it, you can't expect the people below them to abide by it . . . because then they won't be supported."

Many companies today complain that they can't get good people, or that no one is willing to work for low wages, or that the wage pool is undereducated. To those arguments, Isadore retorts "Nonsense." He believes that there isn't a country, a city, or a village anywhere in the world where you couldn't bring together a group of people, give them an opportunity to do their best in a work environment that supports them, and fail to achieve a five-star level of service.

A great example of this truth is Four Seasons Istanbul. Isadore recounts the following story, "In Istanbul, our partners there are Turkish. A few years after the hotel was opened, I was having dinner with the owner and his wife and she said, 'Where did you get these people from?' I said, 'What do you mean?' She replied, 'Where did you hire them from?' I said, 'We brought a few in from other properties around the world, but 99 percent are Turkish people.' She said, 'No, no they are not Turkish people.' I said, 'They are Turkish people, all living in Turkey.' She said, 'I have Turkish people working for me and these are not Turkish people.' I realized that something was being lost in the translation. The general manager, Marcus, was there, and I said, 'Marcus, will you please explain in your native language?' He said, 'These are local people who we've hired and trained.' She said, 'But they are *so* different.' I said, 'They're not different. All we are doing is giving them a chance to be themselves.' This happens over and over again at many of our properties. That's why Disney was successful. He understood the importance of believing in people."

Most employees do not set out to fail. They fail because management does not train them, nurture them, and support them. Management is typically to blame for the failure of employees. When you have people with the same vision working for a cause they believe in and can be proud of and, if and only if, they are given the freedom to perform, the results are always amazing. People simply cannot flourish under paranoid power-hungry leaders who watch their comings and goings like a perched hawk. At Four Seasons, all employees are treated according to Golden Rule tradition.

(Continued)

Living your values can be the difference between providing mediocre service and creating legendary, memorable guest experiences. In Isadore's profound words, "You can write your values on paper, but they are only words . . . the words have significance only if behaved. Behaviors have significance only if believed."

Chapter 4

Never a Customer, Always a Guest

You don't build the product for yourself.
You need to know what the people want and build it for them.
Walt Disney

In an age when consumers all across the country bemoan the state of customer service, The Walt Disney Company is repeatedly hailed as a superior service provider, perhaps the best in the world. On the day Disneyland opened, Walt himself announced the theme park's motto: "At Disneyland, the visitors are our guests." Since then, the bar has continually been raised to new heights in the company's desire to delight its guests.

That visitors should be treated as guests is also a theme that emerges in nearly every movie Walt Disney made. The dwarfs welcome Snow White into their cottage; forest animals care for Bambi after his mother dies; the Banks family invite Mary Poppins into their home; and, of course, "Be Our Guest" is the title of one of the best-known songs from the 1991 film *Beauty and the Beast*. The guest motif is present in every corner of Disney, from the Magic Kingdom to Animal Kingdom.

Walt Disney knew instinctively what his visitors wanted. He didn't need to do expensive research into customer tastes because, as he once put it, his audience was "made up of my neighbors, people I know and meet everyday: folks I trade with, go to church with, vote with, compete in business with, help build and preserve a nation with."[17] Disney's understanding of his customer base coupled with his innate drive for perfection meant that audiences got more than they ever knew they wanted, whether in watching his films or visiting his theme park.

Know your guests, treat them honestly and with respect, and they will keep coming; that pretty well sums up what Walt Disney believed. The crowds that throng the Disney parks today, both here and abroad, testify to the enduring soundness of his belief. During the first week of November 1996, 793,000 people visited Disney's theme parks in the United States alone—and this in a week that didn't even include a school holiday.

Most of the companies we work with and others we have studied have wholeheartedly adopted Walt Disney's belief that customers should be treated as honored guests. Many of these companies are not in the service business per se; they have simply made it their business to provide excellent service. As you read their stories, you will see how an obsession with customers begets the kind of innovation that ultimately spells success.

How Important Are Your Customers—Really?

You're probably wondering which companies don't try to please their customers. In reality, plenty. All too many companies seem to consider customers as nothing more than a necessary nuisance. Oh, they may say otherwise, but they don't deliver. If the road to hell is paved with good intentions, then the road to business failure is littered with placards proclaiming "The customer is always right."

A cavalier attitude toward customers is shortsighted in the extreme. The hard truth is that it costs five times more to attract a new customer than it does to keep an old one. According to Frederick F. Reichheld, director emeritus of Bain & Company and author of *Loyalty Rules! How Leaders Build Lasting Relationships*, a 5 percent increase in customer retention results in a 25 to 95 percent increase in profits.

So if the payoffs are so great, why do companies fail when it comes to dealing with customers? The answer is *lack of leadership*. Without question, the CEO is the primary role model for every company value, and service is no exception. In an example of a leader who just didn't understand his responsibility, the CEO of a well-known rental car company was quoted as saying, "There's nothing more irritating than having the person next to you on a plane say, 'And what do you do for a living?' I used to be polite and tell them about my company, only to have my ear bent about the story of the dirty car in Chicago. Now when people tell me that story, I empathize with them and say, 'I know it's a lousy company. That's why I'm quitting.'"

Shocking, isn't it? Whatever happened to the customer focus of this CEO? Maybe he never had it.

Nearly two decades ago, Tom Peters told it like it is in his revolutionary book *Thriving on Chaos:*

> Each of us carries around a crippling disadvantage: we know and probably cherish our product. After all, we live with it day in and day out. But that blinds us to why the customer may hate it—or love it. Our customers see the product through an entirely different set of lenses. Education is not the answer; listening and adapting is.

The accuracy of Peters' words is borne out by an example with which we are particularly familiar. Bill's uncle, the owner of a newspaper distributorship in Chicago, had only an eighth-grade education and knew nothing about return on investment, asset turnover, or market segmentation analysis. He built his business on the simple premise that his customers paid him to deliver the paper at a reasonable time in readable condition. The customers' happiness was his primary concern. For three decades, Uncle Shorty never forgot the customer's perspective, even if that meant leaving the dinner table to attend to a complaint, which he did on many nights.

After 30 successful years as owner/operator, he sold the distributorship to people who went out of business within 10 years. How could the new owners go under when they had been handed a thriving business of long standing? It's very simple: They did not attend to customer needs and solve customer problems. They made the mistake of operating the business like the monopoly it was, neglecting their home-delivery customers and allowing service to the local retail stores to deteriorate.

The retailers' anger over shoddy service was compounded by the fact that they had no other choice but to buy from this distributor. Eventually, the growing number of complaints made directly to the Chicago newspaper publishers caused the distributor to lose its franchise.

All too many owners and CEOs are like the rental car executive or the newspaper distributor. They feel it is beneath them to concern themselves with dirty-car stories, or late deliveries from their docks, or doing whatever it takes to make a customer happy.

Although a "customer first" policy usually makes its way into most of the mission statements we've read, far too few companies really live those words.

One of our clients, Illinois Power (currently doing business as Ameren Corporation) is an exception, however.

In 1991, this company won the U.S. electric utility industry's top honor, The Edison Award, awarded by the Edison Electric Institute (EEI). In 2002, they won the Edison Electric Institute's Emergency Assistance Award for providing critical assistance to neighboring companies struggling to recover from numerous tornadoes and a devastating ice storm. Their efforts to better the company's relationship with customers and improve service through employee teamwork and empowerment have paid off. Illinois Power president and CEO Larry F. Altenbaumer commented, "This award acknowledges their [employees] skill, professionalism, and willingness to work under tough conditions. This is the same dedication and commitment our employees bring to providing safe, reliable service to our own customers every day."

What really illustrated Illinois Power's commitment to its customer-first policy was the creation of a 24-hour customer center. Remember those Denny's commercials filling our living rooms with that serious voice echoing, "If a restaurant really loved you, it would never close." A service organization is a different animal, though. Being there for customers 24 hours a day proves to us that Illinois Power's commitment to customers is more than just a line on the company mission statement.

Test the Welcome Mat

An innovative way to discover if you are doing a good job of pleasing your customers is to turn your employees into guests. New employees of Four Seasons Hotels are required to spend a weekend at a Four Seasons property to experience five-star service firsthand. John Young, retired executive vice president of human resources told us:

> Orientation is probably the biggest single training program which contains the necessary messages about our culture. It is spread over the first three months of employment. There are seven stages of orientation and the culminating event is the trial stay. Each new employee has the opportunity to stay at one of our hotels as though they were a guest—everyone from the dishwasher on up through the organization. We just believe that's so very important because many of our people have not had the opportunity to stay in a five-star hotel, and they just can't afford to stay at our properties. After

orientation, they have complementary group privileges, so they get the opportunity to stay at any of our properties around the world. In the trial stay, they complete a rather extensive guest service questionnaire that cites our standards. Then they rate how their experience compared to those standards.[18]

And you can be certain that Four Seasons would do anything in its power to solve a problem that an employee encountered just as they would for a noncompany guest.

One of the best ways to know for sure if customers really count is to evaluate how an organization deals with guest problems and complaints. At one of our Dream Retreats, we learned from a participant whose daughter manages a Limited, Inc. store location in Arizona that the company will dismiss a store manager who receives three unresolved customer complaints.

At first, we were somewhat taken aback by the severity of this practice, but after a little research into the effects of customer complaints on the bottom line, we realized that the policy makes very good sense. The Technical Assistance Research Programs Corporation of Washington, D.C., which publishes statistics on customer complaints, has found that for every customer complaint that an organization receives, there are 26 other dissatisfied customers who will remain silent. Each of the 27 dissatisfied customers will tell 8 to 16 others about the experience, and 10 percent will tell more than 20 other potential customers. If you do the arithmetic, you will find that three complaints translate into more than 1,000 potential customers hearing about the poor service a company provided. No company can afford to drag its feet when handling customer complaints.

The results of a recent customer service study conducted by Coldwell Banker indicated "a strong correlation between the quality of a company's customer service and its long-term success." The findings also revealed that a typical consumer switched businesses they dealt with twice in the past three years because of "bad service." When asked to define the differences between great and poor service, consumers ranked the top characteristics of companies with "great service" as follows:

- Resolving questions and problems (66 percent)
- Knowledge of the product or service (49 percent)
- Being easy to reach (35 percent)
- Understanding requirements (35 percent)

We have been wowed many times by Disney's exceptional attention to guest problems and complaints. One example occurred when we were visiting Walt Disney World with a group of clients. After we had all checked into the hotel, we quickly departed for dinner. As we were riding along in one of the in-park buses that shuttle visitors around Walt Disney World, the driver asked us how our rooms were. One of our clients mentioned that the faucet in his bar sink had an annoying drip, and he added that he hadn't had time yet to report it to maintenance.

"Sir, I'll take care of it for you," the driver assured him.

We didn't give it another thought, but when we got back from dinner about 10 o'clock, the faucet was fixed. And then, more impressive yet, shortly thereafter the driver showed up on his own time to make sure that the problem had been taken care of. This is the level of service you should aim for when you ask your employees to treat every customer like a guest in their own homes. The bus driver was truly committed to making the guest experience the best it could possibly be. That is service with a capital "S."

John Dunn is chairman and CEO of Dunn Hospitality Group (DHG), a privately held company that owns and manages 19 Midwest hotel properties, mainly Marriott and Holiday Inn brands. In our work with John, we were impressed by the cordial and most welcoming environment of his properties. No pretense, no stuffiness, but simply a commitment to offering guests comfortable accommodations at affordable prices with a dedicated staff to service their needs. In each hotel room, hangs a framed copy of a so-called ancient prayer for "The Stranger within Our Gates" It reads:

> Because this hotel is a human institution to serve people, and not solely a for-profit organization, we strive to ensure you will experience peace and rest while you are here.
>
> May this room and this hotel be your "second" home. May those you love be near you in thoughts and dreams. Even though we may not get to know you, we hope that you will be comfortable and happy as if you were in your own house.
>
> May the business that brought you our way prosper. May every call you make and every message you receive add to your joy. When you leave, may your journey be safe.
>
> We are all travelers. From "birth till death" we travel between the eternities. May these days be pleasant for you, profitable for society, helpful for those you meet, and a joy to those who know and love you best.

"This piece constantly disappears," says John. "We have hundreds of customer comments on how meaningful this saying was to them. Most of our franchisors do not allow foreign objects in hotel rooms, but we continue to leave it there and accept those 'digs,' if you will, because it's an integral part of who we are."[19]

"The Stranger within our Gates" inspired John to bring his team together to create a Mission Statement and Codes of Conduct. Nearly every DHG management meeting begins with a ritual recitation of both the Mission Statement and Codes of Conduct. DHG Associates who carry the company card inscribed with both creeds are awarded $5. For reciting both the Mission Statement and Codes of Contact, an additional $20 is awarded. "It's not about the money," John admits, "it's about the importance of using the Mission Statement and Codes of Conduct in our daily lives at Dunn Hospitality. Getting everyone on the same page is difficult, but the Dream and Believe principles help us achieve this."

Like Disney, Dunn Hospitality Group has a great reputation for handling complaints. Each DHG employee has very specific responsibilities, but a complaint from a guest is owned by the employee who receives it, no matter whose area of responsibility the complaint involves. If you've ever complained to a front-desk employee about the absence of coffee at your morning seminar or a lack of toilet tissue in your room, the response at most hotels was probably something like "You should talk to the banquet manager" or "Housekeeping takes care of that."

At a Dunn hotel, however, any complaint is solved directly by the person receiving your complaint, from the front-desk manager to a bellhop or a housekeeper. You can count on it.

The Dunn Hospitality Codes of Conduct

We Work while Others Enjoy Their Stay
- We are open 365 days a year in all kinds of weather; convenience for our guests is our aim.
- We are here to make things easier for our guests.

We Create a Friendly Atmosphere
- Two musts: Practice a friendly smile; use courteous phrases.
- Maintain a neat, professional appearance.
- Never complain or comment on operating or personal problems.

(Continued)

We Give the Personal Touch
- Treat each guest as a special individual.
- One personal experience, good or bad, can make the greatest impression.
- Use the guest's name whenever possible.

We Know the Answers
- Any question, find the answer.
- Do not send guests in circles.
- Eliminate call transfers when possible.

We Know Our Roles
- All associates understand and strive to achieve their natural work group goals.
- Maintain uncompromising levels of cleanliness of our facilities.
- Record each incident of guest dissatisfaction.
- Every associate is empowered to resolve a problem of guest dissatisfaction and prevent a repeat occurrence.

We Make Our Facilities Clean and Safe
- Provide a safe environment for guests and associates.
- Notify the appropriate supervisor immediately of hazardous situations or injuries.
- Protect our assets. This is the responsibility of all associates.

We Are a Team
- We believe that our atmosphere needs to be friendly and informal.
- We take our jobs seriously, not ourselves. We create fun in our roles, which creates fun for our guests.
- We communicate openly; we do not promote barriers between people.

No examination of extraordinary attention to customer complaints would be complete without a story about Nordstrom, the Seattle-based department store chain that wrote the book on making customers happy. As the following anecdote illustrates, the slightest dissatisfaction is taken quite seriously.

Bruce Nordstrom, cochairman, was leaving one of the stores on his way to a meeting when he overheard a woman say to her companion, "I've never been so disappointed in all my life." Nordstrom beckoned to a sales associate and asked her to find out why the woman was disappointed. The sales associate followed the two women out to the street and politely asked what had happened to them in the store.

The ladies laughingly explained, "It's not the store. The problem is that we have champagne taste on a beer budget. We fell in love with a dress and it's way too expensive for us."

Now, at virtually every other department store in the world, we would bet that the sales associate would have made a mildly sympathetic comment and wished the ladies a good day. But not at Nordstrom. This associate escorted the two back into the store to a department where they each bought two dresses that cost less than the original find.

Equally important was what happened when Bruce Nordstrom returned from his meeting: He made a point of finding the sales associate to ask about the two customers. By indicating his interest in the outcome, the top man sent the employee a strong signal that service is of paramount importance to the Nordstrom's of Seattle. In the words of Bill Gates, chairman and chief software architect of Microsoft Corporation, "Your most unhappy customers are your greatest source of learning."

Solving Customer Problems Sparks Innovation

A few years ago, Ken Thompson, chairman, president, and CEO of Wachovia Corporation, said in his introductory remarks for Bill Capodagli's keynote address to Ken's staff, "We must rededicate ourselves to solving customer problems. That means we must do what our customers ask of us unless it is illegal, immoral, or unethical. Just do it. Execution is the key."

Customer service is more than just taking care of customer-expressed needs and demands. Companies must also investigate and solve customer problems in the areas of product, process, and service. Before that can happen, however, an organization's leadership has to create an environment that encourages everyone to listen to customer problems and try to accomplish the impossible. It takes effort to do this well.

As we outlined for you in Chapter 3, Four Seasons Hotels & Resorts is one company that does this extremely well. Known throughout the world as a luxury hotel chain, Four Seasons is very sensitive to the needs and problems of its guests, as an incident at Four Seasons Hotel New York amply illustrates.

Just as a guest was being whisked away in a cab, the doorman noticed that the man's briefcase was lying by the curb. Checking inside the briefcase, the doorman located the phone number of the man's firm. He called the guest's secretary and told her what had happened.

"He's on his way to a very urgent meeting in Boston," she said, "and I'm sure he needs the papers in his briefcase."

Without hesitation, the doorman asked for the guest's flight number and volunteered to take the briefcase to him at the airport before he departed. With a substitute on duty, the doorman jumped into a cab and raced to the airport, but he was delayed in traffic and arrived too late.

The doorman again called the secretary, who thanked him for his efforts while expressing regret over the whole situation. But the doorman told her not to worry because he had just purchased a ticket on the next shuttle to Boston and would personally deliver the briefcase to the man at this meeting. Without asking anyone's approval, the doorman flew to Boston and saved the day!

In most companies, one of two scenarios would happen next. Either the doorman would be a hero for solving the guest's problem, or he would be fired for failing to gain the appropriate approvals before flying off to Boston. At the Four Seasons, he was neither a hero nor a scapegoat, because extraordinary service is all in a day's work. Every Four Seasons employee is expected to do whatever it takes to ensure that each guest has a positive and memorable experience. The environment demands it.

Problem solving is so ingrained, in fact, that Four Seasons employees have been known to jump into action long before an individual has become a guest, as we discovered when working with the CEO of a large consulting firm in Chicago.

In preparation for a major retreat where partners from around the world would be in attendance, we suggested using a hotel at the airport to conserve expenses. But the CEO insisted on using the Four Seasons, and he explained his preference by relating an extraordinary tale about the hotel's downtown location.

It seems that the CEO was a board member at a Chicago museum that enlisted Nancy Reagan as the featured speaker at its fund-raising event. The CEO was expected to join other board members in the receiving line to greet the then First Lady. Arriving at the Four Seasons after a hectic day at the office, he noticed that people entering the grand ballroom were in formal attire. Not having checked his invitation for several weeks, he had forgotten that this was a black-tie event.

There he was in his business suit with no time to go home and change. As he stood in the lobby contemplating what he should do, the concierge, seeing the look of consternation on his face, approached him and asked, "Is there anything I can do for you, sir?" After the CEO explained his dilemma, the concierge volunteered, "One of the waiters is off today, and I know he would not mind if you wore his tuxedo."

When the two men went to the locker room, they found a clean shirt but the tuxedo had been taken to the cleaners. The CEO thanked the concierge for his trouble, but the concierge refused to give up. "You can wear my tuxedo!" he offered as he began to disrobe.

Not deterred by the fact that he was two sizes larger than the CEO, the concierge attempted to staple the arms and legs to make them look presentable. And when that didn't work, the concierge called the hotel tailor who came immediately and fixed the tuxedo on the spot.

The CEO took his place in the receiving line and no one was the wiser!

To top the whole thing off, when he returned from the event, he found that his business suit had been pressed and hung neatly on a hanger. The CEO, wishing to express his gratitude, began pulling out all the cash in his pocket plus his checkbook. But the concierge refused to accept any payment, insisting that he had only been doing his job, which was to serve the guests and solve their problems.

"But I'm not even a guest," the CEO said. "I just walked in off the street." To which the concierge replied, "Well, maybe someday you will be."

The CEO was sold on Four Seasons, of course, and decided that the honored guest at the first dinner of the retreat would be that concierge. The CEO presented him with a brass clock, which he graciously accepted while reiterating, "I was only doing my job."

Another well-known name in the hospitality business with an equally well-known reputation for providing stellar service is Marriott International. In our work with one of the Marriott hotels, we got an immediate sense of the company's motto: "Go beyond." Go beyond what your customers expect and surprise them with your ability to solve their problems. An incident at one of the company's smaller hotels outside Seattle illustrates how this value is lived every day at Marriott.

A guest checked into the hotel and began to prepare for the first big speech of her career. When she unpacked her laptop computer to retrieve her speech, she realized that she had forgotten to bring the computer cord and the battery. The hotel management quickly located compatible replacements, but this guest's problems were just beginning.

As she booted up the machine, her hard drive crashed. Any computer user can imagine her panic. But once again, the hotel came to her rescue by allowing her to use a desk and a computer in the hotel's accounting office.

Staff members coached her on using the unfamiliar machine and then enlisted other employees to listen to the guest rehearse her speech. In a final gesture of superior service, they all showed up for the big event, where she was enthusiastically received by her audience.

Innovative problem solving has given rise to centuries' worth of inventions and products, most of which we take for granted and many of which we would be hard-pressed to do without. Consider the ubiquitous Post-it notes, those sticky little squares of paper that decorate every imaginable surface in homes and offices across the land.

No wild-eyed inventor came up with the notion in a dingy little basement workshop. Rather, the product came about as the result of a problem that a 3M employee recognized and solved.

This particular employee, who happened to be a member of his church choir, was annoyed that he often lost his place in the hymnal. One day at work, a solution dawned on him. He experimented with some glue that had been shelved because of its inferior bonding qualities. Not strong enough to serve its intended purpose, it turned out to be just right for holding little yellow squares in place on a hymnal page.

What began as the solution to an individual problem turned into a wildly successful and profitable product line.

Customer problems are sometimes difficult to discern because they surface only under certain conditions or situations. Nevertheless, problems are certainly there for the finding. And while your customers' problems may not open the door to a Post-it note gold mine, they can offer you the chance to provide the kind of customer service that will set your organization apart from the crowd.

Superior Process Equals Superior Service

We continually stress that innovation is needed in every process, not just in products and services. Nowhere is the acceptance of that idea more urgent than at the many companies that deal directly with the consumer market. How many of them have an adequate—not extraordinary, mind you, just adequate—process in place for providing customer service? Few, indeed, if we are to judge by the inordinate amounts of time that most of us waste on the phone waiting for a human voice to respond to a need, or, for that matter, to rescue us from the annoying music we are forced to listen to.

In an effort to help the Mead Johnson Nutritional division of Bristol-Myers Squibb improve its customer service, we facilitated a complaint analysis team.

The team was given responsibility for reengineering the customer service process, specifically for figuring out how to cut the time that callers were kept on hold. At Mead Johnson, mothers might call in because their children are sick and they have questions about the baby formula they are using. No mother with a sick child has the time or the patience to hang on the phone; she needs and often demands immediate assistance.

A surprising statistic that surfaced from the team's work was that a majority of the calls came during the lunch hour. It was obvious that employee lunch hours needed to be staggered, with some taking an earlier lunch, others going later. This simple solution considerably cut the time callers had to spend on hold.

Clearly, innovation in process is alive and well in some organizations. As Dr. William Cross, retired vice president at Mead Johnson, says,

> We have tried very hard to find out how we are meeting our customers' needs and where we need to improve. Putting all the emphasis on the customer's needs and continually improving how we meet those needs—that's how we have been able to eliminate waste from our systems.

Another of our clients, a builder of prefab houses, has found an unusual way to bring his customers into the process. From the initial step of signing the agreement and on through the entire construction process, photographs are taken to record events. Furthermore, a photograph of the family is attached to the work order. As construction proceeds, from digging the foundation to hanging the front door, the camera is present to shoot pictures for and with the family. Besides making the home seem real to the buyers, it also helps to personalize the project for the workers. They are not just building Work Order No. 48, they are building a home for a family they have come to know. Such face-to-face interaction motivates the workers to do a good job and to take pride in their efforts.

In our experience, large manufacturing companies often rank customer problem solving far down on their list of priorities. Senior management, in many instances, believes that middle managers should devote all their energies to strategy, systems, and training issues. Most plant managers seem to be trapped in a world of direct supervision and paperwork.

Besides allotting scant time to customer interaction, plant managers also have little time for determining misalignments between short-term objectives and long-term vision and mission. The Vision Align tool in Chapter 3 provides a method of incorporating the "voice" of the customer into the manufacturing process. We urge plant managers to spend at least 30 percent of their time on customer needs and problem solving.

However, before a company can hope to excel with an innovative product, service, or process, it must know its market. Perhaps most disturbing to us is that the majority of organizations know neither what customers want nor what their problems are. To demonstrate this point, we have asked workshop participants to list the most important features or services needed at a retreat or seminar. Top answers consistently include unlimited coffee and easy access to restrooms. When we ask hotel managers what things most attract business customers to their hotels, they usually say, "Our great food, ample parking, and atmosphere." What's more, this phenomenon is not unique to the hotel industry. From computers to automobiles to restaurants, we have found the same story. Companies all too often simply do not know or understand their customers.

Even Disney has made mistakes when entering new markets. EuroDisney, the 4,800-acre theme park built outside Paris, got a lot of press when it stumbled badly after its 1992 opening. Disney erred by opening a park suitable for an American audience in a country whose culture differed from ours in many respects. For example, originally, no wine was served in the park. No wine? In France? The French have never accepted American culture with wholehearted enthusiasm to begin with, and they sourly regarded EuroDisney as just another example of Yankee imperialism.

Disney soon made changes, however, and today the park, which was renamed Disneyland Paris, is beginning to rank with the other theme parks in popularity and in revenues. Mistakes can indeed be a valuable learning tool if a company ferrets out the causes and then uses the feedback to design appropriate solutions.

Getting Your Company on Track

From the beginning, Walt Disney instilled his organization with the idea that every moment should be magical for its guests. Since nothing is more important at Disney, the company makes sure every employee buys into that belief through its formal training programs at Disney University. New recruits are immediately made to feel that they can play a significant role and be a part of something with a higher purpose.

In most organizations, however, the people who have the primary contact with the customer are usually the least educated, least trained, least respected, and have the least input regarding the direction of the company. And, unfortunately, too many customer service training programs deal only with how to smile and greet the customer, leaving service providers without a clue about how to solve a problem. Treating customers with respect and communicating in a pleasant manner are indeed important, but smiles alone will not improve customer service.

If your organization is among the ranks of the clueless, do the following two things well and listen for favorable customer response:

1. *Become a customer problem solver.* We are convinced that the quality of orientation at most companies would have to increase tenfold to reach the "pathetic" level. Orientation for front-line workers usually consists of how to fill in the time card and how to complete an order form. In rare cases, a 30-minute session on how to talk to a customer is added. Organizations then disguise unskilled front-line employees by hanging a sign on them that reads, Trainee. What that really means is, "Don't expect me to know anything; I'm trying to figure out what goes on here too."

Within the first week of employment, your front-line coworkers should be able to answer the following questions with assurance:

- What products and services do we provide? It is not a matter of being able to point to the catalog and describe the products, but rather of knowing how to solve the problems and fill the needs of the customers.
- What are the organization's vision and values?
- What is the mission for my department?
- Who are our competitors and what is our competitive advantage?
- To whom do I turn for assistance with a problem I cannot solve?

2. *Gain customer feedback.* Customer perceptions are very powerful and often become reality. Therefore, every system in the organization must be evaluated through customers' eyes. Two critical questions to ask yourself are:

- What is the level of ease of doing business with our organization?
- What do we consider to be exceptional service?

Many customer-feedback tools, such as surveys and focus groups, require a considerable investment of people, time, and money to put in place. Evaluate your budget to ensure that you are not skimping on these critical activities. Recognize also that you have a wealth of customer information at your fingertips just waiting to be tapped. Consider anyone who has customer contact as a barometer for measuring both positive and negative customer perceptions. Ask accounting clerks and order entry clerks alike to call customers and ask the simple question, "How did we do on that delivery last week?"

Simple efforts like these let your customers know that you care about their experiences. They also send a clear message to employees about the value of customer perceptions.

In his recent interview with Jan Carlzon, former CEO and turn-around architect of Scandinavian Airlines, Bob Thompson, CEO of CustomerThinkCorp, asked Jan about his application of what he famously termed "moments of truth"—the various points at which the airline's employees came in contact with their customers. Through numerous interviews with his customers, Jan made the startling discovery that the perceptions of his company did not match those of his customers. In Jan's own words, "We asked them about different things: What is your perception about our head office? What is your perception of our technical and maintenance station? What is your perception about our aircraft and so forth? What is your perception about meeting with people? We found out that the only perception they really had was the meeting with people. We did the research to prove a point to the technical and operation people, to convince them that their tools were no longer, perhaps, the most important we have."

The Positive and Negative Power of Perception

The Physics Department at San Jose State University prided itself on having a freshman physics class that was so difficult that 50 percent of the students routinely flunked out of or dropped the class. One semester, a professor decided to do an experiment. In the first of two identical classes, he stated during his opening lecture that 50 percent of the students would flunk or drop out. In his second class, he stated that the normal flunk-out rate was 50 percent, but in looking through the students' transcripts, he was astounded to see that everyone in this class had an exceptional aptitude in math and science.

You can probably guess the results. In the first class, 50 percent of the students dropped out or flunked. In the second class, every student passed with a grade of C or better.

The point of this story is that perceptions really do become reality.

Perception Becomes a Grim Reality

The power of perception takes on a strangely disturbing cast in this story of a railroad worker in California. The man was sent to check on some freight in a refrigerated boxcar. While inside the car, the doors shut accidentally, trapping him inside. When the man failed to check in at the end of the shift, a coworker found him dead in the boxcar. The following words were written on the walls: "No one is hearing my cries for help. My hands and feet are getting colder. I don't know how much longer I can last."

The eerie fact of this story is that the boxcar had been sidelined on a spur because its refrigeration unit was not working. The temperature outside was in the eighties, and although the temperature in the boxcar was slightly lower, it was nowhere near freezing. There was also plenty of air for the man to breathe. So what happened? His perception of freezing to death was so strong that it became reality.

Plumbing & Industrial Supply has a heightened understanding of customer perceptions and a firm set of long-term beliefs. Thus, when an elderly gentleman came to the retail counter area of the company one day, he received a reception that is, we're sad to say, not typical of most businesses.

The apparently lonely old fellow asked a lot of general questions and didn't seem as if he were a serious buyer. "My initial reaction," said the counter attendant, "was to return to my other duties of stocking shelves and processing orders. However, having just attended a three-day retreat in which we talked about treating the customer as if he were a guest in our own homes, I continued to converse with the man for about two hours."

The following day, this seemingly unlikely customer returned to place a $500 order. What's more, he related that he had told his sons, who were taking over his construction business, about the fine hospitality he had received the day before. He assured the counter attendant that his company looked forward to a long-term business relationship with Plumbing & Industrial Supply!

Walt Disney would have appreciated the counter attendant's story, for he always focused special attention on those who dealt directly with theme park visitors—the ticket takers, the waiters, the security officers, and the people who operated the rides and other attractions. That's because he recognized that those people were the ones who made the invaluable direct impression on the Disney guests.

If you have ever visited one of the Disney theme parks, chances are that you've had a cast member stop to chat with you and ask which attractions you've been on, whether you need anything, if you're having a good time, and so forth. In other words, they treated their guests like any good host would.

To ensure that his front-line cast members would always deliver superior and pleasing service to the guests, Walt Disney went out of his way to make sure that employees were satisfied with their jobs and with the company. No one had to tell Walt that workers who are happy take pride in their work and do it well.

"Front line equals bottom line" is still an accepted rule at The Walt Disney Company. Walt also recognized that teamwork is a necessary component of the good show. Many of our clients are utilizing empowered teams and reaping the benefits of more efficient and effective performance. Guests may come first, but cast members are not far behind, as you will see in the chapter that follows.

Questions to Ask

- Do you know your "guests"?
- Are your employees empowered to solve customer problems?
- Do you view your front-line as your bottom line?
- What special training do your front-line people receive?
- What is the turnover rate among your front-line staff?

Actions to Take

- Ask coworkers to experience how the customer is being treated in your organization.
- Recognize and reward outstanding customer service.
- Establish a mechanism for customers to comment on how they've been treated by coworkers.
- Encourage coworkers to regularly visit customers to discuss customer problems and dreams.
- Pay a little more than the going scale for front-line coworkers.
- Encourage every coworker to call two to three customers each week to ask, "How are we doing?"
- Recruit people who like people.

Listening to Customers Pays

You can't expect to have a group of 35 people without a few among them exhibiting a "show me" attitude. "I was trying to establish a culture that was strange to them—a departure from the norm that they had always worked in," Whirlpool's McColgin asserts. Yet in the end, the cohesion of this international team and the prevalent belief in the goals that were set proved the skeptics wrong.

Jerry challenged the team members to utilize their international expertise in discovering and fulfilling the needs of their international clients and suppliers. The members from Brazil, or India, or any other of the countries represented were, in effect, wearing two hats. Professionally, they were engineers or marketing people, but back home they were also customers, who were now sitting right in the room with Whirlpool's American employees. They knew what the needs of their own people were.

Focus groups were also used in this international market to determine customer dreams and desires for the product. Several participants said that they wanted ice trays. Corrosion resistance was an issue in tropical regions. A quiet motor was important in countries where the refrigerator often stood in the living room. And the number of kilowatts per hour—the cost of the electricity—was a major factor in other areas.

Seriously listening to the customer resulted in cost savings and a better product for the team's international customer base.

Our Featured Organization: Griffin Hospital

CHANGING THE FACE OF HEALTHCARE

In the mid 1980s, Griffin Hospital's maternity ward was a nightmare for expecting mothers. Not only was the all-male obstetrical staff growing weary of the stress from working in the department and eager for retirement, but it was also rumored they didn't like women at all. At least one patient described the Griffin maternity ward as a "dungeon." When deliveries had plummeted by 50 percent, the hospital board met over whether to close Griffin's maternity ward and open a geriatric center. Nearly split down the middle, the board ended up listening to its only female member. She had

(Continued)

argued that the community was growing with people of child-bearing age and that if these newcomers did not choose to have their babies at Griffin, they would be unlikely to return to the hospital for other services. In the end, the board voted to save the maternity ward.

According to Patrick Charmel, then assistant administrator of the hospital, this marked the birth of a new patient-centered movement at Griffin Hospital. "Today when patients come here, they expect a superior patient experience. Certainly they expect to have a good surgical outcome, but they also want a good experience. They want a friendly environment that smells good, they want great food, their families embraced, their questions answered," explained Patrick.[20]

At such a critical juncture in Griffin's history, Patrick thought, "I don't know a lot about maternity service, but I know who does: women of child-bearing age, especially those who have had children." That one seed of truth launched the philosophical shift at Griffin, from following old school principles to treating women like guests and finding out what they wanted from maternity units. What seems obvious to many businesses today was not so obvious back in the 1980s. The concept that talking to customers and changing direction based on their input was both a novel and a good idea. In hospitals, however, you'd be lucky if you found anyone who believed that this practice was the least bit acceptable.

Griffin orchestrated focus groups as a first step, but in Patrick's mind, that wasn't enough. So, he and a Griffin marketing manager turned themselves into "secret shoppers." Posing as husband and wife, they contacted several hospitals around the country and pretended to be shopping for an obstetrician and a hospital suitable for delivering their child. Most hospital staff who received their calls were taken aback, stating, "we don't do tours." The rest viewed their request as a bother. After all, people were traditionally supposed to find their obstetricians first. Finally, a number of hospitals begrudgingly extended an invitation to Patrick and his "wife," who stuffed a pillow under her skirt to fake pregnancy.

After several months of visiting various maternity units, they returned with great ideas and began knitting them together into what was to become a state-of-the-art program. Griffin emerged with a patient-centered, educational focus—one that embraced patients' families. Sibling preparation classes, grandparent classes, and intensive programs for both moms and dads were pioneered. Gone were the posted visiting hours that had frustrated both patients and their families. And, the facility's facelift was just staggering with its double beds, Jacuzzis for labor pain relief, and beautiful lounges where loved ones could wait. In came a brand-new staff of young, idealistic male and female doctors who understood what mothers wanted and needed.

It didn't take long for Griffin to double its business and become the talk of the town with its new childbirth center, a place where expectant mothers were thrilled to go to bring their children into the world.

"We looked at that and said, "Wow—now we have seen such great success in using this consumer-research model, how do we take this hospital wide?" recounts Griffin vice president, William Powanda.[21] In keeping with their maternity behavioral paradigm of "patient as guest," they took their employees to off-site retreat locations and asked them what they liked and didn't like as customers of healthcare. They knew that their employees were critical to the success of a new hospital model; after all, they would be the ones to live it each and every day. The retreats were a catharsis for many staffers who had been delivering patient service for 20 years and now realized that they hadn't really been meeting the needs of their patients. Some cried and asked themselves and one another, "Why didn't I see this before?" To be fair, painfully few hospitals anywhere in the world were designed to support nurses in providing true "guest service" to their patients. And, surely there was no need for that in the old paradigm.

Even with the escalating staff buy-in to a new way of life at Griffin, the facility was in such disrepair that fixing would be a daunting task. To begin with, the patients' rooms had no air-conditioning, although many of the nurses' stations did. This was certainly inconsistent with the new model where the goal was to make patients feel at home.

Patrick and the vice president of patient-care services were charged with transforming both the care delivery model and the facility. The primary goal was to build the facility to deliver the best care. On one fateful benchmarking journey, Patrick and his associate discovered a new humanistic model of health care called Planetree, which was alive and well in a 13-bed hospital unit in northern California. The Planetree environment was tranquil, with soft lighting and soothing music, and above all, it supported patient empowerment.

The whole premise seemed to dovetail beautifully with Griffin's belief that creating a warm and caring place where patients are intimately involved in their care and treatment is imperative to delivering quality

(Continued)

healthcare. "Signs throughout the facility encourage patients to read their charts. Between 40 and 50 percent do, once, and about 15 percent do it a second time," Powanda says. When Griffin first proposed a ground-up Planetree construction project, there was something of a "giggle-factor." The state Commission on Hospitals and Health Care would not take the idea seriously. Charmel told us, "They thought it was too West Coast. But ultimately, the commission agreed to fund it as a pilot project, the only restriction being that it not cost any more per square foot than any other health facility would spend for a more traditional renovation." Bill Powanda says, "We tried to be economical in purchasing equipment. For example, our furniture was custom-designed and purchased directly from the factory at a significant discount. I think we got maximum value for the total allowance that the commission gave us." Like Disney, Griffin does not try to cut corners in its "on stage" patient areas, but "back stage" office areas are very Spartan-like. The result is the look and feel of a private hospital or fine hotel, for the cost of a not-for-profit facility.

Having been inspired by its numerous positive effects on patients and their families, Griffin acquired Planetree in 1998. With Susan Frampton as its dynamic president, Planetree now assists other hospitals which are focused on adopting the practices that have brought Planetree international recognition. Under Patrick's leadership, Griffin has developed a unique culture where nurses and technicians walk the halls exchanging supportive comments like "That's very Planetree," and these quips serve to reinforce a culture dedicated to creating only the best memories for everyone who passes through its inviting doors.[22]

Chapter 5

All for One and One for All

Many hands, and hearts, and minds generally contribute to anyone's notable achievements.[23]

Walt Disney

He was renowned for his creativity and superior crafting ability and was successful beyond compare, yet even the great Walt Disney did not presume to be able to accomplish his goals without the contributions of a well-coordinated group working alongside him. "I don't propose to be an authority on anything at all," he once explained. "I follow the opinions of ordinary people I meet, and I take pride in the close-knit teamwork of my organization."[24]

That Walt Disney so readily acknowledged the value of collaboration is a measure of his greatness—or perhaps a cause of it. In any event, his belief in the team concept was such that he promoted it both in his films and throughout his company. In fact, teamwork is a crucial element underpinning the Disney "be our guest" philosophy. To wit, exceeding guests' expectations requires a well-rehearsed cast, with every member playing a significant role.

In the area of feature animation, The Walt Disney Company has traditionally tapped the collective power of its workforce by using a long-standing process for determining the value of various concepts for production. As a first step, the senior leaders discuss ideas from several sources to decide which to pursue.

As the project moves along, directors, art directors, and the head of background production all join in the give-and-take of planning. The dialogue eventually produces a consensus, and company insiders insist that no one ever asserts an attitude of possessiveness. The teamwork continues throughout the long process of animation, camera work, adding sound, and editing until, at last, the film is ready for release.

References to teamwork also are sprinkled throughout Disney films, but none better illustrates Walt's belief in the value of collaboration than *Snow White and the Seven Dwarfs*. For many of us, those seven distinctive little fellows—Happy, Sleepy, Doc, Bashful, Sneezy (originally named Jumpy), Grumpy, and Dopey—are childhood friends. Each was carefully drawn with his own distinguishing characteristics, yet we remember them first and foremost as a team, always going off to work each morning whistling a happy tune. Walt purposely made the notion of cooperative endeavor an integral part of that script, with the dwarfs illustrating how different talents and personalities can be brought together to accomplish shared goals.

Many of the companies we work with have become convinced, like Walt Disney, that it takes a multifunctional team to produce the best possible show. They are using teams in their everyday operations and deriving benefits—such as enhanced problem solving—that help to ensure long-term success. Look to these examples to guide your organization in tapping the latent power of its collective wisdom.

The Signals of a Good Leader

In our seminars, we can't seem to stress enough how critical leadership is in producing a healthy corporate culture where teams can flourish.

The kind of leadership required in the best of cultures has been put in a nutshell by the late Edward R. Murrow, one of the world's most credible broadcasters, whose story was dramatized in the movie *Good Night, and Good Luck,* which was nominated for six Academy Awards. He said, "To be persuasive, we must be believable. To be believable we must be credible. And to be credible we must be truthful." Leaders have to earn their credibility through action and through example. The only effective communication—the only reality—is performance. And leaders must perform in order to earn trust, and before a sense of common team purpose can emerge.

Great leaders such as Isadore Sharp of Four Seasons Hotels & Resorts demonstrate through their actions how maintaining a competitive edge in business can only be accomplished by generating wealth through *human resources*, not through physical assets.

In the 1990s, Isadore sought an opportunity to break into the Atlanta hotel market. Finally, in March of 1997 he got his wish and took over management of the Ritz Carlton in midtown, a 40-year old hotel with a well-known history of changing ownership, contract employees, and perpetual difficulties.

During the week prior to the legal agreement's becoming effective, Isadore brought in an experienced general manager from another Four Seasons property to help brainstorm ideas for creating a smooth transition for the hotel's existing employees. The GM knew that in his hands lay the responsibility for establishing credibility with these employees who were fearful of how the change of management would affect them in the long term. The agreement became effective at midnight, and Four Seasons management was on board for a mere six hours prior to the 6 a.m. arrival of first-shift employees. The GM and his leadership team had decided they had only one chance to set a tone of believability in the value of the team. Their goal was to treat their new team members as though they were coming home to a place that was safe and secure. They needed to paint the picture of a new culture before the employees entered the building that morning. And paint they did. At 12:01 a.m., a painting contractor began to transform the "back of the house" (employee break rooms and locker rooms, or the "heart" of the house in Four Seasons terms) from a drab off-stage area that guests never see, to a bright freshly painted employee lounge rivaling the on-stage guest areas. The transformation was more than just a fresh coat of paint, however. New uniforms awaited the arriving employees, as well as steak and eggs cooked by the hotel chefs. Senior staff served breakfast, and then the GM welcomed them to their new home at Four Seasons.

Nurturing the staff is Golden Rule leadership in action. The leaders of Four Seasons, from Isadore to the GM to the management team, believe that at the end of every day, it is the staff that will either make or break them. "Issy said the front doorman contributes as much as the GM in any hotel—maybe more," remarked Doug Ludwig, former CFO and executive vice president, during our interview with him at Four Seasons corporate office in Toronto.[25]

Such humility and attitude of service are rarely more evident than in the leadership style of the management team of Four Seasons Hotels & Resorts. In the beginning, it's all about the signals a leader sends. It's the actions of the leader that team members see and learn to trust or distrust, the very same actions that cause employees to learn to either love or hate their jobs. Four Seasons leadership is the paramount model for creating healthy teams who achieve great success.

A Common Focus Is Essential

For many of us, the word *team* conjures up images of a football field or memories of the Little League games we played during our school years. In sports, teams have always aroused emotions of intense loyalty and enthusiastic support. By adopting the team concept, we can transport this loyalty, enthusiasm, and commitment associated with the playing field to the business arena. What's more, companies find that when management successfully brings together a diverse, multitalented group of employees to work together in a complementary fashion, the team members both challenge and support one another in a winning synergy that constantly improves the organization.

But to back up a bit, it's important to lay the preliminary groundwork for successful teaming—namely, to instill in the team a shared sense of purpose and commitment.

At Disney, team commitment is fostered in many ways, including the storytelling technique described in Chapter 2. And on movie projects, where teamwork is essential, Disney deviates from the norm in that collaboration is not just a one-time thing, with the participants gathered for one particular film. Many of the teammates are staff members who have worked together before. This is especially true when it comes to animated films, which demand special, well-honed skills. Most important, all the participants have been trained in Disney traditions. Knowing exactly what is expected of them and what the company stands for further strengthens the team spirit.

Besides in-house training, another way to develop a common focus is through a mission statement. A written statement of a team's mission and goals is a necessity to communicate the direction to all team members.

Teams can be crippled by the corporate policy manual, which often distracts them from accomplishing their mission. Any new employee—and many well-seasoned ones—would have trouble absorbing all the policy regulations that these weighty tomes contain. Moreover, burying any kind of mission statement inside what is bound to be a deadly dull recitation of rules and regulations virtually guarantees that it will be overlooked or quickly forgotten.

Not long ago, we were chatting about policy manuals with a well-known business leader who told us the following story. Years ago, as a new, young department head, he was approached by an old-timer who offered to get him a copy of the company's newly prepared, 150-page policy manual. The young man thanked him, weighed the policy statement book in his right hand, and then sat down at his typewriter and came up with a new version.

It read: "Work hard, be clever, have fun, use good judgment." In effect, this insightful new employee reduced 150 pages of ponderous prose to a mere nine words that said pretty much the same thing.

We recommend that our clients follow his lead and keep brevity and clarity in mind when setting policy. Your goal should be to enable the kind of creative environment in which problems are solved, productivity is increased, and teams are empowered. Teams that are burdened by excessive rules and procedures are likely to spend an inordinate amount of time dealing with internal functional issues and not solving customer problems. Creativity will most certainly be stifled.

Bringing the Mission to Life

The best way to give a mission statement meaning is to establish multifunctional teams to carry out the organizational values. Many teams manage to craft mission statements that sound wonderful, but as we mentioned in the preceding chapter, they are often little more than an exercise with no real substance. When we begin working with teams, we point out that the statements are only as good as their execution.

Once a team's mission is developed, and all members have confirmed their buy-in, the team can solve problems more quickly and institute changes more effectively than can a handful of loners working on their own. As we have witnessed with our clients, bringing people together in cross-functional teams often sparks a flurry of new ideas that, in turn, produce solutions to problems. Because such teams constantly draw on the diverse experiences and opinions of a number of people from across the organization, they are better able to look at the company as a whole and suggest integrated product, service, and process improvements. In short, multifunctional teams are much better suited to rethinking the old and leading the way to the new.

In general, an organization's top management must formally lay the groundwork and provide the impetus for a team-based structure, although we have run across teams that seem to form spontaneously. Such an example drew our attention recently at an East Coast utility.

We have done consulting work for many utility companies, usually auditing on a management level. In the process, we look at the cost of materials and how trucks are purchased. Used sometimes in maintenance work, sometimes in an emergency, utility trucks are a familiar sight on suburban streets and country roads. They constitute a major investment for utility companies.

Traditionally, whether the buying is done by a group in the corporate structure or, as sometimes happens, by a special purchasing group, the responsibility has always rested in the hands of white-collar executive personnel. The work crews that operate from the trucks and the people who drive and maintain them have nothing to do with acquiring them.

At our East Coast client, the vice president in charge of materials was new on the job, having spent many years as a purchasing manager for an airline company. When we asked him how he went about buying needed supplies, his honesty and candor were both refreshing and instructive. He readily admitted that he didn't know anything about utility trucks, even though he was charged with buying hundreds of them. So what did he do?

"I got a group of line workers together," he said, "the people who were using the trucks, plus people from purchasing and an accountant, and I said to them, 'Go into a room and don't come out until you can give me the specs for a truck.' And you know what? We saved a ton of money, and for the first time ever, the line workers were really pleased with equipment we got for them."

Contrast that story with one we heard from a group of line workers at another utility. The purchasing department bought trucks without any consultation with line workers, who were forced to come up with their own solution: "When we get a new truck in," they told us, "we cut things off of it and weld things onto it. In two or three weeks, we have that truck the way we want it."

Innovative? Absolutely. Efficient? No way! But this is exactly the kind of thing that happens when management is wedded to the oft-heard principle, "That's the way we've always done things here." Through either hubris or inertia, outmoded and costly methods of operation remain in place year after year, leader after leader.

But this need not be so. Any manager can imitate the innovative vice president at the first utility who organized a multifunctional group of people to work together to find the best possible solution to a problem. Rather than following an inefficient and imprudent practice, however "standard," and ordering a fleet of expensive trucks or some other high-priced item, a manager can take the initiative to change any wrongheaded procedure. But taking that initiative often means bringing the front-line people into the process, people who know what is needed, as in the case of the utility that acquired trucks that met workers' needs. At the same time, this team saved the company a lot of money, planning well in advance of the purchase and coming in well under budget.

When properly structured, teams can improve everything from the bottom line to employee satisfaction with the job. In fact, much of the research we see suggests that in a tight market for the top-notch recruits in technology, production, and other fields that demand both high intelligence and high levels of skills, people are attracted to jobs with the most expansive descriptions and opportunities for advancement. Salary is important, to be sure, but it is often not the first criterion that the best people have in mind when they begin evaluating job possibilities or offers. As R. S. Dreyer stated in an article for *Supervision* magazine, people work not only for the salary, but also "for the satisfaction they derive from accomplishment. They work to be part of a team . . . [and] for the feeling of pride they get out of being employed by a fine organization."

In our work with the Mead Johnson Nutritional Division of Bristol-Myers Squibb, for example, we found confirmation of the greater sense of pride people derive from working as members of a successful team. One line attendant, a production line employee whose job it is to make sure that the line doesn't jam up, told us her story about working at a plant that produces infant formula. This employee was responsible for picking up overturned bottles. It's a bit like being a traffic cop, except that watching the line all day can be monotonous and boring. When she was put on a team, however, her whole attitude about the job changed.

Here's how she explained it: "Before I joined the team, I was always proud to say that I worked for Bristol-Myers, but when asked what my specific job was, I usually changed the subject. The truth was that I was embarrassed to say I was a line attendant. Now it's different; I tell anyone who asks that I'm a member of a team that is responsible for making the best quality product at the most affordable cost for mothers and babies throughout the world."

No longer just a lone worker in a monotonous job, this woman became part of a multifunctional team that met with management in an effort to improve quality and productivity. Having been made to feel that her work and her opinions mattered, she was able to take pride in her new role and to exhibit striking enthusiasm, loyalty, and commitment to the team.

Toppling Hierarchical Barriers

Although no organization can function without a certain degree of hierarchy (someone must be in charge), every company should look at how well its hierarchy performs and periodically question its purpose. Some stratification is vital to the smooth functioning of any business, but too much can, and probably will, kill initiative, smother innovation, and lead to a deadening of the spirit throughout the organization.

Consider organizing teams around processes. If visitors were to have visited EPCOT's METLife exhibit several years ago, they would have come in contact with many different departments: merchandising, food service, attractions, maintenance, and horticulture. To the guest, the barriers to providing service were invisible. But cast members recognized problems in delivering the great service we have come to expect. For example, whose job was it to clean up the Body Wars attraction if someone got sick? Was it maintenance or attractions? So they decided to organize around the process. Everyone associated with the attraction now is a member of one team. Their job is to make sure the guest has a pleasant and memorable experience. The whole team is focused on the guest experience and not on who is responsible for what.

Restructuring an organization's operations around teams goes a long way toward breaking down rigid managerial barriers. What results is a win-win situation. Lower-level employees feel empowered when they are encouraged to voice opinions and make suggestions in a group that includes a manager. In turn, the organization derives the enormous benefit of being able to draw from a valuable source of new ideas and knowledge. The hierarchy remains, but the distance between managers and employees is diminished.

The Walt Disney Company well understands that worthwhile suggestions can be lost because employees will hesitate to make them in a normal hierarchical business atmosphere. That's why the Gong Show exists. But in addition to giving employees specific venues for making suggestions, top Disney executives go out of their way to solicit advice from staff members, those front-line people who hear guests' comments and see their reactions.

In 1994, for example, Michael Eisner was walking through an EPCOT computer technology exhibit called "Innoventions." It was anything but innovative. There was nothing particularly imaginative or inspiring about the technology displays, and the CEO was not pleased with it. So he stopped and asked some of the greeters at the exhibit if they had any ideas about how to liven it up. Told that another cast member by the name of Mike Goames talked a lot about what needed to be done to brighten up the place, the CEO approached him to ask for some ideas. Impressed by what Goames had to say, Eisner asked him to detail his suggestions in a memo. (Goames suggested that the exhibit should look more like a technical trade fair, showcasing new technologies and experimental things like wrist telephones.)

We recently told this story about Eisner and Goames at a public seminar where two employees of the local Disney retail store were in attendance. After the seminar, they approached us and one of them, the store manager, remarked, "Michael Eisner has never been in our store. But if he ever does visit, I really believe that he would want to hear our ideas. That's just the culture at Disney. The company respects the ideas from all cast members, regardless of their level in the organization." By most accounts, Michael Eisner once believed in the power of soliciting input from all levels of the organization.

Few companies seem willing or able to trust and empower employees to quite the extent we have witnessed at Disneyland and Walt Disney World. The Disney approach stems, we believe, from a long history of teamwork and cooperation between management and employees that dates back to the way Walt managed the company in the early days. In fact, the Goames incident is reminiscent of the story recounted in the opening chapter in which Walt added fireflies to his Disneyland Pirates of the Caribbean attraction in response to the suggestion of a construction worker at the park.

An astonishing indication of the depth of employee trust and empowerment at Disney is the fact that its customer service representatives, the people who take the tickets at the theme park entrances, have $500,000 in tickets and cash at their disposal to give out to guests who lose or forget their tickets, run out of money with which to get home, or encounter any other problem that merits attention. That's an extraordinary sum of money to place at the discretion of employees, but Disney obviously trusts these empowered cast members to use sound judgment.

What's more, it's noteworthy because of what it says about how Disney has eliminated turf barriers. How many accounting departments would allow a front-line worker to have such power and latitude? The point is that at The Walt Disney Company, no single department calls the shots for any other.

In most organizations, people are often so hung up on the rules and regulations in their policy manuals that they naturally feel unempowered. This is certainly not true in the ranks of Disney or Nordstrom's. In fact, the entire contents of Nordstrom's Department Stores policy manual reads, "Use your own best judgment at all times." Your company can't be focused on the Believe principle if you are plowing through reams of policy prose. Less policy—as long as it's good policy—brings good results. As we stated in our book *Leading at the Speed of Change: Using New Economy Rules to Invigorate Old Economy Companies*, "policy wonks finish last."

Factors in Successful Team Building

Not every team experience is going to be a success, of course. There are those who complain that when they introduced the team concept in their companies, it didn't work. But when the team approach fails, there is usually a good reason for it.

To begin with, setting up teams is not always easy. Much depends on the selection of a leader, who will play a pivotal role in determining the results. This individual has an enormous responsibility to set the tone for the team, both through personal attributes and through the choice of individual team members. He or she must be capable of exercising firm and fair leadership that respects each member's personal values and understands the role each individual plays. A successful leader will establish and manage a climate that encourages creativity while keeping team members on track to accomplish assigned goals. Finding such a person takes thoughtful consideration, but we've yet to encounter a company without qualified candidates.

The composition of the rest of the team is a major factor in its success or failure as well. You must first determine all the stakeholders on a particular project, then move to find the best representative of each of the needed skill sets. And as basic as it sounds, we always urge our clients to consider the personalities of potential members. Inveterate pessimists should be avoided. Management must also make sure to include detail-oriented people as well as big-picture thinkers. You don't want to end up with a group in which everyone looks at the end result but no one is paying attention to all the little things that will make it happen. Diversity is important, but in the end, it's all about synergy, balance, and raising the bar for one another.

How does a leader create an environment in which team members can thrive? First of all, he or she must encourage the free flow of ideas by letting team members know that no idea is too ridiculous. It stands to reason that when innovation is the goal, radical premises are to be encouraged, not squelched. Group discussion and analysis can often transform a seemingly off-the-wall notion into a sensible and usable tool.

Group discussion can also turn an entire team around if it's heading off in a wrong direction, especially if the team leader loses touch with the team and its problems. Such is the case of a person we'll call John, one of 24 team leaders at a manufacturing company we worked with. John's team always came in last among the other 23 teams, and its members could never hit performance targets quite so well as their counterparts. At one no-holds-barred session we attended, one woman broke down in tears when she addressed John: "You and Steve (the plant's general manager) are forcing us to be a team, and we don't want to be."

We had seen enough of these kinds of sessions to know that seldom do the members of a group collectively decide that they don't want to be a team, even if they are aware that it takes a long time and effort to develop that synergy. No, there were other issues here that needed to be surfaced.

As both the team leader and an individual, John demonstrated tremendous courage in his willingness to listen to complaints and suggestions in such a public forum as this session presented. Encouraged to speak their minds, team members expressed their anger about John's lack of support and direction and his absence in spirit when the team hit a wall and needed a boost to overcome a problem. John sat quietly, taking notes and listening intently.

After months of open communication and repairing some team damage, positive results emerged. The team, with John on board, decided to meet twice a week to discuss issues and to solve problems that were plaguing their internal customers. Gradually the gloom that hung over the entire team began to lift as their positive energy increased. Still the leader, John had become a respected leader in the eyes of his fellow team members.

Over the next two years, this team grew both emotionally and professionally. Completing their next round of self-observations, they found that they had indeed become a team rather than a collection of individuals wearing the same logos on their shirts. From top management to shop floor employees, everyone saw the difference both in attitude and in performance. As for John, his new leadership style received kudos from people inside and outside the plant, and within one year he was promoted to the corporate office—not bad for a guy who just a year or so earlier had reduced some of his team members to tears. Now those same team members were singing a different song, praising not only John's success but also their own for the progress they had made as a team.

When we help to bring together members for a new team, we stress the importance of the individuals functioning as a cohesive unit from the outset. They must not think of themselves as a committee, with one person representing marketing, another there to protect the interests of the purchasing department, and so on. Instead of someone saying, "Well, I've done my design piece," or "I've given my financial statement," and then sitting back to wait for someone else to produce the deliverable, the entire team must ask, "How can we all do this together?"

To foster the necessary cooperative attitude and to increase productivity, we emphasize the necessity of bringing teams together to work in a central location, a process known as *co-locating*. Walt Disney often referred to these locations as "planning centers," and his company has found that its people are much more efficient and willing to take the initiative when they can discuss a problem or ask questions of someone sitting nearby. Brainstorming sessions have a way of happening spontaneously under co-located conditions.

Back in the 1970s, MIT Sloan professor Thomas J. Allen, Jr., who taught managerial psychology for nearly four decades, conducted research on the relationship between distance and frequency of communication in the workplace. For six months, Allen examined the communication patterns among 512 employees in seven organizations. He found that at a distance of 30 feet or less, the quality of communication is five times better than it is at a distance of 100 feet. Allen's research also showed that beyond 100 feet, distance is immaterial because communication is simply ineffective—period. In other words, ease of communication is largely dependent on physical location.[26]

Even before we saw this scientific study, we had reached a similar conclusion from our own experience. When questions need to be asked or issues discussed, proximity enables interaction. It was with the idea of bringing people together to facilitate communication and improve production that Chrysler began in 1990 a five-year plan to redesign its engineering facilities at a cost of $1 billion. Bringing together all major engineering functions into one facility, this physical reorganization contributed substantially to the revival of the company.[27]

But a word of warning: We have seen many companies move their people into open workspaces on the mistaken assumption that they have then created a team. When nothing constructive emerges from this arrangement, they disband the so-called team and label it a failure. They have misunderstood the purpose of co-locating. The open workspace does not, in itself, create a team. It is merely a tool that is used to *reinforce* the team concept. To be successful, a team must also have a mission and goal and be dedicated to fostering the progress of that goal. As on the playing field, the team in a manufacturing plant, an office, or corporate headquarters has to work as a unit, not a collection of individual efforts, no matter what stars you recruit for the key positions. The greatest third baseman, running back, or point guard in the world cannot make a group of people into a "team." That comes only with leadership and commitment to a goal that everyone agrees is worth pursuing,

It almost goes without saying that some type of reward system should be in place to recognize superior performance. However, most managers we encounter feel that a little bit of healthy individual competition is as important, if not more important, than teamwork. They really believe competition is good for the organization and will even boost productivity. Most of us have been encouraged since we were very young to compete with one another in school, as well as in sports. People rationalize that a competitive spirit is a simple fact of human nature.

Alfie Kohn, author of *No Contest: The Case Against Competition,* has spent more than a decade reviewing the effects of competition and cooperation in hundreds of organizations. His conclusion is quite clear: "Superior performance not only does not require competition; it seems to require its absence."[28] David and Roger Johnson of the University of Minnesota report the following results from an educational environment study: 173 studies found that cooperation promotes higher achievement than competition or independent efforts, whereas 13 studies found that competition promotes higher achievement. Another 78 studies found no significant statistical difference.[29]

Red Auerbach, the indefatigable coach of the Boston Celtics, who won 16 NBA championships under his direction, never kept individual statistics on his players. Hubie Brown, the basketball commentator and former coach, remembers the Celtic style that Auerbach helped create: "Red knew how to push the right button on each guy to get him to be subservient to the team. . . . The Celtics understood the maxim, 'There is no *I* in *team.*'"[30]

The benefits of a team reward system as opposed to a competitive one are so compelling that even in a competitive society we must notice. Everyone benefits from feeling appreciated, and team rewards are an excellent way to encourage the hoped-for sense of community and cohesiveness among team members.

In our work with the global team at Whirlpool, we challenged the organization to weight the reward system more heavily toward team performance instead of individual performance. We believe that when teams achieve exceptional results, appropriate bonuses and pay raises should go to the entire team, not just to certain people that the organization judges to be key contributors. Anything else undermines the entire structure of effective teamwork. If everyone is truly working together toward a common goal, then everyone should be rewarded equally.

In the case of Whirlpool, the global team leader was forced to go to bat for the team to ensure equal recognition. He argued that the combined efforts of each and every team member made his group one of the top-rated performers in the entire company. Furthermore, he insisted on equality, and he offered to give up his own personal bonus to get it.

This leader exhibited exceptional integrity and commitment in his battle to secure the proper recognition for his team mates, but it's not always necessary to go to such great lengths to reward team members. In fact, rewards don't have to be in the form of money and prizes. A reward can be something as simple as a pizza party over the lunch hour. In some cases, we've worked with executives who chose to host a barbecue, actually cooking the burgers and hot dogs and serving the team themselves. A personal effort is a particularly effective way of showing appreciation. As Dr. Bill Cross of Mead Johnson believed, "I think that [teamwork] is making the workplace more relaxed, and work ought to be fun, if you can use that term. And we are trying to make work fun and it is succeeding to a large extent."[31]

We also encourage teams to develop their own celebrations. When management is comfortable encouraging this—and certainly not all management can do it—team members gain an added sense of empowerment. They can say, "This is really our team, so let's decide together how we want to celebrate." But whether it's a function of management or of the team itself, the important thing is to plan at the beginning for some type of rewards as team members reach and exceed their goals.

George Zimmer learned the value of celebrations during his college fraternity years in the 1960s by attending coed weekend parties and playing ball on the lawn of Washington University in St. Louis. Adding comedic flavor to the whole experience was fraternity brother Harold Ramis, who cowrote the hilariously funny movie classic *Animal House*. Released in 1978 by National Lampoon, *Animal House* starred the late John Belushi, one of the brightest stars of NBC's "Saturday Night Live," and launched National Lampoon as the dynamo comedy machine of the 1970s. The movie's outrageous story is laced with just about everything that flies in the face of conservative, traditional rules, from beer bashes to toga parties and blaring music.

From the very beginning, George's goal for his own company was to incorporate fun (without the raunchy antics) into an annual event, now known as the notorious Men's Wearhouse Christmas Party. Each year, from early November through the third week of December, in all three company divisions, employees don their finest apparel and head for the grand ballroom of a local hotel where a tuxedo-clad George Zimmer has staged one of the flashiest annual events in corporate history. Everything has been meticulously orchestrated for the elegant soireé, which costs the company nearly 2 million dollars a year. A company tractor-trailer travels across the United States delivering the sound and light systems and party favors to every single venue. There are approximately 50 parties in all, each thrown on only weekend nights. "It's wild," George Zimmer told us. "We even have our own company DJ who works full-time. I consider this to be the best party I go to all year."[32]

Beyond the basic premise of rewarding employees for a year of enduring tough retail hours and delivering unparalleled service, the parties are in many respects a celebration of the multiracial, multicultural flavor of Men's Wearhouse. "This melting pot of humanity on the dance floor gives you a sense that we could get it together on planet earth," says George.

The much-anticipated Annual Awards celebration takes place at the end of the evening when individuals and teams are rewarded for their performance and may receive the coveted Aloha Award, a long-standing symbol of success at Men's Wearhouse. Having traveled to Hawaii for years, George Zimmer knew that most of his employees could not afford to vacation in this American paradise, so every year he rewards employee performance with over 100 marvelous vacations. The rules are few. No one may win the Aloha Award more than once, and no one can win it during the first year of employment. The Aloha Award is based on a demonstrated commitment to making Men's Wearhouse one's career. It isn't unusual for six people at each of these parties to nab the award, which brings a fabulous vacation for two to Hawaii or, nowadays, even Europe or the Caribbean.

"It all comes down to being able to get spirit and enthusiasm from people," remarks George. "It's impossible to measure, so it's been overlooked in business. Enjoying life and celebrating are needed to be enthusiastic about what you are doing 40 hours a week."

Concrete Results

Teams have a variety of roles and potential uses. We have set them up to examine customer complaints and determine their root causes. We have structured teams around process reengineering. We have asked outside suppliers to come and join in discussions about partnering possibilities in purchasing, engineering, and manufacturing functions. We have created steering teams whose role is to oversee the whole team process.

Teams can be set up for a specific, one-time goal, of course, but we always suggest that they continue to function on an ongoing basis after they have fulfilled their primary purpose. Even though the group will probably meet for only about an hour a week, the proper harnessing of this collective energy can produce worthwhile results.

At Lensing Wholesale, we helped set up teams that have functioned continuaously since 1993. The steering team, made up of the owners of the company, sponsors new teams as different needs arise. Some of the teams are issue- and process-oriented, but most are natural work teams that follow organizational lines and take care of specific work problems.

The adoption of the team system has made a concrete difference at Lensing, in its relations not only with suppliers and customers but also with employees, who now feel empowered to voice their opinions when they believe that a process can be changed for the better.

One of the managers, Donnie Montgomery, started his career at Lensing by working as a handler for one of the company's products, Pella Windows. Recognizing this warehouse worker's potential, his supervisor, Mike O'Donohue, proposed him for the manager's job when the previous manager left. Mike initially had a difficult time persuading the company president that Donnie was up to the task. It was, after all, a big jump from handler to manager. But Mike's foresight proved to be absolutely on target.

We met Donnie when the company sent him to us for training as a team leader. It seems that not only had he performed superbly on a day-to-day basis, but also working in a team setting had encouraged him to develop an innovative new trucking schedule. It was this initiative that had so impressed management.

Illinois Power, another of our clients that adopted a team-based structure, also has witnessed results worth noting. After the utility executives decided to introduce total quality management, we helped to set up some 475 teams that brought more than 80 percent of the workforce into the decision-making process. The ideas that emerged from these teams played a significant part in the changed management effort. The teams submitted more than 2,500 suggestions to save money or increase revenue, which, when implemented, produced net savings of more than $18 million per year! Teams also came up with nearly 3,000 ideas for improving the work process or customer service.

Teams have taken on very specific functions at the Mead Johnson Nutritional Division of Bristol-Myers Squibb. Initially, 55 teams were organized, of which 7 were process teams, 10 dealt with issues, 32 were natural work groups, 5 were set up as steering teams, and 1 was to be a catchall for any special issues that came up.

At the start, the unit known as the Track Team established its purpose and its goals: "Our mission is to improve the cycle time involved with tracing and expediting, to increase the quality of the response, and to assure our customers that Mead Johnson provides a reliable service."

Tracing and expediting were handled by different departments, so the team began its work by making flow charts of the process used in dealing with customers' orders. The team discovered that the company had received 2,267 requests to trace an order in the previous year, and that each request had taken more than a half-hour to complete. In the same year, 3,117 orders had to be expedited.

The team also surveyed customers to ascertain their expectations and problems and to hear their suggestions or criticisms. This information was then coordinated on a flow chart, which enabled the team to change the functions of various departments.

Participants recounted instances of needless bureaucratic paper shuffling stemming from the fact that the tracing and expediting system was managed by various departments. When a customer called to ask for information about the status of an order, for example, the request went from department to department, requiring that time be spent filling out multiple tracer forms and resulting in the frequent need to request information more than once.

The team remedied the system's shortcomings by allowing the relevant departments to do their own tracing with private carriers, which saved the company thousands of dollars annually. After investigating true transit times of orders, the team further determined that expediting was unnecessary because regular carriers already offered customers the quickest possible transit time. The team decided that, except in the case of a special customer request, normal order-taking procedures would be substituted for formerly expedited shipments. The benefits accruing from this reform added up to about 1,140 hours and additional savings.

Deliveries that previously would have gone out on Saturdays by Federal Express were eliminated. The team also suggested that the paperwork on tracer forms be omitted since the information was now stored in a computer. All in all, the team's recommendations saved the company thousands of dollars a year.

A summary at the close of the Track Team's report underscored the advantages of implementing change through teamwork:

> This experience has opened the eyes of some non-believers and has confirmed to others that this process and new environment is possible and will achieve success. With the proper guidance through training and experience, a new culture of team building closely associated with trust within the ranks will soon become the norm instead of the exception.[33]

Trust is at the core of the value system of any organization that expects to equip anyone on its payroll at any level and at any time to solve customer problems. Trust is the interpersonal principle that needs to be in alignment with the personal, managerial, and organizational levels in a progressive culture.

Trust cannot exist without people themselves being trustworthy. They must share the values and possess the skills needed to meet and exceed customer expectations. If you want your organization to be truly customer-driven, you must give your employees control in assisting each and every customer they serve. In most environments, however, only certain individuals are entrusted and empowered to this degree.

As Father Carl, former general manager of Abbey Press, put it,

> We are definitely talking more about the customer here at Abbey Press. Our teams are more focused on how to work better together making the best use of their time to try to get something done. They also do a good job of taking assignments away from meetings and working independently or in smaller teams to expedite the process of improving the overall business processes. These are all real powerful benefits.

A Collective Effort or an Effort at Collecting?

Father Carl's is a positive appraisal to be sure, and one that confirms our belief in the power of teams. Yet we would be remiss if we did not recognize that some companies have had mixed results with teams. The synergy just isn't developed, or there may be a lack of energy and inspiration. In fact, some situations simply aren't suited to the team concept at all. These drawbacks raise the danger that cynicism will creep in and overshadow the importance and potential value of teams.

Thus, it's important to recognize that when teams work well, they are spectacularly successful in solving problems and delivering results quickly and cost-effectively. At their best—and we have seen many that rate that superlative description—teams are about harnessing the collective talents of a diverse group of employees. The sum is far greater than the parts, and that adds up to an important tool for companies that want to wind up on the winning side.

A company that has recognized the power of collective effort is primed for the next phase of the Believe principle: Go outside the corporate family to draw on the talents of suppliers and partners. In Chapter 6, we'll look at what secure, long-term external alliances can mean for your organization.

Questions to Ask

- Is the "not invented here" excuse used to block the development of teams?
- Does the physical layout of offices and other work areas prohibit the easy sharing of ideas and the formation of teams?
- Do your teams receive the recognition and rewards they deserve?
- Do some employees have an undue sense of owning a product, an idea, or a process? Do you encourage cooperation rather than competition among employees?
- Is team formation part of any job description or training program? Do you have both natural work teams and cross-functional teams in place?
- Does the company provide the necessary tools, for example, a local area network (LAN), for encouraging people to share their knowledge and ideas?
- Do your leaders demonstrate buy-in to a team culture?
- Have your teams written mission statements or set goals (in writing) that are aligned with those of the organization as a whole?
- Are your teams "co-located" for ease of communication and project management?
- Do you encourage teams to enlist the help of qualified facilitators when necessary?

Actions to Take

- Use multifunctional teams for all product-development or process-reengineering activities.
- Be aware of shared resources; you need total commitment that is co-located.
- Develop team rewards.
- Hire team-creation specialists.
- Study other companies with successful teams.
- Increase organization-wide information sharing.
- Hire and promote coworkers who demonstrate a cooperative style.
- Examine the physical layout of the workplace and co-locate teams in a systematic fashion to make the best use of the space.
- Provide well-trained facilitators upon whom team members can call as needed.

- Celebrate and reward team accomplishments.
- Periodically refocus and rebuild teams in a retreat setting.

Working as a Team

One of the problems that Jerry McColgin had faced in his previous team experience was the fact that the members were dispersed throughout company facilities. This time, he insisted, the entire team had to work within four walls. The company agreed and found four abandoned product-display rooms for the team's use.

The company made a further commitment by underwriting the physical construction of the space. Walls were torn down, new lighting and new carpeting installed, and desks moved. An active noise system (ANS) was also introduced into the large open space. An ANS adds "pink noise," a combination of frequencies that match the human voice to the environment. Noise was an issue. Some of the members were used to working in a private office, and the fact that the place was a modern-day Tower of Babel made it hard to tune out foreign voices. A year later, when the system was turned off as an experiment, everyone begged for it to be turned on again.

Everything was brand new for the team, which, as Jerry noted, "Right from the outset sent a signal that this was a unique project, something different, something that had never been done. Nobody had ever had us all sit together like this."

Co-locating also sent a valuable message to the team itself. Clearly, the company was backing the project completely, which was a welcome signal that they had faith the team could get the job done.

To facilitate the work, the overall team was divided into subteams. These, however, remained cross-functional, so that people still intermingled. "I would walk through the room," Jerry remembers, "and I'd see a manufacturing engineer and a design engineer poring over blueprints, each giving their input. Instead of waiting for a Monday morning meeting, the discussion was taking place there and then, when it was needed. One of the things the team prided itself on was the absolute lack of bureaucracy."

No pieces of paper had to be pushed through the system to be initialed by a management hierarchy. As a matter of fact, as Jerry had promised at the outset, there was no hierarchy.

Our Featured Organization: John Robert's Spa

BRING IN THE TEAM

John and Stacy DiJulius opened John Robert's Spa over a decade ago on a wish and a prayer, with four chairs and a loan from Stacy's grandmother. Today, the John Robert's Spa Collection includes three salons in the Cleveland area that employ 140 people and generate nearly $5 million dollars in revenue a year. From the beginning, John and Stacy espoused a deep personal conviction to build a culture of empowered team members who would carry out their vision of delivering superior service, or in John's words, "secret service."

"John and Stacy inspire teaming throughout the organization," says Eric Hammond, director of operations at John Robert's. "We spend more time on our culture than just about anything else." Eric describes their industry as one that attracts people who enjoy helping others to feel good and develop positive self-esteem. He believes the teaming culture of John Robert's is based on this deeply held belief that service and caring for others is the most noble of causes.[34]

The community outreach program at John Robert's allows team members to give of themselves above and beyond what their everyday jobs require. "We give our teams the opportunity to go to a hospital and interact with people who are not as fortunate as most of us," Eric said. "Doing this helps them take their craft to a new level. It's like, 'if you think you feel good now, you'll feel really good when you come away from that experience.'"

John and Stacy firmly believe in repaying the community for the good fortune bestowed on their company over the years. For over a decade, on one Thursday morning of each month, the entire Spa team donates their services to patients and families of Cleveland's Rainbow Babies and Children's Hospital.

For a young child, there are few scarier places than a hospital. A visit from the John Robert's professionals means that the daily hospital routine of poking and prodding is replaced with hair braiding, manicures, messages, and makeup, bringing smiles and laughter rather than tears and moans. "You just start the day off better, and it makes you feel better," said 17-year-old Ginny Little, a patient at Rainbow Babies.[35]

(Continued)

Jennifer Kinn of Rainbow Babies remarked, "You might mistake them (the John Robert's team) for hospital staff until their 'tools' come out. They're not medical, but definitely 'medicinal.' They are so dynamic and bring such energy to our patients, and sometimes, that's just what they need."[36]

The families of these young patients receive special attention from the John Robert's team as well. "They go through so much—mentally, emotionally, and physically—they deserve a little pampering once in a while," said Felisha Makris of John Robert's.[37]

John and Stacy's commitment to "giving back" is not limited to the Thursday morning hospital visits. Here are a few of their exciting ongoing projects:

- *Locks of Love and Wigs for Kids*—John Robert's supports Locks of Love and Wigs for Kids by providing complimentary hair cuts for anyone donating 10 inches or more of their hair to create wigs for children suffering from alopecia or undergoing chemotherapy treatments, and who otherwise would be unable to afford hair replacement.

- *Denim Days*—You may be surprised to see members of the John Robert's team dressed in jeans rather than in their customary attire on certain days. Any team member wishing to participate pledges a contribution to a charity of his or her choice.

- *Flashes of Hope*—John Robert's makeup artists donate their time once a month for the Flashes of Hope project. Flashes of Hope, a nonprofit organization, provides a complimentary portrait sitting to families of children receiving cancer treatment.

- *Prom Promise*—John Robert's partners with local high schools to promote the Prom Promise. Any high school student who signs the agreement not to drink and drive on prom night receives a complimentary haircut.

Giving back to the community not only provides innumerable intrinsic rewards, but it's also good business. John and Stacy's inspired leadership has produced team members who truly believe in the power and importance of stewardship as a way of life. As Eric told us, "We know that if people are happy and enjoy our culture of helping others, the results will take care of themselves."

Chapter 6

Share the Spotlight

Our Space City is a distant dream. But all such dreams must begin in the minds of men. Men like the scientists, engineers and automotive designers of Ford Motor Company. I hope you enjoyed our show and your ride on The Magic Skyway in a new Ford product as much as I've enjoyed the Fords I have driven through the years.

Walt Disney
(speaking at the 1964–1965 World's Fair)

In the world arena, the United States has watched its competitive advantage slip away over the past half-century or so. Where once the United States had a per capita gross national product 4 times that of Germany and 15 times that of Japan, the three are now, in broad terms, relatively equal contenders.

How did this happen? Quite simply, Japan and Germany used partnerships to propel themselves out of their weakened post-World War II states of economic disarray to become strong competitors in one industry after another. What's more, an even bigger competitive threat is posed by the European Community, and what is this largest of world economic markets if not the product of true partnership?

If American companies are to rise to the competitive challenges that lie ahead, they too must reap the benefits of partnering. Fortunately, according to the Association of Strategic Alliance Professionals, "Strategic Alliances have emerged as a distinct competency over the past decade in the management of the modern enterprise and have contributed greatly to the transformation of the modern corporation." Admittedly, successful partnering does not come easily to most of us. As Broadway composer Charles Strouse's lyrics proclaim, applause is what "we're living for," and top billing makes that applause ever so sweet. But when it comes to getting things accomplished in the business world, the savvy competitor will recognize the value of drawing on the expertise and resources of others. In fact, the wise man or woman already knows that it is a fortuitous combination of talents that most often produces the applause-winning achievement. The key is turning that knowledge into practical action.

The solution lies in examining the methods of companies that are top-flight competitors at home and abroad. The Walt Disney Company is a rich sourcebook of partnering expertise that is ours for the taking.

Partnerships Expand the Possibilities

Walt Disney certainly had his share of individual success, becoming a cultural icon around the world because of his many achievements. But even though he was blessed with creative genius, surefire entertainment instincts, and an astute commercial sense, Walt recognized early on that strong alliances were necessary to achieve what one could not achieve alone.

Were it not for his first partnership with his brother Roy, for example, Walt Disney might have remained an obscure animator and cartoonist. When the Disney Brothers Studio opened in 1923, Roy invested his entire savings of $200 in the venture, and it was Roy who took over the finances—such as they were—in those early days. This family partnership had its rocky moments, to be sure—one breach lasted years. But in the final analysis, the two brothers accomplished much more in partnership than either could have done alone. Without Roy's assistance, Mickey, Donald, Pluto, and the host of other beloved Disney characters might well have remained nothing more than figments of Walt's imagination.

Walt knew, too, that not only must an alliance work for both partners, but also each partner must work at forming and maintaining a successful affiliation. A partnership is, after all, an investment in the future, and just like any other investment, it must be carefully considered and skillfully managed to produce the optimum return. What's more, you must know who your partner is and be sure he or she shares your values.

The latter lesson is one that Walt learned all too painfully in one of his first deals made outside the family orbit, a disastrous partnership with the distributor of his *Oswald the Rabbit* cartoons. Disney originally signed a contract with a New York distributor, Margaret Winkler. Trouble began when she married and her husband, Charles Mintz, took over her business. In a 1926 distribution deal involving Universal Pictures, Mintz persuaded the Disney brothers—whom he always referred to as "the bumpkins"—to create a new cartoon to compete with the very popular *Felix the Cat*. The result was the imaginative and successful *Oswald* series.

Mintz, however, was determined to acquire the Disney studio. When the distribution contract expired, he cut the studio's payments by nearly a third and threatened to take over the operation. After all, according to the contract, he owned *Oswald*. Walt was devastated, but he had no choice other than to comply with the contract.

That contract, however, was limited solely to *Oswald,* and Walt was free to create new characters. In the end, the *Oswald* fiasco proved to be a serendipitous turn of events, because the failed partnership led to the birth of Mickey Mouse. But Walt never forgot that partnering with like-minded people is critical to the success of the relationship. One need only look at the list of highly touted mergers gone awry to understand the value of the lesson Walt learned so early in his career. Philosophical and cultural differences are frequently cited as the reason these unions fail.

Partnerships Take Many Forms

Business partnerships are entered into for a variety of reasons, of course. Some are formed to carry out a specific project, whereas others are joined on a long-term basis, like law partnerships.

One of Walt Disney's first remunerative partnerships was with a small New York stationery firm. He signed a contract giving the firm the rights to sell schoolchildren's writing pads with a portrait of Mickey Mouse printed on them. The firm paid a mere $300 for the rights, but it was 1929 and Disney was broke and eager for every nickel he could get. "As usual, Roy and I needed the money," he said later.

Although on its face the deal was a small one, it opened Disney's eyes to the possibilities of making money through ancillary uses of his creative product. He never overlooked an opportunity to do so from then on, and licensing arrangements became central to his management philosophy. A couple of years later, he licensed the sale of Mickey Mouse watches, which initially sold at the rate of about 1 million per year. Other similar agreements brought in 10 percent of the company's income over a decade-long period.

All the while, Walt kept a sharp eye out for any violations of his copyright, just as The Walt Disney Company does today.

But even Walt could not have dreamt of the multimillion-dollar cornucopia of Disney products that has evolved from that first Mickey Mouse school tablet. The company licenses its cartoon characters to manufacturers, and products bearing the names and pictures of those characters are then sold by retailers around the world. There are company owned and operated stores, as well as a Disney Web site that markets movies, books, art, clothing, jewelry, collectibles, and a host of other products all bearing the likeness of various familiar Disney figures and all produced under license from The Walt Disney Company.

Most of Disney's numerous partnerships were formed for purely business reasons, but one of his most unlikely affiliations stemmed from a creative communion that developed quite by chance. One evening Walt was eating alone in a fashionable Hollywood restaurant when he spotted the famous conductor of the Philadelphia Orchestra, Leopold Stokowski, also dining alone. He invited Stokowski to join him. Stokowski was a giant in the world of classical music, and with his mane of white hair and sweeping gestures, he looked every inch the maestro, whether leading an orchestra or chatting with a friend over dinner.

Discussing future plans, Disney mentioned that he was about to start work on a new Mickey Mouse cartoon, *The Sorcerer's Apprentice*. Stokowski expressed an interest in conducting the score and even offered to waive his fee. Over the dinner table, the two men then discussed the possibility of making an animated feature set to the music of great composers. Out of this conversation grew the 1940 movie *Fantasia*. Disney and Stokowski were equally charmed by the concept.

In the film, Stokowski conducted everything from Beethoven to the avant-garde music of Igor Stravinsky, while animated figures interpreted the compositions through dance. Visual interpretation of orchestral music was a new concept, and *Fantasia* won raves from the critics. Bosley Crowther of the *New York Times* called it "simply terrific, as terrific as anything that has ever happened on the screen," while another critic described it as "a new artistic experience of great beauty." Because it was so unlike any other Disney movie, however, the public rejected it. Today though, the film is highly regarded, especially among film historians.

The partnership with Stokowski served Disney well in a creative and artistic sense, and represented a great step forward in the fusion of animation, color, and sound. And even though the film was, at the time, a financial failure, Walt viewed few things as absolute failures. He knew that even unsuccessful ventures provide valuable lessons, and such hard-won knowledge can be put to use elsewhere.

Taking its cue from Walt, The Walt Disney Company does not consign failed projects to the trash heap. Rather, it considers them to be assets of the company that may be tried again later or perhaps utilized in a different capacity.

Partnerships Can Secure Prosperity

Partnerships were obviously an integral part of Walt Disney's business strategy, often serving as lifelines in times of financial distress. In the 1930s alone, a string of partnerships—ranging from an exclusive arrangement with Technicolor and licensing contracts that put Mickey and Minnie's faces on toys and clothes to deals for a syndicated newspaper comic strip and a deal for the publication of the *Mickey Mouse Book*—pulled the company back from the edge of bankruptcy. At this particular time in Walt's career, the cash flow from cartoons was little more than a trickle (he often had to wait months to be paid by his distributors), and the partnerships were crucial to survival.

During the building of Disneyland in the 1950s, Walt again found himself short of cash. Even though ABC invested $500,000 and guaranteed a bank loan of $4.5 million, the price tag for finishing the park came to some $17 million. Walt cashed in his life insurance policy and then began to search for ways to close the financing gap. The novel solution he came up with was corporate sponsorships, which, in effect, are another form of partnership. Disney signed agreements both Coca-Cola and Frito-Lay, giving them exclusive concessions at Disneyland. He also brought in small, unknown partners, even allowing a corset maker and a real estate agent to set up shop in the Park. Walt partnered with Art Linkletter and asked him to emcee the gala grand opening of Disneyland. In those days, Art was one of the best-known celebrities in Hollywood. When Walt told Art that he would love for him to emcee the event, but that having invested everything he owned in the construction of Disneyland, he was sure he could not afford Art's fees. Art recalls the discussion: "Walt said, 'I'm at a great disadvantage in talking to you. Why don't you have an agent like everybody else?' I said, 'Well, Walt, I just do my own stuff. . . . We're friends. I'll do it for practically nothing.' He said, 'Will you?' I said, 'Certainly. We do things for our friends. Now, for instance, you have some things you are going to contract out. You aren't going to do everything there. Restaurants, and parking, and film for everybody who comes there to buy film.'" At that time, Art owned several Kodak film franchises and asked Walt for the photo concession at Disneyland for the first 10 years. Linkletter recalled: "Walt said, 'Good. It's a deal. Now you see what could get done without agents.' The Kodak people once said to me, 'Mr. Linkletter, you own the world's largest automatic film vending machine: Disneyland.'" Kodak once told Disney that 5 percent of all photos taken in North America are taken at Disneyland or Walt Disney World. One can only imagine the millions of dollars that 10-year concession generated for Art's 90-minute appearance.

In building Walt Disney World, the company took the same tack, entering agreements that gave the likes of Exxon, AT&T, and General Motors pavilion space at EPCOT. EPCOT is, in fact, a testimony to partnerships. And when Michael Eisner and Frank Wells took over the leadership of The Walt Disney Company in 1984, 18 years after Walt's death and 13 years after the opening of Walt Disney World, these original partnerships were still contributing thousands of dollars annually to the Disney coffers.

Although the Disney partnerships have certainly helped it fend off disaster at times, the company has never looked at partnerships simply as stopgap measures forced on it by market conditions. Quite the opposite, partnerships are viewed as long-term investments in the company's future prosperity. Corporate sponsorships and the income they generate support this. But the company continues to exemplify, just as Walt did, the principle that alliances must work for both partners if they are to endure. Company executives must thus be willing to commit themselves to cooperating fully, trusting implicitly, and communicating effectively with partners. Even though the relationship may be a business deal, personal contact will help to cement it.

Personal relationships have helped make The Disney College Program a desirable opportunity for students to be simultaneously involved in both educational and real-world work experiences. The College Program's National Advisory Board includes some of the most prestigious educational institutions in the United States and partners with Disney's College Program Team to ensure the highest standards of learning, using the 47-square-mile "learning laboratory" known as Walt Disney World. Students are encouraged to network with Disney leaders, make professional connections in their specific fields of study, and discover career opportunities available after graduation. The Walt Disney Company and its Educational Partners consider their responsibility for developing young people into future leaders as serious business.

Indicative of how much the company values the personal touch is the three-day get-together Eisner planned prior to the Disney-Capital Cities/ABC merger in 1996. The CEO invited 200 people—executives and their spouses—from ABC television and The Walt Disney Company to the Disney Institute in Florida so that the two companies could build a more personal relationship.

This may have been the last true act of partnering performed by Michael Eisner at Disney. It seems that Michael lost the "pixie dust" that once enabled him to re-instill the magic in Disney's once floundering movie studio. During Michael's last 10 years, he dismantled arguably the most accomplished group of animation artists in the history of the industry and severed ties with Pixar. Destroying this partnership may have proved to be the final curtain on Michael Eisner's stage at Disney. The recently ordained CEO, Robert Iger, has repeatedly stated that he is determined to restore artistic integrity at all levels of Disney. His actions speak louder than words. Mere months after taking the reins of the Disney organization, Iger announced the acquisition of Pixar. Pixar's creative genius, John Lasseter, was named chief creative officer of the animation studios, as well as principal creative advisor at Walt Disney Imagineering. Reporting directly to Iger, Lasseter will lend his expertise in the design of new attractions for Disney theme parks around the world. The verdict is still out, but the Pixar deal could be the catalyst for rejuvenating animation in the tradition of Walt Disney's original classics. By all initial accounts, Iger is a leader who understands the fragility of new teams and intends to carefully protect the relationships he is developing with Pixar.

As we stated in Scene 12 of *The Disney Way Fieldbook: How to Implement Walt Disney's Vision of "Dream, Believe, Dare, Do,"* establishing solid partnerships helps create a "best show" experience for your guests and cast and will lead to profitable financial results. This was certainly true for Mello Smello, founded by husband and wife team Jon and Leah Miner, who teamed up with 3M in 1980 to create and produce "Scratch 'n' Smell" stickers of Disney characters. Over the past 20 years, Mello Smello has developed an innovative variety of other products and has also grown to become a multi-million dollar business and a valued partner to the nation's largest retailers, including Wal-Mart, Target, Walgreen's, and Kmart.

In 1986, the late Evelyn Overton, founder and co-owner of The Cheesecake Factory, learned how accepting the guidance of a larger and better-known branded company could result in a great partnership. Evelyn had always prided herself on her strict methods of creating fabulous cheesecakes. Cleanliness and accuracy were huge factors in each and every step of the operation. When The Cheesecake Factory was about to land its first national bakery account with Darden Restaurants, Darden made some critical observations of Evelyn's kitchen operations.

"Darden looked at our company as an entrepreneurial, West Coast company that had true quality with their cakes," says Max Byfuglin, president of The Cheesecake Factory Bakery, Inc. Evelyn was proud of cracking the eggs, but the first time Darden came to visit us in 1986, they said, "You can't do that." Evelyn was also proud of the butcher tables in the bakery and they said, "You can't use those." After that visit, I got a three-page letter saying that they'd love to do business with us, but first, here's a list of the things we would need to do. We were just building a new bakery down the street, so I was able to incorporate their suggestions in the areas of quality and safety. That was the beginning of becoming a national company on the bakery side. Darden has been a great partner for us."[38] As The Cheesecake Factory discovered, a great partnership can dramatically increase both your reputation and your profitability.

Restructuring Your Business through Partnering

Business alliances, as we said, are formed for any number of reasons. There is partnering between customer and supplier and between managers and coworkers. There is also partnering between manufacturing and service companies; between business, community, and educational institutions; and between government and industry. In our consulting business, we have encouraged a multitude of organizations to consider restructuring their businesses through partnerships. By this we mean a coming together of suppliers, manufacturers, and service providers to support and strengthen one another's positions. We envision quality performance through teamwork. Small companies can join forces to take on the giants of their industries; big companies can form alliances with smaller companies that are less restricted by bureaucracy. These joint ventures or strategic alliances champion the sharing of knowledge, markets, and profits. The Commonwealth Alliance Program (CAP) reports that businesses now attribute approximately 25 percent of all revenue to strategic alliances, estimated at $40 trillion.

Certification versus Partnerships

According to old economy rules, customer and supplier partnerships were defined by a process of vendor certification. The process required the vendor to adopt a new culture that entailed meeting a wide range of quality and product standards. In effect, the vendor's performance was constantly tested against a set of standards designed to conform to the needs of the customer.

Moreover, one vendor was leveraged against another because organizations insisted on having two or three sources for the same item. Often a vendor was required to reduce prices to remain competitive, regardless of the impact on the vendor's organization. The rationale for the price cuts lay in the expectation that the vendor should constantly be improving processes and sharing the resultant savings with the customer.

While certification streamlined the buying process, strategic direction was developed without vendor input. Thus, little was done to improve the competitive position of either the customer or the supplier.

In contrast, true partnerships envision working with vendors to develop compatible cultures. If sole-source relationships are developed, win-win performance measures can be devised that take into consideration the needs of both parties. In addition, sole-source relationships encourage process integration and the cross-company sharing of results. Vendors can more readily be included in strategic planning. The end result is an efficient and productive alliance for both suppliers and customers. Indeed, the term *partnership* presupposes the willingness not only to share the spotlight but also to work out in a straightforward fashion what is best for both parties. Sometimes these arrangements aren't bound by legal contracts and actually bear more of a resemblance to the kind of teamwork we discussed in the preceding chapter.

One of our clients, for example, established an innovative and productive relationship with the company that supplies its packaging. Constant problems and the words "This isn't working" marked the association between the two companies before they decided to set up an informal partnership. Now, teams comprising staff members from each company consult with one another about a variety of issues: the design of the packaging so that it meets precise specifications, the costs involved, the materials to be used, and so forth. Engineers, purchasing agents, and managers from each company now meet regularly to discuss their respective needs. The two companies work so closely together that some of the packaging-supply people have desks at our client's offices, and a new computer network keeps everyone informed of progress on issues of mutual interest.

To confirm that it was on the right track with this informal arrangement, our client compared the costs of using traditional purchasing methods against the costs of its new method. The new procedure won hands down, and it is producing substantial cost savings. Equally gratifying, this collaboration has produced a welcome reduction in material needs, a critical factor at a time when forest shrinkage is reducing the supply of wood pulp.

A close alliance is also producing big rewards for both Wal-Mart and Bristol-Myers Squibb, which supplies the discount retailer with its products on a quick-delivery basis. As the products are sold, Wal-Mart's purchasing department informs the sales department at Bristol-Myers and replacement products are shipped out within 24 hours. The partnership has worked so well that Wal-Mart chose to honor Bristol-Myers as a Supplier of the Month, not because of size, for many of Wal-Mart's thousands of suppliers dwarf Bristol-Myers in terms of volume, but because of reliability.

The Walt Disney Company has long understood the importance of respecting its suppliers and maintaining strong alliances with them. Michael Vance, former head of Disney University, tells the story of when he and Roy Disney visited the construction site during the building of Walt Disney World. As the two men entered the site, the first thing they saw was a large sign announcing, "All contractors immediately report to construction shack 47 upon entering the premises."

Reading that clear and curt order, Roy turned to Mike and asked, "What does that convey to you?"

Without hesitation, Vance responded, "It says that we don't trust our suppliers to be on the property."

"Right," Disney replied. "And who's responsible for communicating the Disney culture and values to all employees on the property?"

As it happens, that is one of the goals of Disney University, so Vance put together a team that designed and built a new reception center. Now contractors and construction workers at Walt Disney World are treated like the valued partners they are. The reception center offers them coffee and cold drinks, telephones, and meeting rooms, all in a pleasant and welcoming atmosphere.

As Roy Disney explained to Vance, not only were company values at stake but also the wider reputation of the company. "We need to be partners with our contractors for the park to open on time, but even more importantly, they have to be proud to be a part of this, so they will call friends and family all over the country and tell them to come down to see what they've done."

Lessons Relearned

Do any of us *always* follow the rules, even though those rules may stem from our own stated convictions? Probably not.

EuroDisney is a case in point for Disney. Even though partnerships have always been central to Disney's business strategy, the company deviated from standard practice when it came to building the French theme park. For example, in the early 1990s at both of its domestic sites, Disney retained a percentage of the hotel rooms (14 percent at Walt Disney World) and also entered into partnerships with other hotels, such as the Sheraton chain. But management avoided partnership arrangements with any French hotels, which meant that the rooms were not furnished to French tastes. For example, the French expect fireplaces in their vacation villas and Disney had neglected this detail. Today, Disney has corrected this problem by retrofitting each room with a fireplace.

One of the biggest mistakes, though, was in naming the park. The French are enormously proud of their country and their culture, and they greatly resented the lack of a French identity in the EuroDisney name. In this instance, the entire population of France was, in effect, Disney's partner, and in forgetting the lesson Walt took away from the Oswald calamity (that is, to know and understand your partner's culture and values), the company made a serious error.

Fortunately, Disney took steps to rectify the problems before the venture failed completely. Today, the park is known as Disneyland Paris, and refinancing has established partnerships within the business community. Not surprisingly, the park has demonstrated clear signs of a successful turnaround.

Disney has suffered the consequences of reneging on the implicit partnership it maintains with employees at home, too. For example, when problems arose with Disney's Golf Resort Hotel (now Shades of Green® Resort, an Armed Forces Recreation Center (AFRC) in Walt Disney World that is owned by the federal government for exclusive use by armed service members and their families), management went through the motions of welcoming front-line input from employees, then promptly rejected it.

To determine why the Golf Resort's occupancy rate hovered in the low 90 percent range while every other Walt Disney World hotel was actually over 100 percent by having guests on a waiting list, management called its reservations staff together. "The problem," the staff said, "is in the name. Most reservations are made by wives. When they see the word *golf,* warning signals go up. They don't want their husbands to spend vacation days on the golf course instead of joining in the family fun at the park. So they request reservations at one of the other hotels."

Management's reaction was incredulous: "You guys don't know what you're talking about." Dismissing the opinions of the very people who dealt with would-be guests on a daily basis, the company hired a marketing firm, which, lo and behold, came up with exactly the same answer. Red-faced and apologetic, management went back to the reservations staff to get suggestions for a new name. The name The Disney Inn was eventually selected as a suitably neutral alternative to The Golf Resort and remained so until the change in ownership.

As the above examples indicate, Disney has occasionally made the mistake of ignoring its standards for working in partnership. And every time, management has had to backtrack when the mistake was recognized and re-embrace its time-tested principles. No matter how big or how successful a company becomes, partnership with other companies, employees, suppliers, customers, or the community is a valuable asset that needs to be cultivated.

Partnerships are being cultivated and used in creative ways by a diverse range of organizations. One of the most novel partnerships we ever participated in occurred some years back when we were working with the School of Nursing at the University of Southern Indiana. A dispute arose over the amount of continuing education that was available to the nursing faculty. The nurses wanted more, but the administration said there was simply no money for such a program.

Having already established a team at the school during a strategic planning retreat, we worked with team members to devise a simple but ingenious solution to the dispute. The school approached a local hospital and offered to staff a unit for one shift a week, using student nurses from the school. The fee to the hospital was less than the hospital's usual staffing cost for the hours involved; the students got credit for practical experience; and the school used the money from the hospital to fund courses in continuing education for the faculty. It was a deal in which everyone came out a winner.

Another result of good partnerships is that they often lead to welcome but perhaps unexpected outcomes. At Asea Brown Boveri of Canada, for example, a partnership with customers helped turn around one of the electrical engineering concern's faltering regional operations. A new manager, who was sent in by headquarters to boost revenues, eschewed the traditional approaches of making changes in product and processes and of downsizing. Instead, he asked staff members to find out the needs and problems of the businesses in their marketing area. He also established partnerships with local business people to explore potential areas of improvement. In only one year, the new manager's unorthodox reliance on a partnering approach with customers began to pay off as the operation returned to profitability.

It almost goes without saying that when people from varying backgrounds and endeavors are involved, some glitches are bound to develop along the way. But if all participants are prepared at the outset for this eventuality, with a little give and take, most such difficulties can be smoothed out. The key to effective working alliances is sustained communication among all the participants and a genuine understanding of the purpose of the association. The overriding value of the partnership must not be tarnished by minor problems.

With that in mind, we urge you to identify your key suppliers and partners and then make an honest effort to spend time with them so that you can begin to understand one another's needs. Organize dream-type retreats where you can identify customer problems and customer dreams. Build long-term relationships in which you share the spotlight with "costars."

Our work with numerous companies large and small has made abundantly clear the power that is generated when two or more organizations direct their creative energies to solving shared problems. Mastering the art of partnering can give your organization the confidence to wholeheartedly embrace the third principle in the Disney quartet: Dare!

In the next chapter, we will look at what it means to take calculated risks and how an organization can thrive on the opportunities that arise when one is willing to accept challenge.

Questions to Ask

- Do you trust the judgment of your employees and treat them as partners?
- Does your organization have true alliances with suppliers?
- Do you routinely meet with your suppliers to involve them in strategic planning?
- Do you believe that the best ideas often come from those outside your own organization?

Actions to Take

- Gain feedback from employees on a regular basis by asking the following questions: (1) How are we doing as a company in developing partnerships with employees? (2) Do we invite your input and creativity on problems and solutions on organizational issues? (3) How are we doing as a company in developing partnerships with our suppliers? (4) Are we considering partnerships with organizations that share our goals?

■ Invite employees to investigate organizational issues by identifying barriers to success and encourage them to develop solutions.

■ Meet with suppliers two days or more per quarter to discuss ways to solve customer problems and fulfill customer dreams.

Suppliers as Partners

Of course, when a radical new design for a product is initiated, the costs are high. Changes have to be made in basic drawings and design. Then bids are put out to suppliers, who must, in turn, redesign their products. "This is going to cost you an extra $5,000 because we have to retool," is often the suppliers' answer.

The Global No-Frost team tried a different and innovative approach. As the work moved forward, the team became involved with the company's capital equipment suppliers, who were supplying the equipment for the plant in India. The structure was to be built on an empty site in the middle of a wasteland on the outskirts of Pune, near Bombay. There were some 10 equipment suppliers, and the company was spending, at the very least, $5,000 with each one.

The team set up an unprecedented two-day meeting with all the suppliers. The meeting opened with Jerry McColgin, the team leader, standing up and informing his audience that, first of all, everyone would have to sign a confidentiality agreement to protect the company. Then, he continued, "Traditionally, you're told exactly what is wanted, but this time it will be different. I want you to understand how your contribution fits into the overall project." He proceeded to explain the whole schedule and where each supplier fitted in. "I pointed out as well that our success was entirely dependent on them."

The response was amazing. They were thrilled to be included and to understand their role in the process. Usually, suppliers' contact with the company is limited to one manufacturing engineer. Now they were dealing with 35 people as a team. To keep them abreast of developments, they were sent a monthly update, which not only included an account of the team's progress but also mentioned suppliers who were on time, and even more to the point, suppliers who had fallen behind schedule.

A true measure of the team's partnership with suppliers came on the question of one part's specifications. When this particular part is manufactured in North America, a thickness of 3.8 millimeters is required. The suppliers suggested that the part could be produced with a thickness of 2.9 millimeters and function just as well and at considerable savings. Without their early involvement and attention to detail, the planned refrigerator would probably have ended up at the required specification, but too large and too expensive.

When it came to inaugurating the new plant, some of the suppliers came to the dedication—at their own cost. That's how involved they felt in the project.

Our Featured Organization:
Downtown School of Des Moines, Iowa

BATTLING STUPIDITY IN AMERICA

In April 1983, the National Commission on Excellence in Education declared the United States "a nation at risk". One staggering report read, "The educational foundations of our society are presently being eroded by a rising tide of mediocrity that threatens our very future as a nation and people." Sadly, over the past few decades, most schools have done precious little to eliminate these crises.

One notable exception is the Downtown School of Des Moines, Iowa. Downtown School was born out of a partnership between the Des Moines Business Alliance and the Des Moines School District. Local business leaders dreamed of a school without failure, where no child is left behind, where students are self-motivated to achieve long-term goals, and where teachers are geared to unleash the potential of each and every student. The partnership team shared the conviction of the National Commission on Excellence in Education.

In February 1990, the Des Moines Business/Education (B/E) Alliance was established as a partnership between the Des Moines Public School System and the local business community. Jan Drees, executive director of the Alliance and principal of Downtown School, spent three years researching what worked and what had failed in other institutions. Her

(Continued)

findings and the backing of the Alliance were the springboard needed for establishing Downtown School, just a few steps away from where the parents of enrolled students worked. The close proximity to their children facilitated parental involvement, which is still the case today.

Downtown School opened with 45 students in August of 1993. The premise of the school was to create a place where real learning could take place, not as an exclusive campus for the children of the Des Moines top executives. Steve Schaaf, Alliance president, told us, "The plan from the beginning was that we would try to match the socio-economic statistics of the Des Moines Public Schools with Downtown School. It's also a school based on the philosophy that everybody is here to learn and can learn. If we aren't careful, and turn this into an elitist institution, we have lost our mission."[39]

Partnering with the business community was only a piece of Downtown School's partnering strategy. Finding the right teachers who would embrace a new way of teaching was the next hurdle. As Jan stated, "I look for teachers who do not want to be the power person in the classroom. I don't want teachers who feel 'I'm the boss, you're the student, now go sit down.' I want teachers who are child-centered!"[40]

While attempting to identify the best teachers for Downtown School, Jan ran head on into a roadblock—the union, the Iowa State Education Association. Its contract requires seniority rules; that is, if two people are equally qualified, the one with seniority gets the job. Jan remembered the anger of a key partner, Roger Brooks, CEO of AmerUs, who said "I don't like the way the school district just takes anyone, no matter how good or bad the teacher may be. I won't support the school if you do it this way."[41] Jan credits Roger for insisting that she hire the right teachers for the job, not who's up next in the Union batting order. "That gave me the power to do it differently; we had to take the best person for the job. I thank Roger every day for his insistence," remarked Jan.

The Union has not yet endorsed Downtown School's teaching philosophy, but it has not publicly opposed it either. Interestingly, of the Core Values cited by the Iowa State Education Association, "We value quality public education" tops the list. It just so happened that one day, a high-ranking Union official entered Downtown School during school hours. Usually, this would spell trouble for the principal, likely resulting in countless hours negotiating a grievance. The official reassured Jan, "Don't worry, I'm here on a personal matter. My granddaughter has applied at Downtown

School, and I wonder if you can help me." Jan held her ground. She had always believed in her duty, and her true desire was to uphold the original credo of Downtown School and the procedures that had been instituted to insure the same socio-economic student mix as the Des Moines Schools. She told the union official that she could not help him. Fortunately, his granddaughter was admitted to Downtown School under normal guidelines.

So what is this new way of teaching all about? When you walk into a Downtown School classroom, there are no traditional rows of desks. Instead, there is a "buzz" about the room, a clear sign that children are alive and active. You may witness a group of students discussing a project, or see a child stretched out on the floor reading, or yet another making a presentation to classmates using histograms and flipcharts—or the classroom may be completely empty. The reason is that all of downtown Des Moines is the classroom. So, if you walk into the local bank, you may see students learning firsthand about business, or they may be doing research at the public library.

Is it working? Tracy Donovan, a Downtown School teacher says, "It's 100 times harder, but 100 times better than the traditional classroom approach. It's just a better way to teach. The students love coming to school and love to learn." Tracy spent her first years out of college in a traditional classroom. When asked if she could ever go back to the traditional teaching process, her answer was an emphatic "No."[42]

The next piece of the partnership model at Downtown School is the partnership between the teacher and the student. You won't find any traditional textbooks in the classrooms. The learning process is built around classroom projects. As Tracy explains, "We start by brainstorming the project with the whole class. Students have ownership in the project."

A recent project was "the changing landscape of Iowa." Some students became interested in what the land was like in prehistoric times, millions of years ago; others were interested in learning about the first settlers in Iowa hundreds of years ago. One nine-year-old girl became interested in soil. She enthusiastically read everything that Tracy could find on the topic. This was the little girl's first year at Downtown School, having transferred from a traditional school. One day, she asked Tracy if she could go to the public library and do some additional research on soil. She told Tracy that she wanted to check to be sure that this would not be

(Continued)

considered "cheating." The child's passion for the subject translated into real learning and, best of all, she wasn't saddled with what the author of a textbook thought she should learn. Tracy explains the direction given to students at Downtown School: "If you want to know something, here's how to find it. I don't know all the answers, and the students won't have someone next to them all their lives telling them the answers."

During our interview at Downtown School, we met a fifth-grade student named Amanda who shared with us her perceptions of her teachers, "Very, very fun. I have never heard them yell. They never talk loud. They are really nice. A lot of my other teachers (from her previous traditional classroom) were nice, too, but they can get a lot louder. So, it's better here." Tracy Donovan believes that children feel this way because Downtown School chose to build an environment where children are treasured and respected.

In the words of one Downtown School parent, "There is a close, personal relationship between the kids and teachers, and the teachers know those kids very well. On the last day of third grade, I came in and saw my daughter Lillian with three or four of her friends crying their eyes out because they wouldn't see each other for six whole weeks. I had a flashback to my last day of a Catholic parochial school where I was shouting Hurray!"

The rich and energized learning environment of Downtown School may indeed have a direct relationship to the surprisingly low incidence of children who are taking medication for a diagnosis of Attention Deficit Disorder (ADD) or Attention-Deficit/Hyperactivity Disorder (ADHD). Today, it is commonplace that behavioral problems in schools are addressed with drugs like Ritalin. *USA Today* reported in 2003 that "Ritalin is prescribed at disparate rates." And, if you live in Louisiana or North Carolina, your child is more than twice as likely to be medicated as children living in New Jersey or California. David Fassler, child psychiatrist, reports, "There is no evidence that ADHD is more common in one region than another." The AMA reports that as many as 5 percent of U.S. students ages 5 through 14 suffer from ADHD and 80 percent of those are medicated. As was reported in Megan Farnsworth's article "Schools a High-Test Formula for Success," Principal Thaddeus Lott of Houston's Wesley School stated recently, "Disruptive children are either bored or frustrated. The easiest way to maintain order is to teach to everyone's appropriate instructional level." But, instead, we have become a nation where it is acceptable to label these kids' "special education status" and pour drugs into them. In most public schools in the United States today, the fastest growing and often the largest department is special education. These children who apparently cannot "focus" in the classroom are perfectly able to spend hours playing computer games, are mesmerized for 90 minutes when watching the latest Disney animated feature film, and spend hours excitedly researching a topic that interests them.

Jan Drees and her team have created a classroom environment where each and every student is self-motivated to learn in an atmosphere of mutual respect and trust. Downtown School classrooms are as engaging as any computer game. Jan and her team believe that if a student is motivated by World War II, then why not use WWII reading material to teach basic reading skills? Principal Ronald Williams of Detroit's Newberry Elementary School narrows this down to a single success factor, "If a child can't learn the way I teach, then I must learn to teach the way she learns."

Jan's daring deviance from conventional wisdom has resulted in five times fewer Downtown School students on ADHD drugs than the national average. Using AMA statistics and Downtown School's current enrollment, Jan should have 11 or 12 students on Ritalin-type drugs, but she has only two at the present time. When a student who has been on a course of ADHD drugs transfers into Downtown School, Jan asks the family to try to eliminate the drug and see what happens. In almost all cases, the student is suddenly cured of ADHD!

The final piece of Downtown School's partnering strategy is its partnerships with the families. Parents, teachers and students all participate in student-led conferences. These conferences are held three times a year and usually last between 45 and 60 minutes. Jan believes that leading the conference helps students take responsibility for their own growth and learning. As one parent explained, "It kind of gives the kid somewhat of a star status, telling you what he has done, instead of the teachers and parents talking over his head."

Is it worth it? Downtown School has been in existence for over 10 years and continues to exceed the state and national standardized test results by more than 10 percentage points. The "experiment" that began with 45 students in 1993 is now nearly 300 students strong with over 900 names on a waiting list. Even more significant than test scores is the passion for learning and problem solving that Downtown School graduates take with them as they move on to sixth grade. For many children in traditional environments, that passion for learning is stifled by the end of their second school year.

(Continued)

The depressing truth is that although Downtown School is no longer an experiment, the Des Moines School District has not totally embraced its philosophy. And when students leave Downtown School after fifth grade and enter a traditional sixth grade class, the evidence of this is crystal clear. One sixth grader, a former student of Downtown School, was given a worksheet with questions to answer on the subject of volcanoes. As she would have done in her classroom at Downtown School, she took the worksheet home, got on the Internet, and researched volcanoes for several hours. She made notes all over the worksheet and gathered her thoughts for a presentation she intended to make to her class. When she sat down in her new classroom on the following morning, the teacher asked students to pass in their volcano worksheets. When the little girl asked if she could present her findings to the class, the teacher denied her request and recorded a "zero" on her worksheet. When the student questioned the grade, the teacher explained that she had failed to answer the questions and that her worksheet was "messed up" with all her notes. However, in a spirit of a benevolent dictator, the teacher gave the girl a second chance to complete the worksheet. That evening, this devastated child took the worksheet home and announced to her parents, "I get it, they don't care about learning at my new school. They just want me to fill in the blanks." For six years, this student loved learning, loved coming to school, and now was poised to become a stagnant, detached rote learner who felt only contempt for the educational system in America. Hopefully, as students and parents experience travesties inflicted by traditional school systems, they will demand an educational environment such as Downtown School provides. If our children begin their education in a place where they become self-motivated and take responsibility for their own learning, where teachers establish a creative atmosphere of mutual respect and trust, and where their potential is unleashed, shouldn't we expect this level of excellence to continue through high school?

Dare

Chapter 7

Dare to Dare

I really do feel—about business and life—that everybody has to make mistakes. And everybody should be encouraged to feel that if they make mistakes, it's okay.

Michael Eisner

Premier players can be found in all corners of the business world, and one thing they have in common is a willingness to take bold risks. They clearly understand that grasping at a dream requires one to reach beyond the sure thing. Even more, they seem to relish the opportunity. Walt Disney was just such a player.

In fact, if there literally were a cornerstone upon which The Walt Disney Company rested, it would have to be inscribed with one short word: Dare. Throughout the 43 years that Walt ran the company, he dared to meet challenges; he dared to take risks; and, ultimately, he dared to excel.

From the time that he decided to produce his first cartoon, Disney pushed the limits of ordinary achievement. He pioneered the use of sound in animated cartoons with *Steamboat Willie*. He signed his contract with Technicolor before the revolutionary process had even been accepted by the industry as a whole and astutely insisted on a two-year exclusive for his cartoons. He originated feature-length cartoons with *Snow White* and defied the odds at a time when no one thought anyone would ever sit through a 90-minute cartoon.

Even Walt's decision to build Disneyland represented a new and risky concept in entertainment. Up to that time, amusement parks had something of an unsavory connotation, an association with the tawdriness of pre-1950s carnivals. It took the vision of Walt Disney to imagine a place that would incorporate historical reconstructions, displays, and rides, and it took the daring of Walt Disney to build it into a world-famous tourist attraction.

The Disney experience illustrates how a company willing to take calculated risks can advance the level of development of a product or service and, in the process, reap huge rewards. But not all corporate executives and managers fall into this enviable category. Too many opt for the safest route because they fear failure or loss. They allow themselves to get bogged down in corporate bureaucracy, which can keep the management process from flowing as it should.

However, such behavior is not written in stone. Companies can change the buttoned-down, risk-avoidance atmosphere that dictates status quo first, innovation later—if at all. We have helped numerous leaders learn to prioritize their objectives and to take a holistic view of their companies, thereby putting risk taking into the proper perspective. In this chapter, we will look at how leaders who dare can take calculated risks and lift their organizations to previously unimagined levels of achievement.

Solid Fundamentals Support Risk Taking

Psychologists might describe Disney as a born risk taker, someone whose fear of failure was outweighed by the need to tackle new challenges. His more cautious brother, Roy, often referred to him as "crazy" or "wacky." But then Roy was in charge of the family cash box, which in the early days his brother depleted with alarming frequency, leaving it to Roy to persuade bankers to agree to new loans or extend old ones.

The key point is that Walt, although politically and personally conservative by nature, accepted no conventional boundaries when it came to his work. He was sure of his values and beliefs, sure of his own talent and that of his cast members, sure of his instincts, and sure that if given the proper chance, this outstanding combination would eventually prevail.

That is not to say that he jumped at every idea that came his way, but he certainly didn't hesitate to take a chance if a concept met his artistic and financial criteria. First and foremost, of course, any potential project had to pass Walt's trademark "entertainment" test. But if he felt that a project fit with his vision, he would leap, often ahead of the pack.

Another business giant who is not afraid to take a chance to realize his dreams is Lee Iacocca. His name is so inextricably linked to the Chrysler Corporation that asking whether a particular car is a Chrysler or an Iacocca is not really all that far-fetched—particularly if the car in question happens to be a Dodge or Plymouth minivan purchased in the 1980s. Iacocca hatched the idea for the minivan while he was president of the Ford Motor Company. In fact, as early as 1974, Iacocca drove a minivan prototype put together by one of Ford's product engineers, Harold Sperlich, and two Ford designers.

Iacocca loved the car's roominess, but to work properly, it needed a front-wheel-drive power train, the components for which would have to be designed from scratch, an expensive undertaking. Henry Ford II, Ford's ultraconservative chairman and CEO, balked at taking on the risk and the expense. Henry was still haunted by the memory of Ford's Edsel fiasco some 20 years earlier.

When Iacocca left Ford in 1978, he got permission from William Clay Ford, Henry's younger brother, to take with him the consumer research he had gathered on the minivan. "I didn't know I was going to Chrysler then," Iacocca told *Fortune* magazine in a 1994 interview, "but I had a hankering to do this car because the research was so overpowering."[43]

Harold Sperlich had departed for Chrysler a few years before, so when Iacocca also ended up there, the stage was set for the birth of one of the most profitable consumer products ever built. But first, Iacocca had to find the money to proceed with the minivan project, a daunting prospect at a company that in most quarters had been written off as dead in the water by the time Iacocca took over. The new CEO diverted the money from another project and the rest, as they say, is history.

Like Disney before him, Lee Iacocca dared to follow his instincts while staring potential disaster in the face. Later, with minivan sales surging and a debate raging over whether to commit several hundred million dollars to expand production capacity, Iacocca stood his ground against the opposition of all of his top executives who feared that the minivan might prove to be just a fad. He was sure he had tapped into a huge unanswered market. "Everyone fought me," Iacocca told *Fortune,* "but that's what makes horse races."

Well, not quite. Iacocca had the backing of the solid market research he had done early on, not to mention the strength of his convictions. He wasn't gambling on the unknown; he was taking a calculated risk based on sound numbers and sound instincts.

Both Ford and General Motors had built prototypes of a minivan too, but neither company had the courage to risk investing enough money to bring the vehicle to market. Because of this hesitancy, they lost out to Chrysler.

Successful cities, like successful companies, are often the result of daring yet trustworthy leaders. Once known as "India-no-place," Indianapolis has become a thriving business hub and tourist destination. This transformation did not happen overnight. It began in 1967 with the dream of newly elected mayor, Richard Lugar, now Indiana's senior U.S. Senator. Yet three years earlier, the notion of becoming a politician was far from his mind; he was merely a concerned parent on the Indianapolis School Board trying to preserve the school lunch program. After stirring things up in this position, the *Indianapolis News* suggested that the city needed a mayor who was not afraid of change, and that Lugar would be the ideal choice. In the election that followed, the Republican Party enthusiastically agreed and drafted Lugar as their candidate.

During his campaign, Lugar began talking about the limitless possibilities for Indianapolis, and his fervor spread with 50-foot billboards of the so-called "walking man": Lugar striking a Kennedy-esque pose with his coat slung over his shoulder. With 25-foot lettering that read "LUGAR" in orange underscored with speed lines, talk on the street was that he "was going to remake the city."

Lugar dared to act out the dream of his predecessor's Indianapolis Progress Committee. During Lugar's two terms as mayor (1968–1975), one of the most notable events in Indianapolis government history occurred, the adoption of Uni-Gov, a merger of the city and Marion County governments. Many units of city and county government were consolidated into one civil government, including the City Council and the County Council that joined to become the City–County Council. The structure of Uni-Gov was divided into three branches similar to the federal government: the executive branch, the legislative branch, and the judicial branch.

With Uni-Gov, the population and tax base of Indianapolis nearly doubled, and more than 2,000 agencies were consolidated into 6. More importantly, the merger had near perfect timing and may have saved Indianapolis from becoming another crumbling urban center surrounded by prosperous suburbs.

This story reaches far beyond Lugar's clinching an election; it is one of powerful diplomacy, teamwork that transcended party lines, and a fight to destroy the racial inequalities that prevailed in the 1960s.

Long known as the "Crossroads of America," Indianapolis has shed its tired image and emerged as an exciting community where people are proud to live and work. In the words of CBS sports commentator, Jim Nantz, "You can't say enough about the vision by the civic leaders, the business community and the government constructing this downtown area over the last 20 years. It is such an ideal setting for the Final Four." And the daring of one leader inspired it all.

Avoiding the Short-Term Mentality

Admittedly, being able to determine whether taking an action or not taking it will put employees and/or customers in jeopardy is not always easy. What's more, some managers are so determined to protect their own turfs that they prefer the status quo to any proposition that might threaten their position, no matter how reasonable. This is akin to the "short-term mentality" that we discussed in Chapter 3, and it is the kiss of death for innovation and risk taking. Many great companies have slipped into decline because of this mindset, which combines an inability to take on challenges with a dangerous self-satisfaction with past achievements.

Walt Disney, of course, exhibited the exact opposite of that mindset. When it came to technological advances, for example, he knew that no one could cling to past achievements and survive, so he always had his antennae out for new technology. When the movie industry stubbornly refused to sell or lease any of its products to the television networks in the 1940s and early 1950s, thinking it could stop the juggernaut, Walt took a different view. He saw television's potential market value, and he embraced the opportunities the new medium offered, realizing that it presented yet another outlet for his product.

Although Disney was clever enough to recognize the potential television held, he still spurned the networks' initial approach. As always, Walt was determined to control the environment in which his work was released, and he feared that the black-and-white screen would not do justice to his color cartoons and films.

When he did make a television deal in 1953, he made it with the fledgling American Broadcasting Company, in part because that network agreed to help finance Disneyland. In return, ABC received access to Disney's backlog of films and cartoons. Thus, just as movie audiences were declining markedly in the 1950s, lured away by the flickering screens right in their own living rooms, Disney was cementing an alliance that would plant his product firmly in the new medium. Today, Disney not only has a string of TV successes to its credit, including its own cable channel, it also owns ABC outright.

In our work with the Mead Johnson Nutritional Division of Bristol-Myers Squibb, we encountered a leader who had to make the courageous decision to focus on the long term in the face of very difficult near-term problems.

When we began our talks with this leader, Dr. Bill Cross, who happened to be the division's vice president for quality, his reception of our proposals for change was distinctly lukewarm. Dr. Cross told us later that his first reaction was, "Why do we need to change?" He knew that his division already had a culture of quality and never let bad products go out the door. Then he realized that more than quality was at stake. Dr. Cross began to get excited about implementing a culture where team members could enjoy working together toward common goals and objectives.

As we were laying out plans for the implementation of the change effort and the initial Dream Retreats, Dr. Cross phoned to say that the division was going to have its first-ever layoff in only a few months. "Should the implementation be postponed?" he asked. We couldn't answer his question, of course, because, ultimately, the decision was his to make. But in the end, he proceeded as planned. "Okay," he said, "I'm going to plunge ahead because I feel so sure about its worth to us."

Thus, when the layoffs came, the shock that everyone understandably felt was mitigated by the fact that a plan was in place to change the culture to one in which people could enjoy and take pride in their ability to meet customer needs and problems.

After the initial teams were well on their way to success, the vice president took the initiative to enlist the entire division in the change process. Now, the new cultural orientation has spread throughout the unit. It was this leader's belief in the change effort and his recognition that the long-term future of the division was at stake that made the success possible.

Another leader at a Fortune 500 manufacturing company with which we work also exemplifies the kind of long-term perspective that Walt Disney showed. Traditionally, manufacturing a new product at this company required the installation of an assembly line costing between $80 million and $100 million. If the product failed, a large investment was lost. Obviously, finding an alternative way of doing things was in the company's best interests.

Deciding to experiment with the possibility of running multiple products on the same assembly line, our client turned to an engineering manager with eight years of service with the company who was known as someone willing to experiment to try out new ideas—in short, someone ready to take risks. When the company approached him, however, he was in the enviable position of being head of the division that manufactured the most profitable product in its line.

Although managing this pioneering project carried the possibility of enormous benefits, success was by no means guaranteed. How many leaders would be willing to give up a sure thing to take on a risky, albeit potentially consequential task? Yet rather than fearing failure, this individual was excited about the ultimate goal of limiting capital risk, and he welcomed the chance to take on a new challenge. He was enticed to accept the company's offer by the chance to spearhead something new. "That's how you learn and how the best products are developed," he said.

The Many Forms of Risk

It is usually taken for granted that risks in the business world are financial, but in our experience, risks come in various forms. A risk might involve change in a leader's personal behavior, management style, or willingness to place more trust in co-workers or lower-level employees. Generally, a number of risks must be taken if a company is to reach its peak performance.

One of our clients was unable to risk making needed behavioral change until he was forced into it by circumstance. He was an executive and part owner of a family company. Within the company, he was perceived as an autocrat. Workers complained about his high-handed behavior and his abrupt way of giving orders. The complaints finally reached the company's CEO after it became clear that the executive in question had completely lost the trust of his workers. The output of his department was suffering, and it was losing money.

During discussions with this executive, we pointed out that discontent with his management style was undermining employee morale, and, even worse, affecting his efficiency. He had a tough time accepting our assessment at first, but in the end, he acquiesced. We encouraged him to take what for him was an enormous risk: He empowered his staff by giving them information on business goals and performance and by asking them to participate in problem solving.

After three years of coaching, this executive was finally able to relax control and stop micromanaging everything in his department. He eventually became so comfortable with trusting his employees that he could even skip meetings, thus giving them more say. Because he was able to take a difficult personal risk, he reversed his department's decline.

Over the years, we have discovered that the risk of changing often holds a company or an individual back until the time comes when it is forced to make a choice. Threatened by competition or saddled with a product that has ceased to satisfy contemporary needs, many of our clients have come to us and asked, "What shall we do?"

A few times we've encountered companies that talked a good line when it came to making changes, only to discover that all management really wanted, in effect, was to throw up a smoke screen. They planned to go through the motions of change by attending meetings with us, but they had no intention of even attempting to implement the suggested actions.

In some ways, however, such behavior is not all that surprising, because it takes courage to accept the fact that you must change. Some companies are never able to do it, and, ultimately, they slip quietly beneath the waves. But others, such as British Petroleum, manage to summon the resolve to do what must be done. As previously discussed in Chapter 2, management admitted that its resources were fast being depleted and that a complete structural overhaul was needed. Circumstances may have forced management's hand, but it still took courage to risk making the fundamental change required to survive.

Shake Up Your Hiring Policies

When a client is truly serious about adopting a management style that encourages appropriate risk taking, one of the things we usually recommend is a change in hiring policies. We suggest looking for people who are not wedded to conventional business paradigms—people who may appear to be a bit radical for the prevailing atmosphere at the company but who possess vision and a willingness to try to bring that vision to life, even if it means that they might not succeed. Seek out those whose breadth of experience may indicate that they've taken an alternative or unique path to your door. The value of having people who are not carbon copies of the leader can't be overstated.

Before Michael Eisner became chairman and CEO of Disney in 1984, he spent eight years as president of Paramount Pictures, a period in which the studio had a string of hits and critical successes. Yet he was rejected for the top job at Paramount because he was thought to be "too childlike." In the years since, Paramount has had its share of successes while undergoing a couple of ownership changes. Its performance pales, however, in comparison to that turned in by Eisner in the first decade of his tenure at Disney.

There is little to be gained from empowering employees whose careers have been geared to obedience and suppressing their individuality as they move politely and gingerly up the corporate ladder. If you want to banish the

"It can't be done here" mentality, support employees who challenge those rules that threaten creativity and stifle imagination.

Sometimes, however, that creativity can turn sour. Several years ago, the vice president of stores at Men's Wearhouse fired an employee for stealing a suit and tie. As soon as George Zimmer learned the details of this situation, he told his vice president to rehire the young man. When the baffled V.P. inquired as to the reason his company needed a thief working among their loyal team members, George provided a rationale that is most uncommon in corporate human resource practice.

First of all, the employee had stolen a suit and tie in his own size, George had explained, so he wasn't selling it on the street. George honestly believed that the employee likely needed the suit and couldn't afford to buy one. Second, the store where the employee had worked was touted as a top-performing Men's Wearhouse for a number of years. And third, the vice president told us that George reminded him that the next person hired to replace this employee might be someone totally incapable of running the business.

According to the written corporate philosophy of Men's Wearhouse, "When mistakes are made, leaders focus first on their coaching role, not their umpire role. Mistakes are opportunities for both mentoring and learning—not for instilling fear into the workplace. Reducing fear draws out our employee's best efforts and most positive attitudes."

George Zimmer isn't blind to people's faults. Within the walls of Men's Wearhouse, it is widely understood just how strongly George believes in giving his team members second and third chances, and that he chooses to focus on the positive aspects of their personalities.

The leader who dares to take risks is often an outsider who doesn't feel constricted by the establishment's rules. Such divergence from the established norm is typical in the arts, and art history is full of examples of innovation prompting outrage among the mainstream. The French Impressionist Claude Monet, for instance, was ridiculed by the art establishment early in his career because his daring experimentation with bright color violated traditional artistic conventions.

It may seem odd to describe Walt Disney as an outsider, yet that is exactly what he was for many years in Hollywood. As the producer of cartoons, he was looked upon as small time, the supplier of filler material shown by movie houses before the "real" feature presentation came on. Even the special awards given him by the Academy of Motion Picture Arts and Sciences in the early 1930s were discounted as something of a public-relations ploy by the industry. Some thought that Disney, with his reputation as a producer of "family" products, was being singled out to counter the accusations of immorality that then dogged the industry. Not until he received an Oscar for the full-length *Snow White and the Seven Dwarfs* did Hollywood bestow any real recognition on Disney.

Throughout his lifetime, Walt continued to maintain a distance from the movie-making elite. He never used big-name stars in his pictures, nor did he invite them to lavish parties or Disneyland events. Walt also shunned deals with big-time agents. Early on, he established his own standards and went his own way.

Make It Fun!

Fun is a bad word in old-economy companies. Their management still believes, "If there's too much fun, there's too little work." In reality, the opposite is true. Companies which champion fun have higher productivity and profitability. American Psychological Association has published surveys about this, and it's a fact. Take the example of Southwest Airlines. The company boldly requires job candidates to indicate on their applications whether or not they possess "a sense of humor."

In our work with numerous organizations, even some whose core businesses are highly regulated by standards-driven agencies, we've seen how a fun-filled workplace builds enthusiasm. And, that enthusiasm leads to better customer service, a positive attitude about the company, and higher odds that employees will stay. "Most business practices repress our natural tendency to have fun and to socialize," says George Zimmer of Men's Wearhouse. "The idea seems to be that in order to succeed, you have to suffer. But I believe that you do your best work when you are feeling enthusiastic about things."[44]

If fun is truly a good thing—for human beings and for business—why are so many workplaces fun-free zones? One reason for sure is because times have changed: the effects of 9/11, a recession, downsizing, and the prevalent "do more with less" mentality. The good news is that companies around the country, from Motorola to Sprint, have discovered the benefits of humor in the workplace. The posture of some executives is traditional business heresy: "I know our company is doing well when I walk around and hear people laughing," remarks Hal Rosenbluth of Rosenbluth International, a Philadelphia-based travel agency that has made the lives of corporate travelers across the country much easier.

The dentist office is just about the last place one could think of to go for a good time. But a visit to Dischinger Orthodontics in Portland, Oregon, would make you think you'd arrived at The Walt Disney World of dentistry. "We have always tried to make our office fun, with fun things happening all the time," says Terry Dischinger. "It is in our mission statement to produce a unique personal experience for those who encounter our office—and part of that is having fun!"[45] Perhaps Terry learned the value of fun as a professional NBA basketball player in the 1960s. He was also a three-time All-American and Olympic Gold Medalist: a member of the winning U.S. basketball team at the 1960 Games in Rome.

Keeping the energy high and incorporating fun takes a little thought, but there are many simple and inexpensive ways to do this. You don't have to fly to Four Seasons Istanbul for a Dream Retreat (although that would be nice!). Even something as simple as a pizza lunch, a "Hawaiian Shirt Day," or a karaoke party can turn poor attitudes during a slow quarter into positive attitudes for the next quarter.

Some years ago, the fishmongers of Pike Place Fish Market in Seattle, Washington, committed themselves to becoming "world famous." To date, the now World-Famous Pike Place Fish Market has never spent a dime on advertising. Their goal is simply to interact with people and give them the experience of having been served and appreciated, whether they buy fish or not.

These fishmongers are the subject of the best-selling book *FISH!*, coauthored by our friend John Christensen (who also penned the foreword for this edition of *The Disney Way*). In *FISH!*, readers learn the benefits of a fun and happy workplace. Some may find the story line and principles—like Play, Be There, Make Their Day, and Choose Your Attitude—elementary. Others, however, find a framework of solid management techniques that can transform a workplace into one where energy, productivity, and incredible teamwork drive out boredom, toxic energy, and burnout.

The *FISH!* philosophy and principles give people a common language, one that empowers and energizes the entire employee base. And here's the best thing of all: as the culture is transformed, new attitudes develop, trust increases, performance improves, and, yes, customers notice.

The idea that work should be fun is not new. In the 1985 book *Reinventing the Corporation*, John Naisbit noted, "Many business people have mourned the death of the work ethic in America. But a few of us have applauded the logic of the new value taking its place: 'work should be Fun.'" That outrageous assertion is the value that fuels the most productive people and companies in this country." And to that, we say amen!

The Sleeping Giant Is Reawakened

When Walt Disney died in 1966, the spirit of adventure with which he had imbued his company seemed to die with him. For almost two decades, the company continued to revere the image of its founder, but the old spark and inspiration were missing. The movies that were made during this time were lackluster in content and poorly received at the box office. Walt Disney World, Walt Disney's brainchild, did open in 1971, but Disneyland in California installed no new attractions, and the parks were not refurbished. Moreover, the cost of the EPCOT Center was a huge drain on profits, and attendance at the park was not living up to expectations.

"What would Walt have done?" became the most frequently heard question at company headquarters. Some employees said they felt that they were working for a dead man. Net income dropped 18 percent in 1982 and slid another 7 percent the following year. The Walt Disney Company, an American institution, was on a slippery slope, and with its low stock price reflecting the company's disarray, it became ripe for takeover by corporate raiders who were circling like vultures.

Enter Michael Eisner. With the backing of Roy E. Disney, Walt's nephew and the son of cofounder Roy O. Disney, Eisner came on board in 1984 as chairman and chief executive officer, with Frank Wells assuming the post of president. Both men won the blessing of the wealthy Bass brothers of Fort Worth, Texas, who owned a sizable stake in the company. The support of the Bass family was crucial because it assured the team a significant period of time in which to rescue the foundering company without interference from outside investors.

Disney's legacy was now in the hands of men who understood how to run the company as Walt had done and how to take calculated risks. It didn't take them long to rekindle the magic. New investment in feature-film animation and a string of live-action hits that reflected the tastes of contemporary movie-going audiences vaulted the company into the ranks of major movie studios, a place it had never occupied before. With the large-scale syndication of Disney's huge video library, the release of animated classics on videocassette, expansion and renovation at the theme parks (the whirlwind of activity was astonishing), Eisner and Wells managed to double Disney profits within two years. The duo had remade Disney into a company that dared to excel. Tragically, Wells died in a helicopter crash in 1994.

Along the way, Eisner and his management team made some mistakes, to be sure, but they did not destroy the culture that Walt Disney instituted nearly 80 years ago.

That is not to say that every new movie has been an artistic and commercial success. For example, the movie *Tron,* released in 1982, was a box-office failure, but in true Disney fashion, it introduced more advanced technology that the company will be able to utilize in future films. "When you're trying to break ground creatively," Eisner commented, "you do sometimes fall short. That's risk, and we try to manage it well."[46]

One of the company's great success stories was the launch of the Disney Stores. What began as theme-park shops where customers could buy Mickey Mouse shirts and other Disney memorabilia has developed into a place where not only a wide array of merchandise is available, but also tickets to Disneyland and Walt Disney World may be purchased.

The idea to expand the company's retail presence into malls and shopping centers came from former Disney employee Steve Burke, now president of Comcast Cable Communications and COO of Comcast Corporation. Steve was able to eventually convince both his mentor at Disney, the well-respected Frank Wells, and Michael Eisner that Disney Stores would eventually yield handsome returns. In November of 2004, Disney sold its mall-based chain of stores to The Children's Place Retail Stores, Inc., a leading specialty retailer of children's merchandise. They currently own and operate over 300 Disney Stores in North America as well as its online store; however, Disney maintains a strict license agreement governing the business practices and ways Children's Place synergizes with The Walt Disney Company. Children's Place has redesigned the Disney Stores to communicate that Disney is forward-thinking, as evidenced by a new sleeker and more modern design. Richard Giss, a partner in the retail services group of Deloitte Touche Tohmatsu in Los Angeles, says, "They've got premium locations, and the Disney name is a good place to start out for any enterprise."

That risk taking is alive and well at The Walt Disney Company is nowhere more apparent than in its dramatic entrance onto the Broadway stage. Disney's first foray, *Beauty and the Beast,* raised skepticism about the wisdom of transferring an animated film to live theater, but after more than a decade, the play still delights Broadway audiences. More recently, the highly acclaimed *The Lion King* has been setting Broadway records.

The opening of *The Lion King* represented bi-level risk taking for Disney. First, the company poured millions of dollars into renovating the dilapidated New Amsterdam Theater on New York's 42nd Street, helping the city to turn around a seedy neighborhood in the process. Then, the theatrical version of the movie musical was brought to life on the Amsterdam's stage. With its innovative staging and imaginative use of puppetry designed by its multitalented director, Julie Taymor, the production broke new ground in the long and glorious history of Broadway. One reviewer said that "as visual tapestry, there is nothing else like it."

Not surprisingly, the show instantly became an enormous hit, proving that The Walt Disney Company still dares to take risks, still dares to excel and, in doing so, still dares to provide sheer magic to its audiences.

Looking ahead to Chapter 8, we'll see how those who dare to take risks to further their dreams implement the final piece of the four-pillared Disney philosophy: Do. To make your dreams come true, you must know how to execute. It all begins with the right kind of training and orientation for every one of your cast members.

Questions to Ask

- Is your culture stuck in paradigms that are no longer effective for your business?
- Do you squelch long-term thinking in favor of short-term rewards?
- Do you avoid micromanagement of employees?
- Do you routinely give employees the opportunity to grow beyond their current responsibilities?
- Do you create an atmosphere where failures are accepted and analyzed for learning purposes and possible future innovation?
- Do you promote cross-functional teams for the purpose of re-engineering outdated processes and procedures?

Actions to Take

- Grant employees the opportunity to develop and implement innovative ideas in all areas of their jobs: product, process, and service.
- Schedule off-site retreats and meetings to encourage breakthrough, risk-taking ideas that may fundamentally change the way you do business.

- Assign cross-functional teams to re-engineer products, processes, and services. Examine projects that failed and celebrate employee efforts, despite the outcome.
- Communicate to employees how the study of so-called "organizational failures" is essential for planning future projects and strategies.

The Spirit of Challenge

When the Whirlpool Global No-Frost project started, Jerry McColgin was faced with a real challenge. Not only was the schedule cut by a third, but so was the budget. He thought he could deliver on time if—but only if—he had the team fully behind him. "I felt it was doable, but the team would tell me if I was right or not. I decided, for my benefit and for the team's benefit, that we had to decide very quickly. We couldn't get halfway through and then realize that we couldn't deliver. This was one of the main reasons I took everyone off for a five-day retreat. We all concluded that the project was feasible within the time and budget limits the company had given us."

Of course, by its very nature, the team took risks all along the way. Inviting the suppliers to work as partners was a major risk. Everyone involved was under a microscope from top management. Management had cooperated all the way—by setting up an international team, by giving the team specially outfitted and expensive offices, and by allowing personnel to be taken away from their regular functions to work full time with the team. All of these moves created some resentment and jealousy among coworkers.

The Global No-Frost team was always under pressure to reach its milestones on schedule. "From a risk point of view," says McColgin, "we were carrying a heavy load."

There were personal risks too. Take the case of the finance manager. When the project began, McColgin interviewed various people within the company and found no one he felt was really right. Then an American, who had been working as a controller in Brazil, came to see him. He wanted to relocate back to his own country. He was offered the job but expressed reservations at the risk involved in taking on a two-year job when he needed permanence. But he accepted the risk and took the job. In the end, he was given a management position in the company.

Our Featured Organization: Ernst & Young

BIG FOUR LEADER PUTS ITS PEOPLE FIRST

No one would argue that it's risky to attempt to change a culture that has been successful for over 100 years. But to publicly announce that you are putting your people ahead of your clients might be considered by some as downright foolish. In 1989, the firms of Ernst & Whinney and Arthur Young combined to create Ernst & Young. Rather than attempting to merge two cultures together as a single entity, the leaders painstakingly worked as a team to create a new culture. As Phil Laskawy, retired chairman of Ernst & Young told us, "Those of us involved saw this as an opportunity to create a better culture than either firm had."[47] Ernst & Young International is one of the Big Four global professional services firms with over 100,000 employees stationed in 700 offices throughout 140 countries. The company audits over 100 of the Fortune 500 companies, consistently posts double-digit growth, and leads the competition in tax services and technology.

Bill Capodagli, coauthor, is a proud alumnus of Ernst & Young (from the Ernst & Whinney side of the firm). Bill fondly remembers his tenure at Ernst and Whinney but believes to this day that the company viewed its clients as more important than its people. Jim Turley, E & Y chairman and CEO, confided in us, "In the past, we looked at our people issues from the 'program-driven' side forward instead of from the 'employees' delight' backward. We never trusted ourselves that if we put our people first, listened to them, and really made them the center of the firm, that they will help drive whatever we need to have from a program or policy perspective."[48]

Ernst & Young's unique "People First" philosophy dared to shake the century-old paradigm which dictated that only clients are entitled to first-class treatment. As Jim stated, "It is not only the decisions that I make that are important; it is the decisions that everyone makes day to day." At most of their competitors, "People are viewed as numbers or like inventory," remarked Phil Laskawy.

Jim Turley personally dedicated himself to championing a "People First" way of doing business. He began by visiting all of his North American senior managers and managers to assess reactions to the philosophy. It would no doubt have been easier to stage a formal presentation to the masses than spend precious time in small group discussions. Jim Turley is the kind of leader who fully understands that such programs and ideas are often viewed by employees throughout corporate America as a "flavor of the month"; therefore, he dared to integrate "People First" as a cultural philosophy, not as a program initiative. In order to accomplish this, Jim continued to meet with thousands of employees in small groups to solicit candid feedback and address their concerns. The big question that came out of this road trip was, "How do you go about changing the behaviors of senior managers and partners in order to achieve a 'People First' culture?"

After "People First" was launched in 2001, *Fortune* magazine invited Jim to participate in a conference panel discussion to present Ernst & Young's "people strategies." This was the very first time the philosophy was discussed publicly. Jim recalled, "I began to sweat. All of a sudden it hit me. I was going to tell 100–150 CEOs, half of whom were our clients, that our people are more important to us than they are." Jim's daring was rewarded when nearly all of the CEOs in the room told him that "People First" was indeed a smart move. Jim made a sure bet that his team of highly motivated and highly satisfied professionals would result in the very best service to clients.

Yet a mammoth challenge lay ahead: how to abandon the "old-school" philosophy. There is the traditional, "I'm partner, you're the grunt mentality," Phil Laskawy explained. "It's the 80–20 rule or maybe the 60–20–20 rule. Sixty percent are going to accept it, 20 percent are going to leave, and 20 percent are going to resist the philosophy. Hopefully that last 20 percent keeps getting lower and lower."

From the massive amount of employee feedback Jim gathered, it was clear that some leadership behaviors desperately needed changing. As a prescriptive measure, the human resources team created "People Point." In this anonymous rating system, every employee in North America receives a request via e-mail to answer one question as it applies to a specific PPD (principals, partners, and directors): "How effective is this individual at creating an environment of mutual respect and encouraging personal growth?" A non-numerical scale allows employees to rank the individual on a scale from "Not," to "Extremely."

The "People Point" review system is completely voluntary. Reviewers are encouraged to evaluate as many or as few PPDs as they wish. Reviewers are also afforded the opportunity to submit additional comments as they deem appropriate. At the onset of "People Point," Jim Freer, vice chairman of human resources, said management speculated that they would receive

(Continued)

10,000 to 15,000 responses. Much to their surprise, they received 30,000. A PPD will receive a report only if he or she has had five or more reviews. Eighty percent of the almost 3,000 PPDs receive reports with an average of 13 reviews. Partners with unfavorable reports are offered coaching to help change undesirable behaviors, while partners with favorable reports are interviewed to discover how desirable behaviors can best be communicated to others.

"People Point" would be a risky endeavor for companies without solid leadership. Even Jim Freer pondered the questions: Are we creating a situation were the only people that can win in this process are the nice people? And, do we want to tell people they can't deliver tough messages or their "People Point" score will go down? "So we took a group of high-performing partners, from virtually every role you can imagine: client service for big clients; client service for small clients; area managing partners; administrative staff. Then we compared those groups. We found that within each group, there were high "People Point" reports and low "People Point" reports, but between groups it did not vary much. What this proved to me was that "People Point" scores are not dependent on whether you have a job that requires you to deliver tough messages. They are much more dependant on the individual, not the job."[49] That is to say that people whose jobs typically required delivering tough messages had the same percentage of low and high "People Point" scores as those whose jobs did not require delivering the same number or degree of demanding communiqués.

So, is "People First" really working, or is it just a corporate slogan? Deborah Holmes, director of Ernst & Young's Center for the New Workforce told us, "Here people talk about how smart the practice is. One partner included her client in a conversation regarding her team's work calendar that includes personal commitments as well as business. The nature of client relationships has changed; they have become much closer, from both a business and personal perspective. We still have our busy season, but everyone pulls together to make sure that important personal commitments are met." Asked what makes Ernst & Young different from the other Big Four, Deborah replied, "A culture of entrepreneurship at E&Y makes it different. It allows people to innovate. No other firm puts people first."[50] Deborah reports directly to the chairman, sending the message that this is an ongoing way of doing business.

The "People First" philosophy was put to an early test on September 11, 2001. Ernst & Young was fortunate not to lose any employees as a result of the horrific acts of terrorism. On that day, hundreds of E&Y employees were working in the New York area, and some of them were on the eighty-second floor of World Trade Center's South Tower. When the first plane struck the North Tower, the employees opted to leave the building. Many were temporarily stranded in the stairwell near the floor where they were working when the second plane hit the South Tower. Twenty-four Ernst & Young employees lost close family members in the World Trade Center disaster.

Ernst & Young chairman & CEO, Jim Turley, was at a global partners meeting in Rio on September 11, 2001. At the end of the day, Jim sent a company-wide e-mail message to his Ernst & Young family and entitled it, Day 1. He expressed his thanks for all who were safe and his sorrow for the loss of employees' loved ones. He urged his people to take great care of themselves in those days of uncertainty. He continued to send daily e-mails, entitling them Day 2, Day 3, and so on. Jim received hundreds of responses to his communiqués. On Day 2, he established a disaster relief fund with the option of payroll deductions. "We didn't have a process for a payroll deduction system," Jim recounted, "but someone took responsibility and got it implemented overnight." Many employees that we interviewed were convinced that Jim's display of deep, genuine concern for his employees as individuals was the glue that held them together during those initial days and nights after the disaster. Jim said, "I was getting credit for all these ideas, but they were actually coming from people all over the firm. It created connectivity with people. It was just people who were thinking about what should be done and not worrying about the cost, and saying, 'Look this feels right; just do it.'"

The other Big Four firms reportedly also conveyed support to their employees in the wake of the 9/11 attacks. As Jim Speros, E&Y chief marketing officer, remembers, however, "Other firms did a lot of similar things, but they were also focused procedurally as to how to continue billable hours and what people could do at home. There was no reference to billable hours in any of Turley's communications; in fact, quite to the contrary. Our chairman was encouraging people not to fly. It was not business as usual, and he realized how people were feeling. On our own time, at our own pace, we would get back to some sense of equilibrium. Just the level of empathy, care, and concern that was shown throughout the organization really said, 'This a place that puts its money where its mouth is.'"[51] That's "People First" in action.

Do

Chapter 8

Practice, Practice, Practice

The growth and development of the Walt Disney Company is directly related to the growth and development of its human resources—our cast.[52]

Walt Disney

Actors, musicians, athletes, and others who perform in public must train and practice. Otherwise, they risk embarrassing themselves and incurring the displeasure of spectators. Of great importance, too, is the teacher or coach who tells the musician that he or she is hitting the wrong notes or advises the athlete about batting stance, running form, and so on. Without such helpful criticism and the benefit of the more experienced mentor's knowledge, a performer's career is likely to be short-lived.

So it is in business. To perform at their best, a company's employees must be thoroughly trained, and they need the help of more experienced staff members. Moreover, to maintain their competencies, training can't be a one-shot thing; it must be ongoing.

Perhaps because of his background as an artist, Walt Disney fully understood the essential part that training and practice play in the development of an individual's talents. Add in his well-known penchant for perfection, and it's hardly surprising that he adamantly insisted on rigorous and continuous training for all of his "cast members." After all, common sense dictates that everyone, from the backstage crew to the performers out front, must be thoroughly rehearsed in order to put on the really "good show." But like so much else at the company Walt built, training takes on a special quality not found at most other organizations. Disney even devotes an entire "university" to it.

The students of Disney University enjoy the most exciting campus of any educational institution in the country: Over 29,000 acres of Disneyland and Walt Disney World and anywhere else the company operates. The required course work is brief, but it's famous for its intensity. The freshmen are all new members of the Disney family: Some are there to prepare for a summer job; others are being readied to assume a permanent position.

Disney University—a process, not an institution—was conceived by Walt Disney himself prior to the opening of Disneyland in the 1950s. Today, every new employee, from senior executives to part-time desk clerks and tour guides, is required to undergo training prior to embarking on her or his day-to-day responsibilities. And in typical Disney fashion, the training process leaves nothing to chance, not only imparting knowledge about specific job skills and competencies, but also, and perhaps more important, ensuring that every employee has a thorough understanding of the Disney culture and traditions.

Thus, what is euphemistically called "human resources" at many organizations—which view training as no more than an expensive but sometimes necessary evil—is given top priority in the Disney universe. That's because Walt considered training an essential investment in the future of his company.

Obviously, not every organization has access to the facilities and resources that comprise Disney University, but every organization can adopt the attitude that underlies the Disney approach to training and developing its culture. For principal Jan Drees of the Downtown School (Des Moines, Iowa), training teachers was a critical challenge in producing the culture she and her Business/Education Alliance team members were trying to create, Disney-style. They knew that breaking the mold of traditional education would be just as difficult in the realm of training teachers as it would be for teaching students. The B/E Alliance created a professional development center, which prepares both new and experienced teachers to foster a learning environment where children are self-motivated and where they can learn and grow in an atmosphere of mutual respect and trust.

Drake University School of Education soon became a valued partner, offering an innovative master's degree program in Advanced Studies in Elementary Education. This program of weekend classes allows teachers to learn the latest teaching techniques and then apply their new skills in classes they teach during the week. Half of students' class time is spent at the

Downtown School. Jan Drees told us, "Focus is on classroom implementation. We all know that the 'gold star' approach to classroom management does not motivate learning. When students develop their own goals and take accountability for accomplishing them, true learning takes place."[53] There are currently 18 teachers enrolled in the Drake School of Education special master's degree program. Another valuable partner is Simpson College, which provides as many as eight student teachers to the Downtown School each year. These undergraduate students spend most of the school year student teaching rather than just the typical six to nine weeks required in traditional school systems.

The traditional school system is not only failing our students, it is failing our teachers as well. The New Iowa School Development Corporation reports that in Iowa nearly 18 percent of new teachers leave the teaching profession after their first year, 28 percent within three years, and 50 percent within the first seven years of their careers. *Educational Leadership* magazine reports that 40 to 50 percent of new teachers leave the profession within five years. Judi Cunningham, executive director of elementary and early childhood programs for the Des Moines Public Schools, admitted, "There's probably nothing more important in the field of education now than professional development. So, if this new center can help the teachers of Des Moines and Iowa, that would be fantastic. We talk a lot about changing teachers, but we have to provide them with some structure and some expectations and some ways to do it. This will be another learning opportunity in addition to the university setting, and it will be a wonderful combination of coursework and teaching. I don't know how many times teachers have told me, 'I learned much more in my 6 or 18 weeks of student teaching than I learned in four years of college.'"

In this chapter, we will help you distinguish between training that is purely perfunctory and the kind that will enable your employees to perform at their peaks.

Training—Whose Responsibility Is It?

Only two days after Disneyland opened on July 13, 1955, Walt Disney called the vice president of casting into his office. Normally the calmest of individuals, Disney was so upset over a situation at Tom Sawyer's Island that he shooed everyone but the casting executive out of his office and closed the door, an uncharacteristic act for Walt Disney.

The immediate cause of Disney's agitation was the behavior of the boy hired to play Tom Sawyer. The red-haired, freckle-faced 12-year-old, who greatly resembled the fictitious Missouri schoolboy, apparently had read Mark Twain's novel and was going to great lengths to imitate the rambunctious Tom. He was actually picking fights with other boys visiting the island!

It was a delicate matter, since Walt himself had suggested the boy, previously a messenger in his office, for the job. The vice president, taking his cue from the boss, had hired the young man on the spot. Now the executive was telling Disney, "The kid is beating up all your guests. We have to fire him."

But Walt's response, from behind closed doors, took the vice president by surprise. The boss was upset, to be sure, but his anger was directed toward the executive for *his failure to train the boy to deliver the "good show."* The youngster was only trying to do his job in the best way he knew how, Walt reasoned. The fault lay with Disney management for not making sure the boy understood what was expected of him.

The incident, which had been forgotten until it was recounted by the then-retired vice president at a celebration honoring the little red-haired boy for his 30 years of service to the company, illustrates the underlying belief that led to the evolution of Disney University into a world-class training program. Because Walt Disney believed so strongly in a company's responsibility for training its employees, students at Disney U now receive a complete orientation called Traditions, which includes an explanation of the company's values and traditions, on-the-job training, and procedures for advancement.

As the story suggests, Walt Disney understood the detrimental effects that the sink-or-swim mentality can have on the workplace. Under this approach, which unfortunately is prevalent at far too many companies today, people are thrown into new jobs and left to discover the rip tides on their own—hopefully before they are dragged under by them. If someone is deemed worthy of being in your employ, why not take the time to pilot him or her through dangerous currents? After all, if you buy a $30,000 piece of equipment, you would likely follow the manufacturer's break-in procedure.

Consider an orientation program as the recommended break-in procedure for new employees. Drawing on the expertise of its veterans, Disney designates trainers in each department to oversee and guide the work of new cast members. Front-line employees at Disney also serve as facilitators in some training sessions, sharing their on-the-job experiences with newcomers. Believing the adage that "to teach is to learn twice," Disney thus accomplishes the dual goal of instructing new staffers while reinforcing company values and traditions among old hands. Such contact with senior staffers also makes clear to new cast members that opportunities for advancement are available.

But perhaps the thing that most distinguishes the Disney training approach is its initial concentration on making each new employee feel as if his or her efforts will make a real difference to the company as a whole. As the head of training and development at Disney University says, "If we want new cast members to deliver Disney, that is, to exceed people's expectations, then for those first few days they're with us, our new people better feel that the company believes the same about them."[55]

New employees who are thoroughly grounded in what is expected of them and who believe that the company has confidence in their abilities will gain an amazing degree of self-assurance. Consequently, they will do their jobs much better right from the start, increasing their value to their employers.

What Kind of Training?

A few years back, *Training* magazine estimated that $48 billion was being spent annually on the training of 47.2 million employees who put in 1.5 billion hours on professional development. That's a lot of money and a lot of people, so it sounds pretty impressive until you begin to scrutinize the numbers carefully. The 47.2 million employees constituted only 37 percent of the workforce in the United States, while 54 percent of the money spent was allocated to training managerial candidates, who make up about 10 percent of the workforce. That's not such a splendid picture after all, and it gives rise to a number of questions:

- Are we training the right people?
- Are we getting the results we need to be competitive?
- Is standard training enough?
- What kind of training should be offered?

First and foremost, we must start training *all* employees, not just the professional managers. That many companies fail to grasp the urgency of implementing widespread training was brought home to us in our work with a client. This company had agreed to sponsor a program designed to teach both management and union employees how to improve performance. At the end of the third day, a mid-level manager came to us and said, "Why are you teaching these union employees management techniques?"

Somewhat taken aback by the question, we explained that we firmly believe that customer focus has to be everybody's job, but *especially* the front-line workers'. The misconception that only an elite group need be privy to a company's customer-focused mission, goals, and strategy presents a serious danger to any organization that buys into it. Without a doubt, such shortsightedness jeopardizes the company's achievement of its goals. For one thing, it deprives a company of a vast source of talent and ideas, and for another, it encourages a division among staff members that can only damage the organization.

To include everyone in training is a crucial first step, but to ensure that true learning will take place, an organization must also give every employee in a focused work environment an opportunity to use what has been taught. Lasting knowledge is acquired when on-the-job experience is used to reinforce what has been taught in the classroom.

Unfortunately, a great many companies employ the "spray and pray" method of training. That is, they spray training on people, then pray that it gets absorbed. That kind of slapdash approach is at odds with what we call the Performance Learning Cycle, illustrated in Figure 8-1, in which the depth of training is as important as the breadth. So all companies must ask themselves, "Are we giving our employees enough of the right kind of training?" That means providing employees with the techniques they need to achieve the desired customer-focused results and then following up with a hands-on situation that offers a chance to practice the ideas and learn from experience what works and what doesn't, all under the watchful eye of a veteran coach.

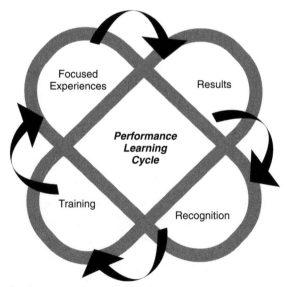

Figure 8-1. Performance learning cycle

The next phases of the Performance Learning Cycle, after training and practice, are the measurement of achievement and its timely recognition. It almost goes without saying that recognizing and applauding an employee's contribution are critical to reinforcing the desired behavior. Without some expression of appreciation, the enthusiasm and hard work required for further improvement are likely to diminish. But someone who is commended for an achievement usually responds by producing even better results. Ultimately, the employer can expect that the results will translate into cost savings, quality improvements, reductions in cycle times, and strengthened customer relationships.

Appreciation means different things to different people, so how an organization chooses to recognize achievement depends on the circumstances involved and the culture of the organization. Disney uses various kinds of celebrations, service pins, distinguished service citations, and other internal excellence awards. A personal word of acknowledgment from a respected leader can go a long way; or small team rewards can help build morale—perhaps dinner at a restaurant or an informal office party. Monetary bonuses are always appropriate, of course, but when cash awards are not feasible, look for other forms of recognition.

When the newly learned skills are reinforced with coaching, practice, and recognition, they become habits; habits that will move your company steadily along the path of improvement. Moreover, a company that embraces employee training as an essential investment in its future will soon see that continuing education enhances the odds for sustained long-term success. (See Figure 8-2.)

To reap the optimum benefits of any training program, however, the entire company must be committed to it, with the main push coming from

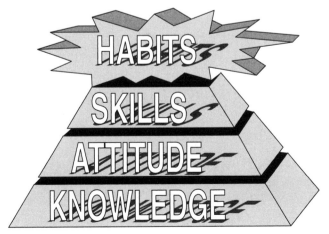

Figure 8-2. Habits

the top. When it becomes clear that top management firmly supports the change effort, impressive results will follow.

When we first began to work with Plumbing & Industrial Supply, for example, the 38-member company had been trying for some time to implement a customer-focused culture, but with minimal success. Among other things, multiple-day Dream Retreats had been held to teach top management the new concepts, after which team members were supposed to relay what they had learned to the lower-level employees. Daily responsibilities required that the implementation be done piecemeal.

Our initial employee survey turned up a telling and disturbing attitude. The typical comment went something like this: "If the program is so important, then how come we're not really trained to do it? We're only getting a couple of hour-long sessions while management goes off for days." The snail's pace of implementation was clearly taking a toll.

Although we relayed the findings to management, we recognized that the company's small size was at the heart of the problem. Whereas a large company can afford to take groups of people off on retreat for three days without disrupting operations, that is not the case at a small company. So we suggested to the president that the training program be conducted on weekends. "Let people take one day off and then ask them to work overtime on Saturday or Sunday."

But the president had another solution: "There is no reason why you can't have three sessions of 10 or 12 people, and we [management] can take over their jobs while they are out. We can load trucks. We can drive their routes. It would probably be good for us to get back to the nitty-gritty jobs while the others are off being trained."[56]

Besides being an excellent sign of top-level commitment to the change program, the president's suggestion helped repair the breach that had opened between management and the workers, who had felt they were being treated like second-class citizens not worthy of training. Within a short time, the customer-centric culture had permeated the organization.

Make Excellence a Habit

The goal of learning is to develop positive habits that benefit individuals and organizations. When learning a foreign language, for example—say, Spanish— first a pupil studies to get good enough to understand and be understood in a social situation. That is a useful but limited skill. If that person goes to live in a Spanish-speaking country, his or her limited skill will at first prove inadequate for new-found needs. The language has to become like a habit, an involuntary reaction, before the student will be fully comfortable with it, but that won't happen until she or he has practiced, and then practiced some more.

Aristotle said, "We are what we repeatedly do . . . excellence, then, is not an act, but a habit."[57] If this is so, organizations that wish to pursue superior performance at all levels must work to ensure that the characteristics that define excellence are practiced, and then practiced some more, until they, too, become an involuntary reaction.

We believe that proper habits grow from obtaining knowledge, attitude, and skills. Knowledge is understanding what, how, and why we need to do something. Skill is applying that knowledge in a practical situation. Attitude is the desire to transform our knowledge into skills and, ultimately, into a habit. A company that claims the corporate value of excellence must therefore establish a specific ongoing process to transmit knowledge and, in turn, improve employees' skills and attitudes.

But for such an effort to produce the desired results, a company must understand that the customer drives the process. Many times, we have encountered training programs for which an organization's human resources department has developed extensive in-depth material that neglects to mention the importance of the external customer. Employees are trained to refine their own skills and perhaps to take care of the needs of internal customers, but the *raison d'être*, the external customer who provides the revenues that support the company's existence, is ignored.

Knowledge of customer needs and expectations can be taught, but not attitude or motivation. These elements are transmitted through the behavioral patterns of employees and are part of the values and sense of mission that pervade the workplace. In fact, Holocaust survivor Viktor Frankl defines *attitude* as "our response to what we have experienced."[58] The process is summarized in Figure 8-3. That is why employee training becomes far more effective when old-timers, who can become role models as well as instructors, are involved.

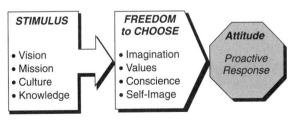

Figure 8-3. Attitude

Their behaviors provide signals to new employees as to the company's underlying culture.

Illinois Power, which invested thought, money, and effort in developing a training program that supports its cultural transformation, exemplifies a company that has reaped the rewards of an organization-wide commitment to customer-focused training.

As an initial step in the implementation, we instituted an intensive training program that included a three-day Dream Retreat and a complete immersion in the concepts of a customer-centric culture. The aim was to improve teamwork, customer service, and employee empowerment. In one small example, line workers were allowed to rearrange work schedules to allocate time more efficiently. By making a point of training its employees in a "customer first" approach, Illinois Power instigated a remarkable turnaround throughout the company. Capping the utility's accomplishment was its 1991 receipt of its industry's most prestigious tribute, the Edison Award.

Another top-flight company that has achieved enviable results with its training initiatives is Motorola Inc., a Fortune 100 global communications leader. In the 1980s, Motorola pioneered Six Sigma, a quality and business improvement methodology that is still revolutionizing industry. Two decades later, in 2002, Motorola achieved the unique distinction of receiving the Malcolm Baldrige National Quality Award for a second time. Motorola became the only company in the world to have received this award twice, having won it earlier in 1988. Motorola is still finding ways to reinvent itself using Six Sigma (a registered trademark of the company), and Motorola University offers Six Sigma Certification and Six Sigma consulting and training services to organizations throughout the world.

At a time when management became increasingly aware that Japanese manufacturers were invading the company's markets with considerable success, Motorola was by no means in bad shape (profit improvement hovered between 5 and 10 percent per year). In 1981, Motorola's CEO announced an ambitious five-year strategy designed to improve process, product, and sales. The measures put in motion included setting a strategic goal for quality (target of no more than 3.4 defects per million products); instituting performance rewards (savings stemming from team recommendations shared as bonuses); initiating senior management reviews (constant reinvigoration of quality programs with results passing through the entire organization); and, most important, training employees (40 percent of training one year was devoted to quality matters). The success of this creative combination propelled Motorola to new heights. Over the past four years, Motorola Inc. beat the S&P 500 by 40 percent, and in their 18 years of implementing Six Sigma, the company has documented over $17 billion in savings. Additionally, Motorola University has helped companies from Black and Decker to Toshiba reap dramatic rewards. This is a great lesson in practicing what you preach!

Beware the Performance Appraisal

One of the favorite devices of human resources departments is the performance appraisal. These appraisals have become something of a constitutionally mandated fact of business management. We believe that these appraisals are, in truth, harmful to morale and unnecessarily costly for an organization to administer. Let us explain.

A few years ago, we asked the CEO of a major company what he considered to be his company's greatest asset. "My employees," he answered without hesitation. "I make certain that we hire the best possible people for the job." He then went on to explain his hiring policy, from the search process to the extensive interviewing of a candidate, the personality testing and, finally, the careful checking of references. It was an impressive list.

He concluded by saying, "My most important job is to make sure that my company is made up of winners."

When we asked him further about the company's performance appraisal system, he assured us that it, too, was carefully structured. Once a year, every employee was evaluated in depth by a supervisor, and the CEO was proud to report that supervisors spent a considerable amount of time and thought on performance appraisals.

Later on, we had the opportunity to chat with the supervisors and employees of the company. When we asked about performance appraisals, everyone, without exception, agreed that (1) performance appraisals were a waste of time; (2) people dreaded the entire ritual; (3) the process did not result in behavioral change; and (4) the outcome was influenced by the recentness of performance.

In the course of a year, we talk to hundreds of people, and the reaction to performance appraisals is universally negative. They are described as one of the biggest barriers to service and quality improvements. Here's why. Most people believe that they are above-average performers. When their appraisal evaluation rates them as average or below, they feel discouraged and misunderstood, and the quality of their work often suffers.

As the late W. Edwards Deming, considered the architect of total quality management, once described it:

> The effects are devastating. Such a system substitutes short-term performance for long-term planning, wrecks teamwork, and nurtures rivalry. It builds fear and leaves people bitter or despondent, unfit for work for weeks after receipt of the rating.[59]

Performance appraisals are highly subjective; they depend on the evaluator's personal attitudes. Suppose, for instance, that an employee has missed two days of work in the previous year. One supervisor might give relatively great weight to the absences, especially if the missed days have been recent, and rate the employee as "average," while another supervisor might completely ignore the missed days and assign an "excellent" rating.

Other factors, too, enter into the assessment of a worker, and they are often situations over which the individual has no control. For example, an employee may have the necessary education for a job and be a hard worker to boot, but further on-the-job training may be needed for the person to perform at the desired level. Some people are hired for jobs for which they do not have the appropriate education; others are evaluated on results that are heavily dependent on factors over which they have no control. Effort and commitment are really the only parts of the equation over which an employee has complete control, but it is impossible to isolate the effects of these factors.

In the final analysis, performance reviews may tempt a worker to try to please the boss at the expense of either fellow workers or, more importantly, the customer. Such efforts can undermine teamwork as well as job performance.

There Is a Better Way

What are the alternatives to traditional performance appraisals? We help companies devise individual development plans that foster an environment of understanding and a commitment to personal growth. If you think about it, the word *development* sends a much more positive message within a company than does the term *appraisal.* A company that wants its workforce to be productive—and what company doesn't?—will find that individual development plans are more conducive to achieving that goal.

When creating personal development plans, the first requirement is that each employee understand the company's vision and its values and how they relate to the individual's responsibilities. Job scope and guidelines for performance must be clarified. Everyone from the mailroom employee—whose speedy and accurate job performance precludes stopping to chat at every office—to the middle manager—whose in-box should be emptied expeditiously—must understand his or her part in the process. It should be made clear that one person's failure to carry out assigned duties has an impact on the whole process and that the organization is only as strong as its weakest link.

One of our clients took an interesting approach to developing guidelines for employees. Rather than defining procedures, the company identified areas of known failure, ideas that had been tried in the past without success. Other than these particular paths, employees were free to exercise their own initiative in order to obtain desired results. Having an understanding of how and why something failed in the past enabled the employees to accomplish their goals more efficiently. With this example in mind, we encourage our clients to go heavy on guidelines and light on procedures, particularly when training employees.

A second imperative for setting up effective development plans is that desired outcomes be jointly defined by management and employees. Avoid specifying methods and means. Doing so only leads to undesirable and unproductive micromanagement. What's more, tightly prescribed approaches give employees a built-in excuse for failure; for example, "I did what you told me to do, so it's not my fault if something went wrong." Often a simple example of what quality output looks like is the best motivator. At the moment of understanding, all those necessary measurable objectives and expected results will make sense to them.

At Disneyland, Jungle Cruise Boat cast members are given a script that suggests telling certain jokes but still allows cruise leaders to inject their own personalities into the performance. By giving cast members guidelines rather than dictates with prescribed expectations for the outcome, The Walt Disney Company is encouraging employees to exercise good judgment, which is a hallmark of empowerment.

A third area of importance in designing individual development plans is an evaluation of processes. According to sociologist Kurt Lewin, effectively changing behavior requires consideration of the environment and the process as well as the person. "Behavior," he observed, "is a function of the person times the environment."[60]

An experience with a former client illustrates the validity of Lewin's observation. The company, which made automobile engine parts, had a milling plant staffed by good but not exceptional workers. Everything went along fine most of the time, but occasionally, product quality levels would drop into the unacceptable range for no apparent reason. During one of these dips, the company's human resources department decided that the plant workers' attitude was at fault. So HR launched a comprehensive training program in interpersonal relationships. Alas, the quality levels did not change. Why? Because this approach wrongly assumed that change comes solely from the individual. In this particular case, further investigation revealed that the quality discrepancies were the result of problems at the raw materials supplier. Deming validates Lewin's concept. He once stated that more than 85 percent of the quality and productivity problems in the United States are the result of the process. Therefore, it is imperative that process improvements be discussed between management and employees. Process improvements may also require changes in management policy. Management needs to assume a proactive role by asking the following questions:

- What do you need from management to reach your objectives?
- How can we both achieve great success?
- How can we remove barriers to success?

Direct face-to-face discussion is key to evaluating the process correctly; contact via memos or e-mail will not ensure that the message is heard and absorbed on both ends. What's more, this dialogue must be ongoing to support continuous improvement.

Finally, personal development plans must include a determination of the positive and negative consequences associated with meeting or not meeting the desired results.

Although the plans should be revisited approximately every six months, or at the least on an annual basis, this activity is not a replacement for regular feedback. We encourage our clients to employ a 360-degree feedback system that constantly updates performance information. Immediate feedback provides the basis for achieving and maintaining excellence because it allows an organization to customize individual development plans. When everyone is helped to achieve personal bests (as described in Chapter 3, these must be aligned with the overall vision of the organization), the organization's overall performance improves dramatically.

As should be obvious by now, an organization's management cannot afford simply to say to new employees, "Here's what we expect of you. Now go to it." A company must be prepared to work with new employees and guide them until they become familiar with their responsibilities and the organization's culture. The former manager of customer satisfaction at Disney summed up the reasons for Disney's success this way:

> Recruit the right people, train them, continually communicate with them, ask their opinions, involve them, recognize them, and celebrate with them. If you show respect for their opinions and involvement, they will be proud of what they do and they'll deliver quality service.[61]

Nothing more need be said. With all employees primed to deliver, we will take a look next at the role proper planning plays in bringing dreams to fruition.

Questions to Ask

- Do you support individual development planning rather than the demoralizing performance appraisal?
- Do you verbalize and demonstrate to employees that you value their partnership in creating plans for their own self-development?
- Are you providing training to the right people in the organization?
- Do you provide training that is tailored to the needs of your employees?
- Do you celebrate the contributions of employees, even when they are not exactly in line with management's thinking?
- Do your managers coach employees to reinforce important concepts after they have been formally trained?

Actions to Take

- Ask for feedback from employees on the value of specific organizational training that they attend.
- Concentrate training efforts on those who need skill development rather than on those who desire training as a company perk.

- Schedule follow-up sessions with employees to reinforce skills learned in a formal training environment.
- Ask employees to engage in regular 360-degree evaluations.
- Institute development plans in place of performance appraisals. Work in partnership with employees to create their own plans.

Team Appreciation at Its Best

All the members of the Global No-Frost team were experts in their fields, but many were philosophically far removed from a culture that endorses teamwork. It isn't easy, we have discovered in our consulting work, for people who are used to working within a hierarchical, conservative structure to adjust to a completely different work environment. Describing his experiences throughout the project, Jerry said, "I could see people's expectations grow and grow and grow. They were pushing themselves on all levels." In the end, people said that they had never felt so fulfilled, so satisfied by any job.

One situation that Jerry faced involved the cultural differences between team members. Even though everyone had a sense of commonality about the work, there were nevertheless differences of behavior and attitude. So we initiated another two-day training session for the team and called in two professional advisors to enlighten us about national differences. They warned the non-Americans that Americans could be brash, sarcastic, and loud. Then they warned Americans that Indians and other Asians often hold back, watching and waiting for signals from their superiors before they contribute anything. On the other hand, Brazilians, they said, can be argumentative and noisy. Gradually, we established what you might call cultural assimilation, a trained awareness and respect for national differences. It was still a gradual process, but knowing what to expect from another member often smoothed the way. It kept people from being offended and created an empathy and appreciation of others that continued to grow throughout the process.

Jerry also felt that he didn't want his team members to know each other only on a nine-to-five basis. To foster the sense of a team identity, he organized after-work events. "Fairly early on, we developed a work hard and play hard environment," he explains, "lots of parties involving families. We had barbecues, cookouts, and trips to local fairs."

There were more formal celebrations, too, when a milestone was met, but these were on company time and at company expense. The impromptu gatherings were more family affairs and really served to establish cross-cultural bonds.

Our Featured Organization: Men's Wearhouse

SERVANT LEADERSHIP IN ACTION

Most retailers don't put training on their "to do" list, and when people fail to perform, they're sent packing. Why bother developing people, when we can pay people with less experience less money and when we know there are people on the street that we can hire? some may ask. George Zimmer, however, and his team at Men's Wearhouse, North America's largest specialty retailer of men's tailored clothing and business attire, know why this thinking is short-sighted.

George has invested years of tending to his culture where "Servant Leadership" rules. This practical philosophy of motivating, supporting, and inspiring (all words incorporated into Men's Wearhouse mission statement) is the foundation for all of the company's training programs. Servant Leadership at Men's Wearhouse is about nurturing people and training them to become the best they can be: "self-actualized" (another word from Men's Wearhouse mission statement). "It's about how much you impact the people below you, not impress the people above you," Shlomo Maor, associate vice president of training told us.[62] Based on teachings of the late Robert Greenleaf who coined and defined the concept in the 1970s, the essence of Servant Leadership is the adoption of persuasive rather than manipulative power. Since leaders must be "authentic" in the mind of George Zimmer, the entire Men's Wearhouse culture has become a caring and benevolent one where leaders know that their business is more about people than about men's clothing.

Seeking out individuals who like other people, who are optimistic, who have passion, and who are trainable is much more important to the leadership of Men's Wearhouse than finding folks with stellar resumes. In fact, many employees of the company are ones who were viewed as failures in their former work lives. Potential new hires who arrive here quickly

(Continued)

discover they don't need to be afraid or ashamed of making mistakes. The focus at Men's Wearhouse is to celebrate successes and mistakes, learn from them, and move on. And, most of all, employees know that this is a place where, like Four Seasons, The Golden Rule is an implicit working principle throughout the organization. "If we take care of them, and that means training and nurturing them, they will take care of the customers," Eric Anderson, director of training, told us in our interview with him.[63] If an employee isn't performing well in the organization, the reaction of Men's Wearhouse leadership is to blame themselves and figure out a way to achieve a win for the employee and the company.

Training is an integral part of the fabric of this uncommonly paternal organization. There are no training budgets and no training measurements. Training is happening all the time, at every level, both formally and informally. Everyone, from senior-level staff to sales associates in the over 500 stores, must be committed to practicing the skills that will help them and their fellow team members grow and excel.

One could debate whether or not it's possible to train people to possess "emotional intelligence" (admittedly an overused term according to Eric Anderson), but it is a coveted trait of salespeople at Men's Wearhouse. It's about developing sensitivity to others, and honing a skill for "reading" the customer.

The formal training and development here affords employees numerous opportunities to learn in a classroom environment, some 40 hours per year. Upon their arrival at Men's Wearhouse, new Wardrobe Consultants typically receive two days of new-hire training by their district managers. The goal is to immerse employees immediately in the culture and the team philosophy. The next step is out-of-store training, Suits High, a more specific regimen that takes place after two to eight weeks on the job.

But the biggest and most anticipated learning experience of all is yet to come. Suits U (officially Suits University) is a week reminiscent of leaving home for the first time or going off to begin college. And, for some Wardrobe Consultants, being on a plane for the first time in their lives is an experience they will remember forever. The week-long training is filled with energizing classroom activities, and vacation-like fun takes place on a beach in California. This perfect mix of education and team-building is exclusively for employees approaching their one-year employment anniversary.

And they are about ready to meet the man of the hour, Men's Wearhouse's legendary and masterful teacher, Shlomo Maor. We were lucky enough to witness Shlomo in action with a mesmerized group of students of Suits U at the Fremont, California, corporate offices. These students were "wowed" by a stage play depicting the fine art of selling acted out by the man who once broke all company sales records in his Men's Wearhouse years in the field. On this very first day of training, Shlomo makes disciples out of all who enter his sanctum. "Shlomo has uncovered specific principles of retail that seem so obvious that you wonder why every company wouldn't do it, but few are," remarked Eric Anderson.[63]

How Shlomo Maor communicates those principles is the stuff of corporate legends. One minute he is bellowing about the importance of timing when greeting the customer: "Do you think you should stand by the door, and after the customer has spent 45 minutes driving in his car, just jump into his face and ask, 'May I help you?' No. That's wrong." To Shlomo, retail is theater, and the greeting is the opening action. He alerts his students to the fact that the best salespeople set the stage before they utter a word to the customer. Then all at once, Shlomo becomes the reverent pastor in keeping with the Servant Leadership model. He describes the synergistic environment, that the whole is always greater than the sum of any group of individuals. Participants hear over and over again that at Men's Wearhouse there is no such thing as a zero-sum game, where someone wins and someone loses. In the end, he reminds them that the ultimate goal is for the company and the employee and the customer to win. History has proven that countless more empires have been destroyed from within than from the outside. After witnessing the interaction of Suits U students with Shlomo, and with one another, it is almost impossible to believe that this empire could topple!

Clearly, the best predictor of a successful Men's Wearhouse store is not a great salesperson, but rather a successful team. Moreover, the company goes all out to motivate and reward team performance by staging frequent contests and linking bonus targets to team goals. There are volume bonuses on sales, plus weekly and monthly bonuses based on store performance. Eric Anderson is convinced that achieving the goal of working collegially in teams at Men's Wearhouse is paramount to the success of the entire team of nearly 8,000 employees. And to add certainty to this, he states with conviction, "Ours is a culture where training will never finish last."

Chapter 9

Make Your
Elephant Fly—Plan

The way to get started is to quit talking and get started.

Walt Disney

Vision without a means of execution is like a plane without wings or Dumbo without his ears—it just won't fly. No matter how deep a company's resources are, progress of company projects greatly depends on the strength of execution, and proper execution requires thorough and detailed planning, a reality that Walt Disney understood completely.

No wand-waving or intonations of "abracadabra" preceded the building of Disney's Magic Kingdom. The cartoons, movies, theme parks, and all the rest of the delights that took shape in Walt's prolific imagination came into being through a precise process of planning that he employed from the very beginning of his career. Making a movie is a costly undertaking, but because animation is especially expensive and labor-intensive, Disney *had* to plan carefully to control costs and successfully execute his ideas. Out of necessity was born a nine-step process that takes a "blue sky" idea and turns it into reality.

Dumbo, the perennial animated favorite about the flying baby elephant, was itself a product of this rigorous Disney regimen. By putting process in creativity—in this case, using a straightforward script and story and resisting the temptation to experiment with expensive new technologies—Disney and his animators produced *Dumbo* in just one year. As one Disney executive has described it, the system says, in effect, "Within these boundaries you will create. This is the budget, these are the limitations. Make it work within this framework."[64]

And work it has, as consistently successful and profitable flights of fancy from *Dumbo* to *Aladdin* attest. While our clients may not be staging magic carpet rides, we have seen diverse companies devise their own methods, both formal and informal, to ensure that a workable idea will actually come to fruition. In this chapter, we look at both the Disney "blue sky" process and the variations crafted by companies in a range of industries.

Carefully Managed Creativity, The Disney Way

There have always been two basic schools of thought on business creativity. The first insists that researchers and other in-house innovators be given the loosest rein possible, allowing new ideas and projects to develop on their own momentum with a maximum of independent decision making. The second approach demands that the reins be kept taut, that the generation of ideas be part of the corporate process, and like the other parts, that it be carefully managed.

Walt Disney was definitely of the second school. Although his famously forceful and controlling management style was largely attributable to his personality, there was also a practical consideration: the cost of making animated pictures. Makers of live-action films could shoot extra footage and then piece together their final product through artful cutting in the editing room, but animation costs were such that cartoon makers couldn't even consider this whittle-down approach.

So to keep costs in check, Disney exercised extremely tight control of the creative process itself by instituting a rigorous, nine-step regimen for project management. Only by demanding that his people follow this standard procedure could he continue to turn dreams into tangible products, whether he was dealing with films, amusement parks, television shows, or any of the other Disney enterprises. In the Disney system, nothing was—or is—left to chance. Figure 9-1 illustrates the planning process.

In schematic form, the process looks like this:

Step I—Blue sky

- Ask "What if?" rather than "What?"
- Learn to live for a time with the discomfort of not knowing, or not being in full control.
- Take a trip through fantasyland; start with the story.

Planning Guidelines

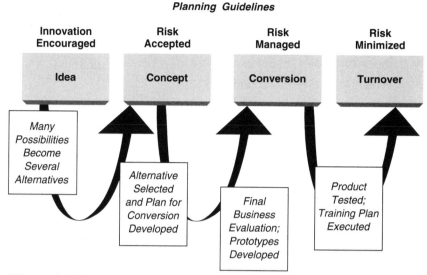

Figure 9-1. Planning guidelines

Step 2—Concept development

- Develop research.
- Evaluate alternatives.
- Recommend an idea.

Step 3—Feasibility

- Reconcile scope.
- Prepare pro forma.

Step 4—Schematic

- Finalize master plan.
- Outline initial business processes.

Step 5—Design objectives

- Finalize design details, equipment, and materials.
- Develop implementation strategy and budget.

Step 6—Contract documents

- Prepare contract documents.

Step 7—Production

- Construct site infrastructure and develop work areas.
- Produce show elements.

Step 8—Install, test, adjust

- Install the show.

Step 9—Close out

- Assemble final project documents.
- Monitor performance.
- Get sign-off letter from operations.

We like to add a Step 10: Celebrate a job well done!

Although managers at many companies fly by the seat of their pants, Disney executives follow these guidelines for aligning the company's long-term vision with short-term execution. Not only is the company kept on track from project to project, but costs are cut and production is faster. Such strict adherence to a set of production standards and processes enables Disney to deliver consistently successful products and services.

The Process in Practice

New technology of every kind intrigued Walt Disney, but railroading held a special fascination for him. So when he could finally afford it, he built his own miniature train on his Holmby Hills estate. He spent hours driving it around, dreaming and planning. So when the time came to build Disneyland, it was only logical that Disney would be drawn to the idea of installing a monorail. Because Disney's single-track vehicle was the first ever built in the United States, there weren't any American engineers with the knowledge or training to construct it. So Disney turned to German engineers to help with the job.

When the monorail was completed at the end of six months, the Germans congratulated him on the amazing accomplishment. Walt Disney had finished in only half a year what had taken six or seven years to build in Germany. The Disneyland monorail represented planning and execution at its best.

Before planning or execution, of course, must come the vision. Without a vision, or "story," as discussed in Chapter 2, there is nothing to plan. The first step, then, is the generation of new ideas, ideas designed to satisfy customer needs or solve customer problems. A team must be prepared to suggest, discuss, argue about, and try out any number of diverse ideas. If one or more ideas fail, no real harm is done. We remind the teams we work with that although Babe Ruth hit 714 home runs, he also struck out 1,330 times. So striking out a few times doesn't stop someone from eventually setting a record.

Trying out ideas, perhaps putting parts of several ideas together to produce a prototype, helps develop an overall concept and determine whether or not it is workable. A prototype can be evaluated and market tested, and it can serve as the centerpiece around which the process is developed.

When Lee Iacocca came up with the idea of reintroducing convertibles into the Chrysler product line, he began by asking his engineers to make him a prototype. After some figuring, the engineers came back and told him they could do it, but it would take nine months. The exasperated Iacocca, wondering why a prototype of what he had in mind should take so long to make, responded in effect: "You just don't understand. Go find a car and saw the top off the damn thing!" Within a few days, Iacocca had his convertible, which he then drove around Detroit, conducting his own version of a marketing study. People stopped and waved at him, shouted encouragement, or just turned and stared in wonder. Iacocca counted the stares, the shouts, and the waves that his prototype convertible elicited. After he had received a certain number of these responses, he decided that Chrysler should go ahead with a line of convertibles.

In some ways, the vision and idea-generation steps are among the simpler parts of the project-management process. Any number of people can sit around a corporate conference table and spin out a set of ideas and objectives for their company. The real difficulty is in determining how to go about reaching those goals.

Implementation of a project demands a carefully thought out structure that establishes specific guidelines, from the initial "blue sky" idea up to the final stages of completion. Certain milestones along the way must be specified, points at which management is appraised of overall progress. Those who work on a project need to know what is required at each step and how to measure their headway. Efficiency dictates that nothing be left to chance. Barring unforeseen acts of God, managers carefully plot every step on the chosen path.

We recognize that in today's business climate, a forceful ruler patterned after Walt Disney might generate no small amount of enmity and have a harder time maintaining control, particularly if the company involved has a somewhat free-wheeling culture. And, in fact, a strong argument can be made for giving creative minds the maximum amount of freedom. But most companies find that an approach that falls somewhere between absolute control and complete freedom works best for them.

We recommend that each company design its own procedures for turning a dream into reality. Such a process works best if it grows naturally out of discussions among management and employees rather than being imposed from the outside. That way, it can more adequately reflect the company's culture, history, traditions, and structure.

Many of our clients have successfully adopted rigorous processes similar to the Disney approach but tailored to manufacturing and service businesses. At one company, for example, the first phase is called the *Idea*.

In screening the Idea, the company initially asks:

- What is the compelling customer benefit?
- How is the Idea going to increase shareholder value?
- Does it fit strategically into the organization?
- What resources are required to move the Idea into the next phase?

Next comes the *Concept* phase. The questions asked at this stage include:

- What is the market assessment?
- Is the Concept technically feasible?
- What is the business analysis?
- What are the preliminary design specifications?
- What plans and resources are required to move to the third phase?

The third stage is *Conversion*. Here the questions are:

- What is the business case?
- What critical process and product elements can we identify?
- What is the plan of execution, and how can we make it happen?
- What costs and benefits will be associated with the final phase?

And, as the company moves into the final *Execution* phase, it asks:

- How do we release the product (if there is one)?
- When is the process going to be implemented?
- How do we get the product to the customer?
- Do we have a feedback mechanism in place to gauge the success of the product?

With carefully determined guidelines and milestones, teams or departments can proceed on their own. Micromanagement is avoided because the company does not have to keep track of what everyone is doing every minute of the day. There is no need to ask how the project is going. Instead, management can safely trust that the team is keeping tabs on progress and that appropriate appraisals will be forthcoming at specified points along the way.

Project leaders understand, of course, that if problems arise that threaten deadlines or if some assistance is needed, management is there to help. Otherwise, the message from management should be, "You're on your own until you've finished this phase of the project." An interesting sidelight about Disney's planning process is that many times a project may not receive the necessary funding to continue. In most companies, when this happens the team is viewed as a failure.

At Disney, they look at these projects as assets that may be dusted off and continued midstream as funding or technology becomes available. The story-line for the legendary movie *The Little Mermaid*, released in 1989, really began in the late 1930s with the amazing pastel and watercolor sketches of illustrator Kay Nielson. The Disney team recently pulled some pieces out of the studio archives and created the musical jewel that will soon be transformed with live characters for Broadway. *The Little Mermaid* was the last Disney animated feature to use hand-painted cells and analog technology. The animators received such inspiration from the Nielsen story sketches that they gave her a "visual development" credit on the film. The movie was hailed as the phoenix of big screen feature animation and was the first to spawn a TV series. The movie's music earned the Academy Award for Best Score. Additionally, "Under the Sea" won the Academy Award for Best Song, the first Disney tune to win since "Zip-A-Dee-Doo-Dah" from *Song of the South* won in 1947.

A Planning Center Facilitates Communication

One of the most effective tools we've found for managing a project and bringing an idea to its successful fruition is a planning center, a room where all the various elements of an entire project and its progress can be assembled.

When The Walt Disney Company was still small—some 1,200 employees—management pinned rough drafts of drawings and story ideas to the walls of a planning room so that the exact status of a project could be quickly ascertained. Walt Disney didn't care much for meetings or written reports. He preferred to wander into the planning center alone, usually late at night, and scan the walls for samples of work in progress. Comparing the visuals to the vision he held in his mind told him instantly whether a cartoon or feature film project was on the right track.

A similar type of planning center was established when we worked with a large South African company that had 54 plants throughout the country. The complex assignment involved installing a materials management system over a three-year period. The first step was to figure out how to manage the relevant mass of material. Borrowing from Pentagon jargon, a "war room" was set up that allowed the project team to keep abreast of what was going on and where. The room was approximately 25 feet by 35 feet, with 15-foot-high walls where information could be displayed. So as not to waste valuable space, the room was windowless.

On one wall were pinned the plans for the project, which enabled everyone to know at a glance when training would start, when the software would arrive, when the next general meeting was to take place. A special section of the planning wall was reserved for messages. This became the communications center. We have found that although people often ignore e-mail and telephone messages, somehow it's harder to ignore a message when it's printed on a card and openly displayed. Perhaps the public nature of such communication makes it more difficult to disregard.

Another wall of the center was dedicated to keeping everyone up to date on what other team members were working on and how far along their individual pieces of the project were. When a segment was completed, that fact was posted in a special section. Another place was set aside for anyone who had a problem. The project manager could walk in and see immediately what difficulties lay ahead, then take the appropriate action. If someone was having trouble getting accounting department approval of a costing method, for example, the manager could step in and move the process along.

Occasionally, people who are greatly attached to their computer system complain that all plans can be tracked online. "Why do we need a visual display?" they ask.

The whole point of a planning center is to allow people to see a holistic picture of the projects and activities throughout the organization. What's more, when two or three people congregate in an area where the significant work of the company is visually displayed, often an impromptu meeting takes place. People communicate better face-to-face; and, as discussed in Chapter 5, MIT research supports this conclusion. The quality of communication improves markedly with proximity. Close contact encourages questions and discussion, which is the kind of interaction needed to move projects along.

The planning center proved to be a valuable tool for a team we know that ran a testing laboratory. Any team member could walk in and scan the wall for information on all of the company's major projects and their stage of development. If the head of the testing lab noticed, for example, that one department was experimenting with a new product, he could be pretty certain that sooner or later his lab would be asked to perform certain tests. Previously, he probably would have received an unexpected call saying, "Hey, tomorrow I'm going to be sending you a part, and I need 47 tests done on it right away."

The new information alerted the lab manager to find out approximately when the work might arrive so that he could schedule someone to be ready to do the testing. For the first time, the engineering and the lab staffs were working together in a meaningful and cooperative manner.

Unexpectedly, the planning center also turned into a morale builder. It brought employees together and gave them a sense of involvement in all aspects of the company's processes. People began to feel that they had a voice in developments outside their own departments. Compartmentalization gradually disappeared.

Planning centers are useful when working on side issues within projects—or projects within projects. One client's cross-functional team was charged with evaluating internal planning barriers and developing solutions that would promote buy-in from all stakeholders in the main project. The symptom, or "pain," as we call it, were pretty clear from the start: Many people were angry about being left out of the planning and communication loops on a project that required their input in order to be successful.

The planning center is a practical approach for targeting the status of any one of the myriad pieces in a company process or for viewing the overall picture. The physical size of the center and the breadth of information displayed can vary, of course, according to specific needs. All that matters is that project leaders and participants have a way of keeping abreast of individual and overall goals, making specific progress toward those goals, and dealing with any problems or needs encountered at various stages of a project.

Another form of the planning center is embodied in the concept of co-locating, which we discussed previously in conjunction with teaming (Chapter 5). When the Whirlpool technology team decided to co-locate people from around the world to work in its Evansville, Indiana, facility, a subteam was charged with coordinating the co-location activities. To facilitate small-group interaction, the subteam's leader went to great lengths to create just the right environment.

This leader worked closely with two furniture suppliers to put together smaller functional areas within the total space allocated for the entire team.

He also installed an active noise system that effectively tripled the perceived distance between individual team members in terms of the privacy it created. In the case of this Whirlpool global team, the illusion of greater distance was particularly important because many of the team members had a difficult time adjusting to the open-room style. In addition, the multiple languages spoken by the participants made the system imperative. Since people tend to listen when others speak a different language, it would have been virtually impossible for group members to tune out one another's conversations.

The effort involved in putting together the co-location space paid off for the Whirlpool team, which put together and executed a project that ended up surpassing everyone's expectations. The ease of communication that both planning centers and co-locating promote goes a long way toward keeping a project on track and ensuring its ultimate success.

Taking the Holistic Approach

Thinking holistically is counterintuitive for those schooled in the principles of corporate Darwinism, where only the so-called fittest survive and where the law of the jungle guides most decision making. To overcome those blocks and to help people accustom themselves to the concept of the holistic company—where everyone works for the common good of the organization—we conduct an exercise called Broken Squares (See Scene 18 of *The Disney Way Fieldbook: How to Implement Walt Disney's Vision of Dream, Believe, Dare, Do in Your Own Company*) in which clients sit in groups of five at separate tables. We hand each person an envelope with pieces of a puzzle. The goal is for all players to finish their puzzles; but to succeed, they have to trade pieces without saying a word.

This is not a competition, but as the game progresses, invariably some players begin to compete, hoard pieces, and strive to finish their own puzzles—and their group's—before anyone else does. After the experience, the participants who have pitted themselves against one another begin to understand that success comes from not hoarding pieces, either individually or within a group. The fastest way to win—for all players to finish their puzzles—is for everyone to collaborate across "organizational" boundaries, in other words, to think and to act holistically.

As you set about using the tools described in this chapter to design your own planning procedures, we must add one word of caution. Don't get so involved with making plans that they become the be-all and end-all. Some teams are so proud of the fine plans they craft that they forget about implementing them. They begin to look at the plan as their deliverable. Get in the habit of thinking *execution* immediately after you say the word *planning*.

One way to help you keep the process in perspective is through your system of rewards. Set it up so that idea generation is rewarded, to be sure, but save the biggest rewards and the largest celebration for the successful completion of the overall project. That way, employees will be encouraged to keep their eye on the ultimate goal.

That objective will be closer to your reach after you master the storyboarding technique that we will describe in the next chapter. Using it has helped our clients to conquer seemingly insoluble planning and communication problems. Once you learn how to storyboard, you will find it useful in solving a range of problems.

Questions to Ask

- Do organizational boundaries inhibit your planning processes?
- Do you have one or more planning centers in your organization where leaders and employees can work together on processes and projects?
- Do you have a designated communications center where employees can post their project timelines and critical aspects of their projects?
- Does your organization have a specific process for project implementation?
- Do you encourage the development of prototypes to help develop an overall concept and determine whether or not it is workable?
- Do you avoid micromanaging employees who are working on projects and champion their adherence to determining guidelines and milestones?
- Do you celebrate specific milestones and the completion of projects?

Actions to Take

- Develop a process for project implementation that is used throughout the company; provide training on the process and champion its use.
- Create planning and communication centers for project and process activities.
- Allow individuals and teams the flexibility to work on projects without management interference.

- Set up cross-functional project teams on a routine basis.
- Develop quick and inexpensive prototypes to test products, processes, or service ideas.

All the Right Stuff

We were really enlightened by the Global No-Frost team for a number of reasons. We often work in conservative situations where we cannot really experiment or try new approaches. This team gave us the chance to do just that, and in Jerry McColgin we found the ideal team leader. He understood his role.

Right from the start he announced that although he was the leader, hierarchy meant little to him. "I'm not going to sit in a closed office, and no one is forbidden to come in to see me. I want to hear from anyone who has a concern, a problem, or an issue." As he says himself, "I tend to be a proactive, risk-taking, cheerleading, inspirational type. Facts and do-it-by-the-book are not my way of working." His personal experiences working in amateur theatricals and on charity drives had also taught him how to lead groups of people. He realized early on that the team offered an extraordinarily high level of capacity, and he came to realize that his job was to harness these talents and to guide and direct them. He was not there to design a refrigerator; the engineers and designers could do that. In other words, Jerry understood that he was macromanaging the team, not micromanaging it. So long as the milestones were reached, he could preside and guide, leaving the details to his competent staff.

Very early on, at the first retreat, Jerry made a speech that was very influential in laying out the fundamentals of teamwork. Every individual at Whirlpool goes through an objective appraisal process that determines future raises and the size of the year-end bonus. The team would work by a different norm. Each member would be judged not on individual achievement but as part of a team, holistically. "I pointed to the marketing guy," Jerry remembers, "and said, 'You will only succeed if the manufacturing guy gets the equipment designed on time.' To the purchasing guy, I said, 'You will succeed only if the performance of the airflow system is up to par.'" Jerry's message was that the success of the team depended on the sum of its parts—everyone working together at the highest level possible.

During the early retreat, the team began using storyboards to develop an entire 18-month plan so that people could see what had to be done and could negotiate their schedules. Someone said, "This is January and you expect me to get this done by April. I can't do this unless engineering produces its blueprints for this part by mid-March. I'm dependent on them. How can I do this?" With these kinds of comments, we walked through the whole process and established everyone's role and when they had to deliver a certain part of their output.

Our Featured Organization: The Cheesecake Factory

A WELL-BAKED PLAN

The Cheesecake Factory chairman and CEO, David Overton, is a master dreamer and a meticulous craftsman. He is, piece by piece (no pun intended!), building an empire composed of restaurants that have become legendary for large, something-for-everyone menus that serve huge portions to vast numbers of people. After nearly three decades of business that began in Beverly Hills, California, the company has reached $1 billion in annual sales and 110 restaurants, including 103 Cheesecake Factory stores and seven Grand Lux Cafes. Oh, yes, and two Cheesecake Factory Express units inside DisneyQuest® indoor family entertainment centers (in Chicago, Illinois, and Orlando, Florida).

How does he do it? For starters, David Overton has hand-picked a "passionate, dedicated, hard-working group of people with good values and who put one foot in front of the other," in David's words.[65] Those traits were the same as those of his entrepreneurial parents, Oscar and Evelyn, who started a small wholesale and retail bakery business in Detroit over 50 years ago. Having built a reputation for perfect cheesecake that could be made anywhere, and growing weary of Detroit, Evelyn and Oscar headed to Los Angeles in 1971 to start fresh. In California, everything seemed more difficult—even the professional ovens didn't arrive for seven months, forcing Evelyn to use her own oven which held only four cakes at a time. The process of filling orders was often an all-day and all-night ordeal.

(Continued)

It wasn't long before son David left San Francisco, where he had been living at the time, to lend his business acumen to his parents. David was troubled by the fact that the restaurants buying his mother's cheesecakes didn't appreciate them as he thought they should. He knew that people loved the cheesecake, but he also knew he must demonstrate to restaurateurs and prospective foodservice customers that having a great dessert program was a sure path to success.

David's grand plan was to take "cheesecake" to the next level by opening the first The Cheesecake Factory restaurant on Beverly Drive in the heart of Beverly Hills. With nine investors willing to bet on David's dream, the deal was locked in. Or so he thought. A new landlord had just recently purchased the property, which included four stores, and David had his eye on one of them. David was ready and eager to lease the 3,200 square foot space, but the landlord hesitated and asked, "What are you going to build here?" With nothing to show him, David told the landlord he was welcome to visit the factory, the bakery operations in North Hollywood, if he wished.

A few days later, David and his father were on their way to the factory in the bakery truck, after having made a sales call together. When they entered the building, David saw the landlord talking to his mother, Evelyn. He walked over to the baker to communicate an order, and then went over to greet the landlord, still not knowing if they had a deal. Happily, the landlord did agree to lease the space to The Cheesecake Factory for its new restaurant concept.

"Three or four years later," David told us, "I was talking to him and he told me this story. Of course, I didn't know this at the time. He said, 'When I went down to your factory, I wasn't planning to lease you the place because there was nothing I could see and I was very worried. But when I saw you go over to the baker and take care of business before you came over to me, I knew you would do a great job. That's why I leased it to you.'"

The lesson is clear. "If you take care of business and are dedicated, you can do it," said David.

On reputation alone, The Cheesecake Factory's first restaurant opened with great fanfare in 1978. People stood in line for a table, and they are still standing in line 28 years later! "Our guests are the happiest in the world—Disney-style," former executive vice president and company secretary Linda Candioty proudly told us prior to her retirement in 2002.[66] Forget about getting a reservation, however, as the company does not accept them, based on a belief that it would be unacceptable if a guest's requested dining time couldn't be honored.

Without great people, David knows, it's impossible to achieve great things. Early on, he found perhaps the best team member of his career—good friend, loyal baker, and first-class hostess, Linda Candioty. Linda worked in the original LA Cheesecake Factory bakery experimenting with recipes for mousse pies and fudge cakes alongside Evelyn Overton. Today, Linda's famous Fudge Cake is still one of the chain's most popular menu items.

David and Linda were a match made in "cheesecake heaven." In the new restaurant, their roles were carefully planned: David took care of the business and Linda took care of the people. David was always testing and perfecting new menu items, and people continually raved about the quality and the choices he made. Linda was practicing the "Never a customer, always a guest" Disney credo even then. "Our guests choose us. They are in our home. They need to be comfortable." says Linda. "If the coffee is cold or they don't like it or they want another table, that's what I'm here for. There's never any other way to look at it in my mind." For years to come, new staff learned Linda's style of taking care of people, and although she is now retired, her legacy is valued to this day.

The Cheesecake Factory grew slowly, even though they had a huge hit on their hands and a formula that worked. He could have opened up new stores at any time in the first five years, but David's plan was to make sure everything was in place before jumping to new sites. By 1988, The Cheesecake Factory was operating in only three locations, all in California. In 1994, David decided to test a market in far away Washington, D.C. on the advice of a good friend. Having done no formal market research and no advertising, David held his breath to see what would happen. Once again, people showed up in droves. In D.C., or in any other location for that matter, the company has never deviated from its policy of "no reservations," much to the dismay of notable U.S. senators and distinguished executives who pleaded for the best tables and no waiting. "I told them we are very democratic at The Cheesecake Factory," Linda said, "We seat our guests in the order they arrive."

According to the masses that swarm to their doors from opening to closing, The Cheesecake Factory restaurant experience is worth the wait. This leading chain was one of the first to provide pagers for their guests, allowing them to shop or mingle while waiting for an open table. A new

(Continued)

system will likely soon be in place to allow for guest notification of available seating via cell phones.

Many other restaurant chains also have great concepts, but often when they go public, they weaken under the stress and pressures of Wall Street. There's a great temptation to grow too quickly, thereby increasing the risk of ending up in a death spiral trying to salvage success by cutting food quality and increasing prices.

Not so with The Cheesecake Factory. "Our niche is nearly impossible to describe and impossible to duplicate," says Peter D'Amelio, president and COO of the restaurant division.[67] No one has yet duplicated this successful core concept, with the exception of The Cheesecake Factory itself. Few companies can clone themselves with any success, but The Cheesecake Factory launched a second brand in 1999, the lavish European-style Grand Lux Cafe. Grand Lux's first-year sales topped $18 million, nearly twice the impressive per-restaurant average of the company's flagship concept. David and his team creatively and carefully plan Grand Lux locations in the same market areas as existing Cheesecake Factory restaurants, and they coexist beautifully.

"When you sit down and do your planning each year, you think about balance. I'm a producer and it's a juggling act. How much do you give to the creative side and how much do you give to the business. I ask myself, 'Is this going to be feasible?' If you don't hit it, you'll either lose the project or it will be a lousy project. As restaurateurs grow, they often look inside at the numbers and stop looking outside at the customers, the competition, staying fresh," David commented.

David has never deviated from his plan—methodical and controlled growth with no money spent on advertising in any market to date. The Cheesecake Factory is one of the most profitable restaurants in the upscale casual dining market. "They've evolved with this highly complex menu combined with a highly efficient kitchen," says Denis Lombardi of Technomic Inc., a food-service consulting firm. "They're somewhat intimidating to the industry." From all accounts, few entrepreneurs can match David Overton's patience, fortitude, commitment, and passion to stick with it and end up on top.

Chapter 10

Capture the Magic
with Storyboards

*Layer upon layer, we create a patchwork of sketches and words that
color the original idea. Funny, fantastic, diverting, enhancing, persuasive,
serious or not, our visualized thoughts begin to chisel away and uncover
the diamond in the rough.*[68]

Disney Imagineers

Like many ingenious concepts, storyboarding takes a simple technique—visual display—and uses it in a unique way to help companies
solve complex business problems. It is a structured exercise designed
to capture the thoughts and ideas from a group of participants. Their thoughts
and ideas are put on cards and then displayed on a board or a wall. The result,
an "idea landscape," is more organized than the output from brainstorming,
yet it retains the flexibility that project teams need as they work their way
through the various stages of problem solving and idea generation.

Walt Disney originally conceived the idea that eventually became known
as *storyboarding* as a way to keep track of the thousands of drawings necessary
to achieve full animation of cartoon features. By having his artists pin their
drawings in sequential order on the studio wall, Disney could quickly see
which parts of a project were or were not completed.

From its genesis in animation, the technique has spread to many other
areas. Advertising agencies now use storyboarding to sketch out commercials
before they shoot them. Scenes from feature movies are often storyboarded for
the next day's camera work. Editors and art directors utilize storyboards as a

tool in producing picture books. It allows them to visualize what the final page will look like and to make sure that one page leads logically to the next.

But storyboarding is not limited to artistic endeavors. We suggest to companies that storyboarding is an effective method to conceptualize their mission statements, to develop best practices for manufacturing control systems, and to produce technical plans for improvements. Posted ideas or suggestions become the first step in the analysis of barriers, the investigation of their root causes, and the creation of team solutions. Any process can be mapped out in this way.

Storyboarding is a creative and efficient method for generating solutions to complex problems—those that can sometimes feel overwhelming—because it breaks situations into smaller, more manageable parts and focuses group attention on specific aspects of a problem. When ideas and suggestions are displayed on a wall where they can be read by all and moved about as storyboarding participants see fit, the confusion that can stymie breakthrough ideas is dissipated.

No other planning technique offers the flexibility of storyboarding. In this chapter, we explain exactly how storyboarding works, and we look at a number of examples of the technique in action. As you read how companies in various settings are successfully using it to solve a range of problems, think about putting the technique to work for your organization.

The Birth of a Technique

When Walt Disney came up with the forerunner to the storyboarding technique in 1928, cartoon animation bore faint resemblance to the complex web of movement and color we know today. Full animation of cartoon features was still just a dream, but it was one Disney was striving to realize. To that end, he produced thousands more drawings than state-of-the-art animation required at that time.

The finished drawings were arranged in piles according to a predetermined narrative sequence. Then the cameraperson would photograph them, and the staff could watch them in a screening room. But with the prodigious output of drawings, it didn't take long before piles were stacked up in the studio. To bring some sense of order and to make it easier to follow a film's developing story line, Disney instructed his artists to display their drawings on a large piece of fiberboard that measured about 4 feet by 8 feet.

Not just finished drawings, but early rough sketches were pinned on the board. If there were problems with the story line or if a character wasn't taking shape as Disney wanted, changes could be made before the expensive work of animation was begun. The storyboard made it possible for Disney to experiment, to move drawings around, to change direction, to insert something he thought was missing, or to discard a sequence that wasn't working. And he could do all this *before* the animator had spent countless hours painstakingly putting in the final details.

Decades later, in the 1960s, the display technique was picked up by Disney's employee development program when the staff recognized its value for generating solutions to problems and enhancing communications in other areas. The refined storyboard concept has since been adapted to a variety of problem-solving situations in which the introduction of the visual element makes interconnections more readily apparent. As the participants pin cards to the wall, the team begins to develop various alternatives to solving the problem at hand.

Why doesn't a flip chart on an easel, a method often used in brainstorming sessions, work as well as a storyboard? On a flip chart, participants can see only one step at a time and therefore fail to get an overall picture. Moreover, flip charts can quickly become virtually unreadable as new ideas are inserted, old ideas are scratched out or moved around, and large arrows are left pointing nowhere. In addition, the lack of anonymity in brainstorming—participants must voice their ideas publicly—contributes a certain unease that discourages contributions. Our experience with both storyboarding and brainstorming allows us to make concrete comparisons in this regard: Whereas a 60-minute brainstorming session with 14 participants produces, on average, 42 utterances (questions, ideas, or comments), a storyboard session of the same size and duration typically produces anywhere from 150 to 300 utterances! Our studies have shown that in a typical 14-person brainstorming session, 5 participants produce 80 percent of the utterances, 5 participants produce 20 percent of the utterances, and the remaining 4 participants are observers of the meeting. In a storyboard session, all members of the group are active participants.

Anyone who has participated in the traditional, inefficient problem-solving meeting knows the drudgery of endless discussion, time-wasting repetitions, and lengthy explanations. Since only one person can talk at a time, most people's minds wander from the topic being discussed to the job waiting for them back at their desks. And invariably, a single participant tends to dominate the discussion. When the meeting finally drones to a close, it is virtually impossible to remember much of what was said.

Storyboarding, however, works to reverse this outcome. It is a fully participatory activity that places the entire sequence of a project, a company policy, or plan of action clearly in everyone's line of sight.

Overcoming Skepticism

We generally acquaint clients with the concept of storyboarding early in our association. Even though we emphasize its enormous value, acceptance is not a foregone conclusion. The idea of congregating around a space decorated with rows of cards on the wall seems totally outlandish to people who have never witnessed a storyboarding session.

A utility that we worked with in Indianapolis, for example, had spent almost two years trying to devise a plan for changing their culture. After untold hours of management meetings, brainstorming, and arguing, the executive team still couldn't agree on a plan. When we arrived with a stack of cards and dozens of markers, the group listened politely as we explained storyboarding, but they were clearly dubious about the whole approach. Nevertheless, they agreed to give it a try.

The group appeared far from convinced at the outset of our session that tacking cards on a wall would do anything to solve those problems that had baffled them for two years. We began by asking them for their ideas for potential solutions, which they wrote out and we put up on the board. As the cards were moved around and new ideas added, a structure for their implementation plans gradually developed.

The storyboarding process is like building a house; it entails a logical progression. Just as a house begins with the architect's conceptual rendering and then moves through the various stages—foundation, subflooring, walls, and roof—so, too, the storyboard process starts with the "concept," or the problem to be solved, and moves along in a creative interplay of ideas and suggestions until the desired solution has taken shape.

And that is exactly what happened in the session with the utility after only two hours of storyboarding. The once-skeptical executives were astounded. One of them admitted to us afterwards that the group initially thought story-boarding was, in his words, "a real Mickey Mouse technique." They couldn't imagine that it could be of benefit in their situation. But more progress was made in two hours of storyboarding than the group had made in the previous two years of endless meetings and unproductive wrangling. Everyone agreed that the storyboarding technique had crystallized the overall concept of what management wanted to achieve, clarified the necessary action steps, and defined the progression of tasks.

Many people wonder how something so simple can possibly work to unravel complex questions. After all, a five-year-old can be taught to put cards up on the wall. Yet to paraphrase a line of poetry, simplicity is elegance, and it usually takes just one session to convince people of the richness of the storyboarding technique. The power it has to engage and stimulate people and to unleash their productivity is remarkable.

We believe that the high level of participation demanded by storyboarding is one reason that it works so well. Instead of the typical meeting situation in which the troops are forced to endure endless and often garbled rhetoric, in a storyboard situation the facilitator engages all people in a focused discussion.

This approach also heightens the concentration of individual group members as they become immersed in the problem at hand. Participants begin to embellish and expand on one another's ideas, unlike what often happens in brainstorming, when rather than adding to the proposed idea, half the people in the group are busy marshaling their thoughts to rebut it. "That's not going to work," they think, or "My department will never buy that."

In addition, the initial anonymity (people don't have to sign their names to their idea cards) encourages free expression and critical thinking. The value of anonymity was brought home to us in a focus group we conducted for Illinois Power. That group, composed of folks from the community, was set up to help the Illinois Power economic development team become more effective.

Originally scheduled to run from 8 a.m. until noon, the session was conducted just like a conventional focus group, with people brainstorming and putting things on flip charts around the room. When we realized after two hours that no new ideas were emerging, we assumed that everyone had said everything they wanted to say. To our surprise, however, several of the team members pressed us to try the storyboarding technique that we had previously described to them. So instead of ending the meeting early, we spent the remaining two hours doing a storyboard process. The result: at least three significant new ideas emerged concerning ways in which the development team could better serve the community.

As it turned out, some of the focus group participants had been reluctant to verbalize their ideas in front of the group. In our experience, that is often the case. Many people are simply frightened by the thought of speaking their minds in public. But stimulated by the discussion and given the chance to express themselves anonymously, they too can provide valuable input.

Storyboarding, then, can be an inestimable tool for getting to the heart of customer problems, and innovative response to customer problems is the stuff of business legend.

Solving the Communications Dilemma

Intracompany communication is a hot topic these days. People fret about it in management meetings; employees complain about it around the water cooler; and everyone agrees on the need for more and better dialogue. But several questions remain: Is anyone really communicating? How many organizations have a formal plan to facilitate better communication?

One of our clients, Whirlpool, understands better than most the importance of formalizing communications. At its Lavergne, Tennessee, manufacturing plant, the company has developed an entire center devoted solely to increasing the level of interaction between management and production employees. The center, which is actually located on the manufacturing floor, contains several museum-quality display booths that disseminate division and union news, highlight corporate initiatives, and answer employee questions using storyboarding techniques. In addition, people on the plant floor have direct access to a communications manager.

More important, the center is part of a much broader communications plan that encourages face-to-face interaction between management and production people, proposes electronic communication technology, oversees written communication, and holds managers accountable for communications in their performance process.

A formal plan is important because not everyone responds to the various forms of communication in the same way. Some people like it written; some want information delivered face-to-face; and some don't care about the method, but they do care about the quality and the frequency. Obviously, meeting the needs of a diverse work group requires experimentation with various options—quarterly town hall–type meetings perhaps, or skip-level meetings that allow top management to hear from people once or twice removed from the usual information chain, or implementation of a 360-degree feedback approach. The point is that management can't depend on a haphazard communication system. It must consider the various styles and needs of its work group audience and then devise a formal plan for delivering information.

Storyboarding is an ideal way to share ideas and concepts, throwing them into the public arena for discussion and tapping a team's collective creativity to figure out where and how an idea might work in any given function or department within a company. The technique helps break through interdepartmental barriers because it promotes face-to-face communication and a lively give-and-take among diverse personalities focused on a common goal.

Working with various client teams, we have repeatedly noticed that storyboarding enhances a team's cohesiveness. The interplay of meaningful communication has a way of binding people together. This is especially true of cross-functional teams, like those we set up at Whirlpool and at Bristol-Myers Squibb.

Members of a cross-functional team are often near strangers to one another. That's because they work in different departments and receive different training; even their outlook is different. But once team members participate in a storyboarding session together, employees from manufacturing or accounting or purchasing or any other department often find that they are not as far apart as they once thought. To solidify a team, we suggest that the group storyboard. That way, any ideas that come out of the team belong to the group, not to individuals.

The bonding element inherent in storyboarding worked to particularly good effect with a Whirlpool global team. The members of the team spoke several different languages and came from wildly different backgrounds—not just different job descriptions, but different countries, continents, and political situations. For example, among them was an engineer who had never been outside communist China before finding himself set down in the midwestern United States. How could such diversity be melded into one high-functioning group of men and women? Storyboards helped us overcome the hurdles.

We storyboarded national character traits and had team members decide which traits they liked and which they disliked. As it turned out, there was a high level of agreement on what people liked as well as what they didn't like. The best learning of all, they said, was the discovery that they all disliked "arrogance" in others! The storyboarding experiment helped to clarify the team concept for everyone. And that was no small accomplishment considering that many of the participants came from countries in which orders come from above and are followed without question. In such situations, the team concept is totally alien to the culture.

Storyboarding, then, can help a company improve communication and planning at all levels. What's more, establishing storyboarding as an integral part of planning brings clarity to an organization's internal workings.

At Illinois Power, for example, we suggested using storyboarding to help ease the transition to a new culture emphasizing teams. The plan to introduce teams and to increase the participation of the workforce at all levels amounted to radical and far-reaching change for the traditionally structured utility. Top management recognized that such an organizational metamorphosis would require a thorough re-education program. Employees would have to reassess their views of the company as a whole as well as their individual roles within it. But determining how an implementation should be constructed was no easy task.

Storyboarding uncovered potential barriers to the transition, which could then be addressed in the plan. Among the items dealt with in the session were management and employee resistance, closed lines of communication, rigid and hierarchical bureaucracy, and outdated facilities. This particular storyboard ended up serving as the foundation for Illinois Power's implementation plan for the new team culture.

Getting Started with Storyboarding
Supplies

- A meeting room with plenty of blank wall space
- An unbiased facilitator
- Pin boards and pins or drafting tape
- At least ten 4 × 6 index cards for every participant
- Water-soluble felt-tip markers in blue, black, and red
- Several different colored press-on three-quarter-inch dots

Procedure

- Facilitator asks leading questions, and group agrees on "topic card." (See Figure 10-1.)
- Participants record their thoughts regarding the topic on index cards.
- A facilitator gathers the "detail" cards, discusses each card with group, and clusters them by topic.
- Once three to four detail cards are in a cluster, group determines "header card" that describes the cluster. Header card is then printed in red.
- Once all cards are discussed and headers created, facilitator determines the number of "priority dots" to be given to each participant. Priority dots identify most significant headers and most significant detail cards.
- Storyboard is either left on the wall for group reference or typed and distributed to all members.

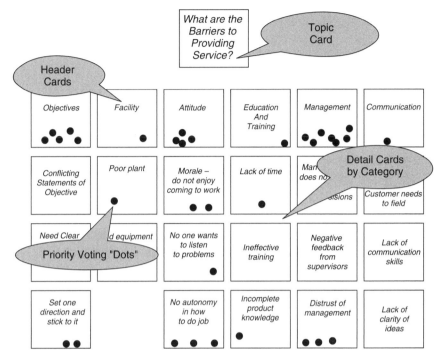

Figure 10-1. Storyboard example

Guidelines

- Facilitator prepares leading questions beforehand.
- Only one idea per card.
- The more ideas the better.
- No criticism of any idea.

Criteria for Good Questions

- Induce curiosity.
- Encourage positive thinking.
- Strive for consensus.
- Prevent termination of discussion.

Facilitator's Role

- Create pleasant, informal atmosphere.
- Lead discussion to mobilize group's creative energy and resolve conflicts.

- Question conclusions or answers in noncompetitive, nonhierarchical way.
- Provide positive feedback.
- Keep the process moving.
- Stimulate group to work on its own.

Things to Keep in Mind during Session

- What has been achieved so far?
- Where do we stand?
- What still needs to be done?

Storyboarding: The Process

In our work with organizations, we have seen every imaginable variety of storyboard technique, some using nothing more complicated than a bunch of index cards and a fistful of markers, others utilizing charts, pictures, drawings, or computer-generated printouts, and some dependent on information technology networks.

While electronic storyboarding is fine for collecting ideas and even for some degree of brainstorming, it cannot generate the creative energy that is sparked by in-person storyboard sessions. In these sessions, you are likely to see people jumping up from their chairs to point at various pieces of the puzzle. Some may even move a card from one place on the storyboard to another in order to prove that a particular idea fits better elsewhere. The increase in spontaneity and enthusiastic communication moves the meeting along at a fast pace. And because everyone is working from the same road map, it's easier to build consensus.

From a procedural standpoint, storyboarding evolves in a logical progression as mentioned above. First, the team identifies the topic to be defined or the problem to be solved, and this is written on a card and posted at the top of the storyboard. Then it establishes a "purpose," meaning the reasons for pursuing the topic. The facilitator allows the participants time to sit and answer the question or problem, jotting down their thoughts, one idea per card. The facilitator then collects the cards as participants continue to write more thoughts and may choose to sort the cards moving duplications to the back of the stack. When the group has completed the writing exercise, the facilitator reads each card aloud, invites discussion, and asks the participants to suggest how the cards might be clustered or positioned on the wall. As the discussion proceeds, all miscellaneous ideas that don't seem to fit anywhere else are held onto and placed in one section of the board. Nothing is discarded, no matter how useless it might seem, because you never know when the idea offered at 10 a.m. will prove to be the perfect piece for solving the puzzle at 2 p.m.

There are four main types of storyboards:

1. The idea board, which is used to develop a concept.
2. The planning board, which is an outline of the steps required to reach the desired result.
3. The organization board, which determines who will be responsible for what.
4. The communications board (highly visible as the process or project is carried out), which allows a person or group to organize and communicate daily activities to those who need to know.

Regardless of what storyboarding is being used for, one thing remains constant—its role in nurturing creative and critical thinking.

When it comes to the mechanics of storyboarding, people often ask the practical question, "How much space do we need to adequately storyboard?" There is no cut-and-dried answer because it depends on how many people will be present at a meeting. Two people can storyboard very satisfactorily in a small office for the purpose of visualizing their ideas or mapping out potential solutions to a problem. In our experience, groups of more than 25 often suffer from the old mindset of the typical classroom where the teacher speaks and the students are silent. This type of rigor mortis kills the intended participation of storyboarding.

Every storyboarding session needs a facilitator, whose job it is to bring everyone into the discussion with stimulating questions. The facilitator should, as much as possible, let the participants run the meeting while still maintaining control and not letting the discussion get out of hand.

Criticism should be avoided, no matter how off-the-wall the suggestions might seem. An informal atmosphere and encouraging words will produce the greatest number of ideas. To that end, the facilitator strives to promote positive thinking and to create a consensus, although he or she must be careful not to terminate a discussion. Ideas must flow freely to their logical conclusions.

An American architect once mused that there are very few inferior people in the world, but lots of inferior environments. "Try to enrich your environment," he advised.[69] Storyboarding is a tool that can enrich the environment of any organization, no matter the specific needs. Storyboarding can be adapted to fit so that anyone can capture the magic.

Having examined planning and problem solving, we turn our attention in the next chapter to the third element of successful execution of The Disney Way. As Walt knew so well, grand ideas are nothing without proper emphasis on the details.

Questions to Ask

- Do you formalize communications through the utilization of storyboards?
- Do teams of all sizes use storyboarding as a way to visualize their barriers, goals, problems, solutions, and project plans?
- Do you promote the use of storyboarding in meetings involving sensitive topics?
- Do you offer assistance in storyboard facilitation to teams in need?
- Do all employees know how to conduct a storyboarding session and in which situations this technique is particularly useful?
- Do you invite your customers and suppliers to participate in storyboarding sessions to gain their feedback and assistance in planning and problem solving?

Actions to Take

- Train all employees in the technique of storyboarding.
- Provide teams with areas to storyboard and the flexibility to leave them visible for as long as needed.
- Use storyboarding in planning sessions to develop timelines and project assignments; use the storyboard as a dynamic tool which can be changed, revised, and updated as needed.
- Use storyboarding to gain anonymous input from all meeting participants, particularly when there are sensitive topics at hand.
- Use storyboarding to gain feedback from customer groups.
- Develop a formal communication plan that defines who, what, when, and how communications are made to all employees. Schedule storyboard sessions with all employees to gather ideas for improvement.

The Mighty Marker

Storyboarding was used throughout the two-year life of the Whirlpool Global No-Frost team. Everyone participated. We kept cards and markers on hand, and we would hand them out whenever scheduling or other questions arose. The cards were particularly effective with cross-functional teams as people's different functions seemed to encourage participation. According to Jerry, "A bunch of engineers in a room will produce few cards, but when they are joined by manufacturing, purchasing, and marketing, diverse points of view come up on the boards, and discussion can become extremely lively, heated, and finally productive."

Storyboarding, Jerry found, was a valuable way to get ideas and reactions out of team members. If a deadline was under discussion, he didn't want the team members sitting back and saying silently to themselves, "This will never be." He told them he wanted everybody's opinions on the cards because only when the barriers are spelled out is it possible to overcome them. "They don't want to stand up and talk about their doubts, so storyboarding is a way for people to get their thoughts on cards anonymously. It's a tremendously helpful technique for seeing a way of eliminating barriers." It was also a way for the team to reach a consensus and to figure out exactly where each subteam stood within the overall schedule.

Our Featured Organization: John Robert's Spa

A NEW STYLE OF VISUALIZATION

The Disney organization performs a balancing act in three areas: a quality cast experience; a quality guest experience, and a quality business experience. As an avid implementer of Disney's method, John DiJulius, cofounder of John Robert's, credits the storyboard process for helping his team achieve that balance. "We have weekly meetings on Tuesday mornings where our managers storyboard," said John. "We actually stopped doing this at one point and said 'Let's go to a monthly meeting,' but we found out that was a bad experience."[70]

(Continued)

Every year, John Robert's uses storyboarding to identify 24 items that are critical to the organization's overall success. Once a month, the entire staff meets to discuss and reinforce these strategic initiatives.

Taking storyboarding to the next level, John teaches all new employees how to use visualization to help accomplish long-term goals. His Dream Retreats have evolved into a training ground for what he terms "the picturization process." As John described them, "They require a lot of homework. Employees must come to the process with their goals, pictures of their dreams, even their eulogy." The Dream Retreat affords people an opportunity to learn how to see the value of visualizing and setting personal goals through activities such as producing a scrapbook of self-promotions. They band together in "Dream teams" and vow to hold each other accountable for achieving their goals. The grand finale is an awards dinner where everyone is required to dress according to how they envision themselves in five years. Some rent costumes, some wear Tommy Bahama shirts with a tie; whatever their "character," they must remain true to their role during the event. On the previous day, John calls employees to find out which "roles" they have chosen. He gives each employee an award based on their personas. Awards may be "father of the year," "new entrepreneur of the year," "best-selling author," and so on. John told us, "Each employee must make a detailed five-minute acceptance speech on how they accomplished their Dream."

As John Robert's discovered, the storyboarding process serves as a springboard for unleashing creative energies, and ultimately contributes to achieving positive results for employees, customers and business alike.

USING STORYBOARDS TO CAPTURE CUSTOMER FEEDBACK

Many of our clients are unable or unwilling to spend thousands of dollars on professional marketing studies to find out just what customers are thinking and what they really want. In our Dream Retreats and "Creating the Magic with Dream, Believe, Dare, Do" seminars, we teach a relatively simple variation of storyboarding to accomplish this goal within structured groups.

Here are the steps for obtaining customer feedback:

1. Invite a group of 15 to 20 customers whom you believe have a vested interest in helping you improve one or more of your products

or services. Plan to provide refreshments, a light meal, or a gift certificate to compensate for their time. We have found that most people, especially loyal customers, welcome an opportunity to provide feedback in areas that directly affect them.

2. Present a brief overview of the mechanics of storyboarding. Distribute the supplies to the group: 4 × 6 index cards, blue (or black) and red water-soluble felt-tip markers, three-quarter-inch blue and red removable dots, masking and drafting tape for creating the "board." (Use masking tape to anchor the top and bottom of 4-foot tape strips that are placed sticky-side out in rows of 12 to 14 per board.)

3. Ask the group to storyboard, answering the question: "What elements create your ideal customer experience in the area of _____(fill in your product or service)?" For example, if you are in the hotel business, you might ask your customers, "What elements create your ideal hotel experience?" Explain to them that this step is to really identify what the ultimate experience should "look like." Write the question you have asked on a 4 × 6 index card. This is the "Topic Card."

4. Once you have collected, read aloud, and posted all the Detail (response) and Header cards (Figure. 10-1), distribute three "red dots" to each participant and ask them to place their dots on the three cards that they consider to be most important.

5. Distribute three "green dots" to each participant and ask them to place their dots on the three cards that they believe are your strengths, or things you are doing well

6. Distribute three "blue dots" to each participant and ask them to place their dots on the three cards that they believe are your weaknesses, or things you could improve.

In a 60 to 90 minute session, the storyboard will be complete and you'll have a snapshot of what really matters to your customers and how you measure up to their criteria of an "ideal" experience with your organization. Figure 10-2 is an actual example of a customer feedback storyboard from one of our clients, a residential healthcare facility.[71]

It is not uncommon to discover that some of the things that customers believe you are doing well are unimportant to them. If you discover an obvious conflict between what you think is important and what the customer thinks is important, consider this a serious red flag. If you don't change

(Continued)

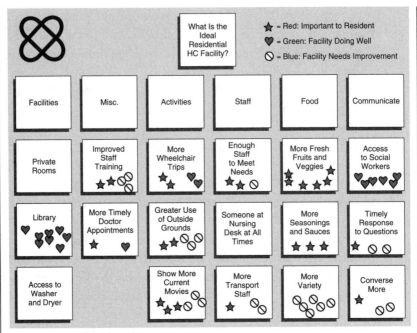

Figure 10-2. Customer feedback storyboard

direction, your organization might be spiraling toward disaster. In Figure 10-2, you will notice that the residents considered the library and access to social workers as the two best attributes of their healthcare facility. However, not one of the residents felt these two items were important.

We recommend storyboarding with three or four different customer groups and then comparing the results. If you want to take this process a step farther, ask the same question to a random group of front-line service providers and to the top management group. It may surprise you which group really has a better understanding of the customers' needs, desires, and dreams.

Chapter 11

Give Details
Top Billing

*There are two words that make [operations] work around here . . .
quality and pride. If you design, build, operate, and maintain with quality,
people will take pride in what they do.*[72]
Dick Nunis (Retired Chairman, Walt Disney Attractions)

Business people of every stripe place a great deal of importance on
seeing the "big picture" or coming up with the grand idea. But seldom understood is the fact that details give the big picture depth;
they bring the grand idea clearly into focus and produce pride in workers'
skills. Paying attention to the little things is what turns the vision into a top-
quality product or an outstanding service. As the great architect Mies van der
Rohe once put it, "God is in the details."[73]

No one had to tell Walt Disney the significance that seeming trifles can
have when excellence is the goal. Perhaps because he possessed an artist's eye,
he recognized that attention to detail was the key to complete realization of
his dreams. As a result, the company he founded has no equal when it comes
to creating the thousands of intricate drawings needed to produce nonpa-
reil animation, bring together the mind-boggling number of parts required
to build a Disneyland or a Walt Disney World, or carefully attend to the
numerous small details that make every guest's experience a magical one.

Often overlooked in Disney's awe-inspiring success is how the company
as an organization has managed to give extravagant attention to detail without
bankrupting itself. It has achieved a careful balance between the competing

demands of the bottom line and the quest for perfection. The key to this balancing act is contained in the Disney philosophy that everyone—from the groundskeepers at the parks and the animators in the movie studio to the number crunchers in the accounting department—is responsible for doing whatever it takes to deliver the "good show." Even Bob Iger has "trash collecting" in his job description when he's visiting one of the theme parks! When all parties are convinced of the importance of their individual roles, nothing will be left to chance.

Most of the companies we work with are far removed from the Disney environment of entertainment, yet they too have recognized that obsessive attention to detail can pay huge dividends. Thus, they are calling on "casts" of employees to present their own version of the good show to an "audience" composed of suppliers and customers, and in doing so, these companies are consistently delivering quality products and services to their target markets.

A Relentless Search for Perfection

There is a photograph in the Disney archives of Walt and 10 of his animators standing around a studio table. In the middle of the table are five live penguins. The birds are all turned toward Walt Disney as if they know where their next meal is coming from. This arresting and charming image perfectly captures so much of the Disney ethos and magic—the element of surprise, the embrace of the animal kingdom, and always, the relentless search for perfection.

Disney, who was determined to exceed customers' expectations, was dissatisfied with the movements of his animated movie animals. They were good, but they weren't perfect. Up until that time, his animators had relied on photographic stills or movie clips to give them the models for their figures. It was clear to Walt that the animators could do better if they were able to copy the real thing—ergo, the penguins.

"How can we do better?" is the question Walt Disney asked at every turn. But then complacency is unnatural to the perfectionist. He strove continually to improve the quality of his products. "Whenever I ride an attraction," he once said, "I'm thinking of what's wrong with the thing and asking myself how it can be improved."[74]

The story is told that after Disneyland was already up and running, the boss stopped in to take a ride on the Jungle Cruise attraction. He emerged furious. The ride was advertised as taking seven minutes, but he had timed it at only four-and-a-half minutes. The very idea that a guest might be shortchanged was antithetical to the Disney culture and to Walt's vision of quality;

he ordered the ride lengthened immediately. Moreover, he made it clear that carelessness toward details would not be tolerated, for such an attitude might cause guests to start doubting Disney's trustworthiness, the heart and soul of his management philosophy and personal credo.

Meticulous attention to detail is also characteristic of the Disney animated films. In *Snow White,* for example, viewers don't see drops of water just dripping from a bar of soap, in itself an unusual level of detail in animated films. Instead, they see glistening bubbles that actually twinkle in the candlelight.

Creating such film magic required a staff of skilled animators, of course, and here, too, Walt refused to leave anything to chance. To make sure that he would always have a sufficient number of talented artists to meet his demanding standards, Walt began in-house training courses and eventually made a deal that brought teachers from an art school to work with his animators.

In fact, no corner of the organization escaped Walt's obsession with perfection. Thoroughly convinced that no detail was too small to be ignored in order to provide his guests with an exceptional experience, the boss made his touch apparent everywhere. He determined that garbage cans should be spaced exactly 25 feet apart all around Disneyland. He ordered that the highest-quality paint be used on rides and buildings, going so far as to specify that real gold or silver be used for any gilding or silvering. He even hired someone whose job it was to patrol Disneyland twice a month to make certain that all the colors in the park were in harmony!

The master entertainer instinctively knew that the whole package—colors, sounds, smells—had an impact on how guests received the show.

If this holistic, integrated approach to entertainment seems excessive, one need only think of a promising restaurant experience that went awry because of one disagreeable factor. Perhaps the food was first-class, the service pleasant, and the decor attractive, but the background music assailed a diner's ears and made it impossible to enjoy the meal. One jarring element can undermine a host of favorable impressions in a restaurant or anywhere else, and Walt Disney wasn't about to risk such a misstep.

That's why street cleaners at Walt Disney World are given extra training at Disney University to ensure that they respond in a positive and helpful fashion to questions from departing guests. It might seem strange to train street cleaners in customer service, but the company learned a few years back that these employees receive the greatest number of unstructured questions from park guests. An exhausted couple with three hungry children in tow might ask where they can get a quick, inexpensive dinner, for instance. To make sure that a guest's last impression after a wonderful day in the park isn't ruined by a don't-ask-me-it's-not-my-job attitude, The Walt Disney Company decrees an extra three days of interpersonal skills training for the clean-up crew. They take a proactive approach to head off potentially damaging situations. The Disney organization realizes that the entire "whole show" is critical; the way the street cleaner treats the guest is as important or even more important than the way the guest is treated on the Tower of Terror.

Maintaining a Delicate Balance

When it came to pursuing the often elusive ideal of perfection, Walt Disney spared no expense. The previously mentioned reworking of the Jiminy Cricket character in *Pinocchio,* after the costly animation process was already well underway, is but one example. When it was discovered that a merry-go-round at Walt Disney World was installed two inches off center, the company insisted that it be moved. "Who would notice?" you might wonder. The Disney folks not only noticed, but they reasoned that if the carousel were not set right, thousands of guests would take home vacation pictures that provided an imperfect memory of their visit to the park

You may think that this was much ado about nothing. However, the Eastman Kodak Company once estimated that 4 percent of all amateur photographs taken in the United States were taken at the Disney theme parks, and many of those taken at Walt Disney World were from an angle that captures the carousel in the background. For example, guests often are photographed as they stand in Cinderella's Castle with Fantasyland as the backdrop. Looking through the doors of the castle, the carousel is perfectly framed at the center of the opening. Since an off-center merry-go-round would make those pictures look strange, Disney naturally decided that the imperfect carousel had to be moved, despite the hefty expense involved.

But we must make clear that "sparing no expense" has never meant profligate spending. Walt Disney was always well aware of the bottom line, and he expected that the money spent would be returned in customer satisfaction and employee loyalty. The way Walt saw it, meticulous attention to detail provided a level of quality that cast members could take pride in, and he knew that when workers are proud of their product, it is reflected in the kind of service they give to customers.

But when it came to spending on items unrelated to providing the good show, the boss was actually known as something of a penny-pincher. He never built a splendidly pompous, ego-enhancing headquarters building, nor did he ever spend a nickel on advertising his theme park. Disney reasoned that his television shows provided advertising aplenty, so why waste money paying for it? In today's environment, The Walt Disney Company has a large advertising budget, but still does not waste money on backstage areas.

Walt also kept a sharp eye on financial arrangements and partnerships, not hesitating to protect his own interests. Although a licensing deal in the early 1930s brought in $300,000 the first year—with Walt's share providing half of the company's annual profits that year—he quickly discovered a major drawback. The deal called for his percentage of the profits to increase as more items were sold, but since novelty items sold fast and then faded from the market, the licensee would make a lot more money than Disney would. Walt canceled the arrangement and set up an in-house marketing division.

Today, Disney executives ask cast members to balance what they call "quality cast experience," "quality guest experience," and "quality business practice." The product should deliver value in all three areas: pleasing cast members, customers, and corporate bean counters and balancing them as needed. The company firmly believes, as Walt did, that obsessive attention to detail in all respects is the key to delivering a sterling experience that will keep guests coming back while holding costs to a level that still maintains profit margins.

In our experience, successful companies like Disney balance business and creative needs by insisting on strict adherence to a set of core values, emphasizing the importance of details in exceeding customer expectations, and encouraging innovation and risk taking within a specified set of boundaries. Disney makes no bones about its belief that creativity works best within a specified framework. In a 1996 interview with *Fortune* magazine, Peter Schneider, president of the film division, called deadlines "a key ingredient to creativity."[75] They force people to focus on the project at hand, to produce *something*—good, bad, or indifferent—that will at least serve to spark the next idea, he said. And, of course, deadlines also keep costs from spiraling out of control.

Many of the companies we advise have devised winning strategies that similarly balance top-of-the-line quality with innovation and bottom-line performance.

John Dunn's hotel properties consistently rank at the top in opinion polls because of his insistence on quality and attention to detail. Employees end up caring for the properties as much as they care for their own homes, picking up trash dropped on the floor, straightening a lampshade as they pass by, and tidying newspapers left scattered about the lobby. Everyone from the desk clerk to the banquet manager is trained to react rather than overlook.

One of Dunn's managers insists that every item on the breakfast bar—coffee, juice, rolls, butter—be placed in exactly the same place every day. Now you might ask what difference it makes if the coffee pot is on the left or the right. But the manager recognizes that repeat guests, and particularly the targeted business traveler, will appreciate not having to hunt for the decaffeinated coffee or figure out which is the apple juice and which is the orange.

At BellSouth, attention to details means that when an installation and maintenance crew is at a particular location, members know they should make the appropriate preventive repairs that will head off future problems and save another time-consuming, money-devouring visit at a later date. Just as with the Dunn hotel employees, being proactive is an important ingredient in balancing quality and costs.

Measuring for Success

Paying attention to detail also means measuring results. This concept seems almost too rudimentary to mention, but experience has taught us that many organizations make little or no effort to assess results, either in terms of operating objectives or in terms of performance standards and customer satisfaction.

In our Dream Retreats, for example, we frequently ask participants, "How many of you feel that you would be more successful if you made fewer mistakes and produced your product more quickly?" Everyone always raises a hand. But seldom does even one hand stay in the air when we follow up with, "How many of you are making quality and time measurements for your key business processes?"

YMCA Camp Kern took the question to heart. YMCA Camp Kern is located between Dayton and Cincinnati, Ohio. This 420-acre facility located along the Little Miami River outside of historic Lebanon, Ohio, was founded in 1910. Camp Kern offers year-round programs serving as host to over 30,000 guests a year. Programs include: Summer Camp, Ranch Camp (Equestrian), Outdoor Education ("Hands-on Learning for Every Season"), Conferences

& Retreats, Leadership Adventure Programs, and a variety of family programs. Camp Kern is a $2.5 million branch operation of the Greater Dayton YMCA.

In 2002, YMCA Camp Kern had a summer camp retention rate of 29 percent, meaning that out of 10 children attending Camp Kern for the first time in 2001, only 3 campers returned in the summer of 2002. The national average rate of summer camper retention (campers who return after their first year experience) is approximately 50 percent. Additionally, Camp Kern had a retention rate of 34 percent in conferencing; and staff retention was at an all time low for seasonal Summer Camp and Outdoor Education staff; and a whopping 40 percent turnover for full-time staff.

That same year, Jeff Merhige arrived as the new executive director, determined to change the culture and philosophy of YMCA Camp Kern. "*The Disney Way* model seemed to be a perfect fit for what we needed to accomplish," noted Jeff. Jeff and his staff team at Camp Kern would strive to become the best in reputation, program delivery and development, relationship building, facility, and work culture.

A Camp Kern *Staff Guidebook* was developed and new staff training was designed for all employees, educating them on the new operating philosophy of "Guests and Kids First," as well as its program goals, mission statement, and staff expectations, which included a staff commitment to excellence contract. Staff evaluations were also created to assess responses to questions such as: (1) What can we do to help you be excellent? (2) What would you change to help us all be excellent? (3) What do you think should be kept the same or modified to be excellent?

By the end of 2005, the all-inclusive sharing of dreams and goals among Camp Kern staff resulted in a dramatic improvement in staff energy and motivation. Camp Kern's retention rate of summer campers had jumped to 71 percent in 2005. And conferencing today celebrates a 92 percent retention rate.

In the past three years, Camp Kern has received donations and gifts totaling over $2 million, renovated five buildings, and built four new buildings—including a 300-person Assembly Hall and Conference Center.

Staff retention: There has been no senior staff turnover in the past two years (9 positions), seasonal staff retention has grown to 65 percent for summer staff and seasonal outdoor ed staff, and full-time staff retention has grown to 85 percent.

The process of Dream, Believe, Dare, Do created a map that made it easy for me and my team to chart a route and make it to our destination of business success, unity, and fun for all of us, and most importantly, our guests and children.

JEFF MERHIGE, EXECUTIVE DIRECTOR YMCA CAMP KERN

We can't emphasize strongly enough the importance of implementing some system for gauging quality level, process time, customer satisfaction, and product cost, as well as negative elements such as errors of judgment and process mistakes. All too often, companies give little thought to measuring processes in their entirety, even though doing so need not be a complicated task. But without measurements, an organization cannot possibly know which processes are working efficiently and effectively, what products and services are meeting quality standards, and whether or not customer requirements are being satisfied.

Identifying processes and mapping the functions involved are keys to increasing efficiency. In many organizations, however, processes seem to be hit-or-miss affairs, the result of haphazard growth. When a team takes the time to map the details of a process, the results are usually an eye-opener. "Why would anyone design a process like that?" baffled executives ask. No one did design it, of course, and that's just the problem. The process simply mushroomed in all directions as well-meaning managers added a step here and required a memo there. Before long, what once was a relatively smooth-functioning process has turned into a Hydra-headed monster.

Dr. William Cross, the vice president with whom we worked at Mead Johnson who was first mentioned in Chapter 4, found this out when teams in his department decided to take a look at certain key business processes. They uncovered many redundant and non-value-added elements that had been built into the system over the course of several years. Dr. Cross was astounded to discover that mapping a single work process related to releasing a new product produced a "flow chart that when it was all put together end to end, was about seven feet high and about two and a half feet wide, and was in very small print. So it was extremely complex."[77]

By mapping out the details of the complex process, however, the team was able to determine which steps could safely be discontinued. The new streamlined process reduced the usual cycle time for a product release by about two weeks.

Something similar occurred when Bill Capodagli was working with the South African utilities company mentioned in Chapter 9. After every step in the procurement process had been documented, more than 100 square feet of a wall in the project-planning center were covered with index cards. Needless to say, the process was hopelessly complex and very often redundant so that capital materials procurement was taking as much as a year and a half, with seven or eight months of that eaten up by the internal bureaucracy.

Astonished company executives could only wonder how it had happened that pieces of paper were going back and forth for months on end, and for absolutely no reason at all. Once the process was streamlined, the savings in time and money was considerable.

When we work with a team on a strategic initiative, a willingness to become immersed in details is a must. At Mead Johnson, for example, the exhaustive process began with the creation of a complaint analysis team to determine the path traveled by product complaints, either from an individual or from another company. It took us three to four months to complete the flow chart documenting each step involved. The team interviewed every department along the route, and when the flow chart was done, each department was asked to check it for accuracy.

Simultaneously, the team followed one sample complaint through the entire handling process and clocked the amount of time each step took. Multiplying the time factor by the department's charge-out rate allowed the team to assess costs. The team discovered that a single complaint traveling through the analysis system took an average of 30 days and cost the company up to $910 from beginning to end. Having established its data, the team was then able to draw up a new flow chart for an ideal system.

One change drastically reduced the number of complaints that were still being stored after the process was completed. Before the analysis, all complaints were being held for four months, even though most of them were never looked at again. The team logically determined that only those complaints that posed a potential legal threat—packaging that had allegedly been tampered with—or those that involved a federal, state, or local government agency needed to be retained. This one simple change of process saved the company considerable time.

Not all of the team's proposals and recommendations could be instituted immediately because some depended on decisions in other divisions. But initial forecasts pointed to eventual savings of $123 per complaint. Dr. Cross said, "The teams have saved in dollars thus far tens of thousands which have already [produced] a payback."

The message for management, then, is to look at your business in a holistic manner the way Disney looks at its show. Carefully examine all the details that affect the way your product or service is provided to customers. In other words, go the extra mile, or as the folks at Disney might say, "Bump the lamp."

This cryptic phrase originated when the movie *Roger Rabbit* was being made, and it relates to a scene in which someone bumps into a lamp, causing the shadow it casts to wobble. Initially, there were no shadows in the scene, which the animators immediately spotted as being unrealistic, so they went back and did the hundreds of drawings needed to bring perfection to these few seconds of the film.

"Bump the lamp" has become shorthand at Disney for doing things the right way, down to the tiniest detail. The Walt Disney Company has raised the bar of performance—to "bump the lamp," despite their well-publicized management blunders of the past decade. In the next chapter, we explain how CEO Bob Iger is re-creating the "magic" throughout The Walt Disney Company.

Questions to Ask

- Do your cross-functional teams map all the critical details of processes in order to determine which steps can be safely eliminated?
- Do your employees and teams make quality and time measurements of their critical processes?
- Do your employees routinely ask, "How can we do this better?"
- Do you include meticulous attention to detail as part of your organization's values?
- Do you reward people in your organization for detecting inconsistencies or defects in the products you produce?

Actions to Take

- Appoint a "details squad" to get fanatical about the details that make a difference to your customers.
- Continuously evaluate the effectiveness of your processes.
- Make attention to detail a part of organizational values.
- Evaluate how "little things" can make a difference in the way you serve customers or turn out products.
- Don't assume you can wow a customer with the big picture at the expense of details.

Three Big Wins

Team rewards are an essential component of all good teamwork. As we mentioned earlier, we had spontaneous celebrations and we had official parties. Along the way, Jerry McColgin often took members out for a game of golf after the completion of an especially grueling project. But the big award was, of course, the year-end bonus, and herein lay a problem—how to calculate a fair bonus for an international team whose members were usually paid under a variety of bonus structures. With the help of the company COO, Jerry finally worked out a solution for the first year's bonus. But when the final bonus was to be paid, there was such a generally critical and unpleasant attitude among other members of management in the company that Jerry felt he should offer to forgo his own bonus, not only to preserve others' rewards but to maintain team morale and focus. In the end, it all worked out, and Jerry received his bonus too, but we have always felt that Jerry's offer was proof of his commitment to the team.

"One of the things we encouraged from the beginning," Jerry recounts, "was to celebrate failure. I'll never forget the first time someone said that his subteam had failed in a design task. My response was to say, 'It's great to discover this now and not once we're in production.'" This was part of Jerry's way of building trust so that people were as open with their failures as with their successes.

For Jerry, looking back after the team's work was finished, this project was the best job experience he had ever had. "I looked out on the horizon and asked, 'How can I top this?'" What Jerry learned, though, is that there is no recipe. There are no hard-and-fast rules for a successful team project. Each team is different in its makeup, in its goals, and in its leader. If you change all the ingredients, you can't use the same recipe. Putting people first is essential. The deliverables will follow if the team is cohesive and dedicated to the goals. In the case of the Global No-Frost team, it was 10 months before a pervasive sense of unity took hold, so patience is required. The team, with its diverse staff, its time pressures, and financial limits, ended its project with a memorable triumph.

"We came in ahead of schedule, under budget on investment, and with a lower product cost than promised," Jerry recounts with justifiable pride. The achievements of the team were, indeed, astounding.

Our Featured Organization:
The Cheesecake Factory

GOOD BUSINESS IS SHOW BUSINESS

The Dalai Lama once said that simplicity is the key to happiness in the modern world. He apparently has never met David Overton, CEO of The Cheesecake Factory. David has made a career out of creating a "show business" restaurant concept where managing complexity is the name of the game. When the doors open at 11 a.m., the curtain is up, so to speak. Every detail—the lighting, the music, the temperature, the cast in perfectly-pressed uniforms—is shining.

If you were going to start a restaurant and sat down with a blank piece of paper, you probably wouldn't dream of the details that David dreamed. The idea of offering over 200 made-to-order menu items and over 50 varieties of cheesecakes and other sumptuous desserts would leave most entrepreneurs cold. Not to mention that every single Cheesecake Factory restaurant is custom-designed under David's supervision. We asked David how he decided to create such a complex menu. "I didn't know any better. You see, I never worked in the restaurant business before we opened," replied David. "Today, it is a competitive advantage."[78] There is no cookie-cutter approach in use, at least not when it comes to executing the concept of outstanding quality with a high degree of customization. "We are masterful at taking something that couldn't be done and doing it well," says Peter D'Amelio, president of restaurant operations. "We bring in weird ingredients for three items. Nobody else does this."[79]

The classic restaurant chain model is grounded in simplicity of concept and simplicity of execution. The Cheesecake Factory thrives on complexity. Every Cheesecake Factory employee understands the all-consuming and intense environment in which they make their living, and most are energized by it. They are required to work harder than the average restaurant worker, but the rewards are also greater. Most tell us that they stay because of the high quality of food, the atmosphere, and the people on their teams. "Cast members" know their lines; they are players in an orchestrated show that is staged up tempo every hour of the workday.

"Our store openings are unbelievably organized," David told us, "people are impressed by this and they naturally team." A difficult challenge for him, however, is deprogramming employees who have worked at other restaurant chains. Most are accustomed to having five tables in their stations, but The

Cheesecake Factory believes that four tables translates to the guests receiving better service. "It costs money and takes time," says David, "but the guests are happier and it's proven that servers make more money if they please the guest." It's a form of "cheesecaking," the verb, always making things best for the guest.

Food is one of David Overton's greatest passions. And, strange as it may seem, he has what his staff terms, "a perfect palate." He apparently has the ability to detect ingredients in nearly every dish he tastes. He periodically stages what are known as "food tours," which are not to be confused with boondoggles. No, in fact there are lessons to be learned on each one. Once on the food tour with his management team in Providence, Rhode Island, David ordered a white pizza that the team quickly devoured. Several months later when he was back at the Calabasas Hills corporate office, he asked Peter D'Amelio to taste a piece of pizza and then asked him, "Where did you have this before?" After a moment, Peter remembered the trip they had taken and the pizza they had loved so much. David had duplicated the pizza from memory!

Food tours are as carefully planned as the restaurants themselves. There are perfect itineraries, each and every time. They'll go from place to place ordering lunch at 11, 1, and 3, and then dinner at 5, 7, and 9. David insists that everyone order an appetizer, salad, entrée, and dessert at each seating. He takes them to trendy places to see what is coming into the market and to more traditional, established places as well. He never goes anywhere to steal an item. It's about judging it, changing it, perfecting it. "David, from the very beginning, is the one person who understands what people will respond to in a positive manner," remarks Robert Okura, vice president of R&D. "We use anything and everything as inspiration. It's a multifaceted process and it takes a long time."[80]

Every item on a Cheesecake Factory menu is a slight variation on a traditional dish. David believes that if the items are harder, people won't be as likely to duplicate them. "Our struggle for all these years has been to manage to the success of the concept, and not bring the concept down to our level of management."

Food, Service, Décor, and Location—these pillars of the restaurant business all have to be top-notch to achieve Cheesecake Factory results. "I'm continuing to take pride in building an excellent company, bringing people up to run it, and sharing the great success of The Cheesecake Factory with all those who have worked very hard to help build it," David says with quiet conviction.

Chapter 12

Re-Creating
the Magic

All the adversity I've had in my life, all my troubles and obstacles,
have strengthened me . . . . You may not realize it when it happens,
but a kick in the teeth may be the best thing in the world for you.
Walt Disney

Our professional passion for The Walt Disney Company began in the early 1980s, when many of our consulting clients were asking us to benchmark "best practices." Disney would consistently emerge as one of the "best of the best," not only in their legendary customer service but also in the areas of training, maintenance, and even production. (Disney owns and operates one of the largest laundry facilities in the world, the largest in the United States. It's a production facility that processes thousands of costumes and linens every day.) Since the early 1990s, we began working with clients to create their own Dream, Believe, Dare, Do cultures.

During the past quarter century, we have witnessed a number of monumental events in The Walt Disney Company: the blocking of two hostile takeovers; an increase in the number of theme parks, from 4 to 11; a catastrophic helicopter crash; emergency bypass surgery; the re-birth, and then death of the classic 2D cell animation of the 1930s; the birth of the 3D computer animation; the acquisition of a major television network; fights in boardrooms and courtrooms; the company's corporate image as both "prince" and "villain" of Wall Street. This list sounds like the making of a new ABC prime-time soap opera, "Desperate CEOs."

From Zero to Hero to Zero

After Walt's sudden death in 1966, his brother Roy postponed retirement to complete Walt's last dream: the building of Disney World. Roy later insisted that the name be changed from Disney World to Walt Disney World, in honor of his brother. On October 1, 1971, Walt Disney World opened its first theme park, the Magic Kingdom. On December 20, 1971, Roy died, almost five years to the day after his brother passed on.

After Roy's death, the financial and creative growth of the company came to a standstill. During the 18 years between Walt Disney's death in 1966 and Eisner's entry as CEO in 1984, a simple question would be asked among the ranks before any decision was made: "What would Walt do?" To be sure, this approach rendered the leaders indecisive, especially when Disney executives had no idea what Walt would do. Asking this question ad nauseam paralyzed the company. (See Figure 12-1.)

Then in 1984, Roy E. Disney, Walt's nephew, convinced the board to hire Michael Eisner as CEO and Frank Wells as president and COO. Eisner and Wells were consummate decision makers. They quickly began to transform the sleepy little movie studio into a global entertainment enterprise now worth over $50 billion. (See Figure 12-2.) They had the Midas touch, turning everything in the company to gold, from television to baseball to book

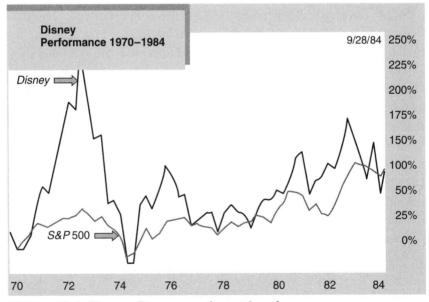

Figure 12-1. The pre-Eisner years financial performance

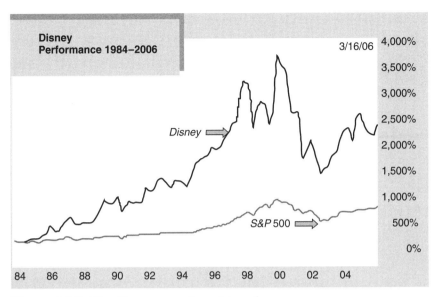

Figure 12-2. The Eisner years financial performance.

publishing to retailing—and, to the delight of the Big Apple, Broadway shows. Here are the results of the Eisner years:

- Revenues from $2.5 billion to $30.8 billion—up 2,000 percent
- Income from $294 million to $4.49 billion—up 1,600 percent
- Cash flow from $100 million to $2.9 billion—up 2,900 percent
- Market value from $1.9 billion to $57.4 billion—up 3,000 percent
- Stock price from $1.33 to $28.40—up 2,100 percent

When compared with the other five media giants that now control the entertainment industry, Disney's success attributed to Michael Eisner is even more heroic. Between 1984 and 2005, the combined reported losses of the five competitor companies exceeded $171 billion: Time Warner—$99.7 billion; Vivendi-Universal—$40.6 billion; Viacom—$21.2 billion; News Corporation—$7.2 billion; and Sony—$2.7 billion. Disney did not have a single losing year during this time period. Most CEOs would give their eye teeth for these results during more than a 21-year reign.

So, why wasn't Michael hailed as a hero like Jack Welch in his retirement, instead of being relegated to the pile of discards as was Richard Nixon? Was it

Wall Street's obsession with short-term results? In 2000, the Disney stock price was up a whopping 3,500 percent from the 1984 price, not the mere 2,100 percent as it was upon Michael's retirement in 2005. His critics fail to realize that in March 2000, the U.S. economy had slumped, causing a mild recession that was shortly followed by the horrific acts of September 11, 2001.

Was Eisner a victim or a villain? Did Roy Disney demand his resignation because of poor investment returns or was it because Michael was like the "wicked Queen," feeding Roy's family namesake company the poison apple?

It's sad to think that this creative, childlike executive of the early 1980s could possibly turn out to be the biggest villain in Disney history. Could the same person who showered the world with unforgettable tales of tribulation and grandeur told through captivating animation and music—*The Little Mermaid* (1989); *Beauty and the Beast* (1991); *Aladdin* (1992); and *The Lion King* (1994)—have also given us such mediocre and, for the most part, forgettable stories as *The Emperor's New Groove* (2000); *Atlantis: The Lost Empire* (2001); *Lilo and Stitch* (2002) (which some might consider a moderate success); and *Treasure Planet* (2002)? Could the same man who once welcomed new ideas, not only from his staff but from anyone at any level in the organization, have hired a visionless array of MBA yes-men to fill creative posts that launched these disappointments of the big screen; have dismantled what was arguably the most accomplished team of storytellers and artists ever assembled; and, in addition, have severed ties with Pixar, the only Walt-like creative enterprise that the company could turn to after totally destroying its in-house animation capability?

Our goal here is not simply to recount the events of the past that led to Michael Eisner's transformation from "hero to zero," but rather to share our insights regarding his actions as well as the reasons for his demise. (For a provocative, detailed chronology of the "fight of the century," CEO Eisner versus Walt Disney's nephew, Roy, read James Stewart's *Disney War.*)

The Eisner "Paranoia"

Merriam-Webster defines *paranoia* as "systematized delusions of persecutions or grandeur; a tendency toward irrational suspiciousness and distrustfulness of others." This definition seems to fit the Michael Eisner persona from the late 1990s until his grand exodus in 2005. After Frank Well's tragic death in a helicopter crash in 1994, Eisner's inability to trust anyone became transparent in his reluctance to name a replacement for Frank. The whole

Jeffery Katzenberg saga is a prime example. Jeffery had been Eisner's protégé at Paramount and followed Eisner to Disney to head up the film entertainment division. Katzenberg wanted to be the company savior and replace the beloved Wells. One might reasonably chastise Jeffery for his inappropriate timing and total lack of respect for the late president. It is reported that he barged into Eisner's office on the very day of Wells' funeral and demanded to be named as his successor. Eisner claimed that Jeffery was not the right fit for the job, despite his apparent savvy in running a major portion of the business and launching one of Disney's biggest hits of all time, *The Lion King*. The outraged Jeffery promptly exited the Disney organization, hauling it into court and forcing it to fork out hundreds of millions in unpaid bonuses due him from *The Lion King*. (By the way, Katzenberg appears to be doing just fine running DreamWorks SKG.)

We believe the seeds of Eisner's paranoia were really planted at Paramount. (Who knows when it really began? Maybe he felt rejected being sent off to camp every summer.) In 1976, Michael became president of Paramount and aspired to be named CEO when his friend and mentor Barry Diller left the position to run Twentieth Century Fox. However, Paramount's parent company, Gulf & Western, had other plans for Eisner. They said he would never be CEO of Paramount because he is too "child-like." In 1984, Michael was terminated and went to the company that could best utilize the talents of a "child-like" executive: Disney.

But Michael's paranoia continued at Disney. The seeds were fertilized during his initial negotiations with the company. The Bass family, one of Disney's largest investors, wanted Frank Wells to be CEO and Eisner to be president. Eisner argued that the top spot should be a creative type like himself, not the typical numbers type like Wells. Much to Michael's surprise, Frank agreed, and the two of them convinced the board of directors as well as the Bass family that this decision would be best for Disney. But there was one important detail that is overlooked by many. The board insisted that, as president, Frank report directly to the board rather than to Eisner. In many respects, Frank and Michael were true partners much like Walt and Roy were in their years together. Even though Michael's public persona was that of "top dog," in his heart he knew he was really sharing control of Disney with Frank.

Not only was Eisner envious of Wells's coleadership position, but one could make the point that Michael was also envious of Frank's business and financial acumen. Frank was a former entertainment lawyer and a Rhodes

Scholar. Now, a healthy and secure person seeking to understand the financial workings of the organization may have asked his CFO for a crash course in reading the financial reports. But Eisner didn't want to reveal any of his inherent weaknesses, and even made an attempt to enroll his wife in a local college's hotel financial management course. When she refused, Michael ended up taking the class under an assumed name. Creative, yes; secure, no.

The Eisner family heritage is that of American royalty. Michael's parents were the upper crust of society living in a sprawling apartment on New York's famed Park Avenue. Both of Michael's grandfathers had been successful self-made businessmen. On special occasions, young Michael was chauffeured to Broadway shows. Yet, prior to becoming Disney's CEO, Michael confessed that he had never seen a Disney movie or visited any of the Disney theme parks. This could have been both an asset and a liability. On one hand, it afforded him an opportunity to be both critical evaluator and undaunted creator, aided by his reputed childlike eyes. On the other hand, his lack of familiarity with all things Disney might have exposed the brand to attack. Frank apparently would often squelch Michael's ideas, reminding him that they would not fly at Disney.

To make matters worse for the psyche of Michael Eisner, Frank was known as "the popular guy," the one to whom everyone turned upon fearing the wrath of Eisner. It seemed that only Wells was able to handle Michael's frequent tantrums and excessive ego. The unflappable and loyal Frank applauded Eisner's creative genius and graciously positioned him as the sole savior of this one-time modest studio. Frank was content to remain in the background and let Michael take center stage.

But, some may say Wells was the ultimate enabler. Creating this larger-than-life character in the person of Michael Eisner fooled everyone for a time, perhaps even Michael himself. Wells may indeed have facilitated Michael's delusions of grandeur, believing he was a deified Jack Welch–like figure. In reality, Eisner, like his grandfathers before him, was a born entrepreneur: creative, impulsive, and a hands-on decision-maker. While these are desirable skills in start-up and turn-around situations, they could reap havoc in a massive, multifaceted, world-wide corporation.

One can only imagine what The Walt Disney Company would be like today if Frank Wells had lived and remained a key player. Katzenberg may not have left, which would have prevented millions from being drained out of the company coffers. DreamWorks would never have come into being, securing Disney's monopoly in the animated feature film arena. Michael

Ovitz would never have been hired, which would have eliminated another costly and embarrassing fiasco. The animation department would still be intact, and the string of mediocre films would have been replaced with modern classics in the tradition of *Beauty and the Beast* and *The Lion King*. And finally, Disney would have purchased Pixar during its start-up days for millions rather than the billions Disney ended up paying.

Like Walt and Roy, Michael Eisner and Frank Wells tended to the creative and business operations, respectively. Together, they produced a rare formula, allowing for the coexistence of a childlike entrepreneurial environment and a business-driven multinational corporation. As evidenced by Michael's last 10 years at the helm of Disney, hard as he may have tried, he was unable to maintain this balance. It is interesting that Michael changed his stripes and gave way to his latent hard-core business drive. He became the tight-fisted bean counter, sacrificed quality, abolished creativity, and released unimaginative sequels such as *The Lion King 1½*. However, there were several flashes of creativity that emerged during Michael's last 10 years: the creation of the Disney stage show along with the renovation of Broadway, the Animal Kingdom theme park, and the *Pirates of the Caribbean* film.

It's refreshing, however, that in an era of the Enron and Arthur Andersen scandals where corporations have failed because of criminal mismanagement and fraud, the boardroom battle at Disney was about the culture and maintaining the legacy of its founder Walt Disney. In the end, Michael Eisner realized that only one man in the history of the "most magical place on earth" could capture the hearts and minds of people everywhere, and that man was Walt Disney.

Bring Back the Magic

Each year, we spend a good deal of time at Walt Disney World and Disneyland in a variety of activities from keynoting conferences to sharing the "magic" with clients, family, and friends. During the last years of Michael Eisner's tenure at Disney, we had detected a slight decline in the level of service at the theme parks. Although this change may not have been discernible to the casual observer or occasional tourist, it is certainly apparent to those of us who have considered Disney as the pinnacle of service standards for years. When we questioned cast members about the boardroom battles between Michael and Roy, many reported to us that it was "an embarrassment" to the company but had little effect on their day-to-day roles and responsibilities. Our first trip to Walt Disney World after Eisner's resignation was in January 2006. Bob Iger had been at the helm of the company for just over three months. Surprisingly, in this short period of time, we observed an increase in the level of service: it was as if someone had recovered the "pixie dust." When we inquired about Iger's impact on the organization, cast members responded enthusiastically, stating how he had publicly thanked them for their hard work, something they seldom if ever heard from Eisner. In our attempt to validate cast member perceptions, we were unable to elicit a response from one of Disney's key executives. Understandably, he was protecting the Disney brand and attempting to close the book on the Eisner years. However, the Disney corporate office is amazed at the candor we unleash from cast members at the parks, many of whom have shared their thoughts and dreams with us for nearly a decade. It may sound corny, but loving what you do and loving the company you work for might mean the difference between providing good service and great service. Even though there were no immediate operational changes after Iger arrived at Disney, cast members seemed to regain the pride in their company and truly responded to one of the "suits" taking time out of his whirlwind schedule to compliment them on a job well done.

Can Iger bring back the magic? It's too soon to respond accurately to such a question, but clearly he is saying all the right things out of the gate. In a recent interview with the *Wall Street Journal*, Iger cited "Five Tips for Managing Creativity":

1. Don't take a hierarchical approach.
2. Don't create an approval process that's unduly rigorous.
3. Be careful not to water ideas down or lose people's passion.
4. Let those directly in charge make decisions.
5. Put the spotlight on the company, not the individual.

Having been on the job for less than four months, Bob Iger surprised the business community by purchasing Pixar for $7.4 billion. Iger explained that the revelation to purchase Pixar came to him while watching a parade at the opening of Hong Kong Disneyland:

Disney, home of Mickey Mouse, Snow White, and Cinderella, hadn't created any recognizable animated characters in the past decade. It really hit me hard that we had had 10 years of real failure. Keeping animation strong is incredibly vital. Animation creates more of a ripple effect. Characters from Pixar's *Toy Story* create opportunities for merchandising and theme-park rides, such as the Buzz Lightyear Astro Blasters ride at the Hong Kong park.

Iger also announced that John Lasseter, founder and creative genius at Pixar, will become the creative head at Disney. Lasseter is charged with reviving the Disney animation department, whose staff was cut by almost two thirds during the Eisner cost-cutting rampage, when the animation staff plummeted from 2,200 down to 800. Disney studio chairman, Dick Cook, who worked closely with Pixar during their 15-year partnership, commented, "I was talking to a group of animators when the announcement came out, and they let out a big yell. The reaction has been genuinely huge. John is that rarest of talents. Everything he touches becomes better. He is selfless in his desire to make things great."

Will Bob Iger and John Lasseter become the Roy and Walt of this era, a perfect blend of business pragmatist and creative genius? We can only hope. It remains a mystery if Apple CEO Steve Jobs (who became Disney's biggest stockholder after the Pixar purchase) will be content to be a Disney board member—where he can continue to provide visionary thinking with introductions like iTunes and the sale of short films, music videos, episodes of smash hits like ABC's "Desperate Housewives," and "Lost" for downloading onto video iPods and other mobile devices. Or, will he want more control in the day-to-day running of the company?

There are many unanswered questions, but Bob Iger is already making his mark on Disney. There are lessons to be learned from the Disney brothers, ones we hope Bob will take to heart. First, as Walt believed: never compromise quality. Today, the Disney mission statement reads: "*We create happiness by providing the finest in entertainment for people of all ages, everywhere.*" That means producing the "best of the best" stories, music, theme parks, animated feature films, television programming, and so on. Finest means superior in quality, not acceptable or as good as the competition. Our final hope is that Bob Iger also gives credence to Roy's words, "When values are clear, decisions are easy."

Perhaps Bob realizes he has more than the keys to the kingdom. He is the quintessential protector of an American icon. Disney is as much a part of the American landscape as Mount Rushmore. May he never forget the true meaning of the dedication of Disneyland spoken over 50 years ago:

> To all who come to this happy place: Welcome. Disneyland is your land. Here age relives fond memories of the past . . . and here youth may savor the challenge and promise of the future. Disneyland is dedicated to the ideals, the dreams and the hard facts that have created America . . . with the hope that it will be a source of joy and inspiration to all the world.

—WALT DISNEY, JULY 17, 1955

The culture that Walt Disney created over three quarters of a century ago has withstood the test of time and history. Now, Bob Iger has a formidable challenge and responsibility for upholding the Dream, Believe, Dare, Do principles that were part and parcel of Walt Disney's success credo. All eyes are upon him.

Chapter 13

Dream, Believe, Dare, Do

We keep moving forward, opening new doors, and doing new things, because we're curious and curiosity keeps leading us down new paths.
                                                                    Walt Disney

By now you know that Walt Disney made a practice of envisioning the untried and impossible; that he understood that success comes from the entire team and is enhanced by solid partnerships; that he refused to follow the paths of others; and that he was a master at creating detailed plans that not only ensured results but inspired the entire team to act: Dream, Believe, Dare, Do. The result: "the happiest place on earth" where guests return year after year to relive the magic that Disney created.

Thankfully, Walt's legendary success credo is inspiring companies from New York to California, in industries light years away from the majesty of Disneyland and Walt Disney World. It is here behind the scenes of our seven featured organizations that "show business" emerges as a way of life and is not exclusively reserved for the most powerful entertainment organization in the entire world. Like Walt Disney before them, *The Cheesecake Factory, Downtown School, Ernst & Young, Four Seasons Hotels & Resorts, Griffin Hospital, John Robert's Spa*, and *Men's Wearhouse* have raised the bar from simply meeting customer needs to a demonstrated passion for fulfilling the dreams of those they serve as true guests.

As if in a dream, when we watched the curtains go up on these seven organizations, we nearly forgot that there was another world out there where old economy theories of management are still very much alive and thriving. Yet, in our travels, we are continually reminded that the level of excellence attained by these seven is only within reach of those who are brave enough to relinquish power and become servants to their employees, their teams, and their customers. Most of all, these iconic leaders are smart enough to exercise their "magic" each and every day by empowering others, from the boardroom to the front line, to live their dreams; create new avenues to the future guided by their values; dare to make a difference; and, most of all, never to be satisfied with the status quo. Remember the inspiring words of Walt Disney: "All our dreams can come true, if we have the courage to pursue them."

The Cheesecake Factory
Dream

David Overton must have had an inner voice that said to him, "If you build it, they will come." In 1974, he left the music scene of San Francisco to fulfill the dream of building a showcase for what his mother had created: the "ice cream of cheesecakes." All he knew about cheesecake, per se, was that his mother, Evelyn, made the best cheesecake west of New York (and now one could argue, *anywhere*) and that everyone seemed to love it. He remembered folding pink bakery boxes with his sister Renee to earn their allowances of a penny a box. (Fact: The boxes are still hand-folded!) David also remembered being in elementary school and bringing only one cheesecake to a bake sale, where his principal was literally standing on the steps waiting to buy it.[81] And to this day, people are still waiting with pager in hand for more than just a slice of the over 35 flavors of cheesecake. Yet, guests never really have to wait for The Cheesecake Factory experience to begin: as soon as they walk through the grand entrance into the glistening palace-like banquet room and absorb the magic of the rich Egyptian columns, hand-painted murals, and gently swaying palm trees, they have entered a fairytale world and left the real world behind.

David didn't let the fact that he had no restaurant experience stop him from starting a little restaurant in Beverly Hills in 1978. He was a businessman with a keen sense of what people liked, and they certainly liked cheesecake. But, what else could he offer them besides cheesecake? For David, this was more like figuring out what to fix for guests for dinner on Saturday night than it was for opening up a restaurant. As Linda Candioty, retired vice-president recalled, "David was sitting on a very old saggy couch in a teeny office surrounded by cookbooks, mountains of magazines, and things he had torn out. He had stacks of things everywhere. He dreamed of making things better.He didn't want to bring out something that wasn't unique and innovative."[82] If you've ever tried the Thai Lettuce Wraps on the menu, you'll know what she means.

Before the little restaurant opened in the world-famous city synonymous with wealth and celebrity, an ounce of fear entered David's mind. He had never set his sights on opening with the fanfare of the Disneyland band or having the who's who of Hollywood enter on the red carpet as if approaching Mann's Chinese Theatre. In fact, he really didn't want to be open at lunchtime at all. "I put a small sign in the window, 'Open at 2 p.m.,'" David told us. "At 1:30 p.m., a line had already formed in front of the restaurant, and by 2 p.m., the line reached well beyond our property to the next store. I told Linda to go out and entertain these people. She was a wonderful cheerleader." And, for the "money's no object" Beverly Hills clientele, you'd better be prepared to "razzle-dazzle 'em. David once said, "New Yorkers can be very straightforward in their demands, but Beverly Hills is a tougher group to really please. In a sense, we were trained by the best customers in the country."

David seemed perfectly content to let Linda take center stage. His role as consummate producer and director of a one-of-a-kind culinary institution was and still is reward enough. And, fortunately, both of his parents lived to see his extraordinary success.

Believe

Every generation seems to blame the one before it for something, and in families everywhere, this certainly rings true. It's an uncommon and refreshing exception when adult children publicly credit both of their parents for helping formulate their fundamental beliefs and values. David Overton is such a person. "My father was total perseverance," said David. "He could go and call on a restaurant account six or seven times and never take no for an answer. With my mother, I think I got just the straightforward quality, the sort of desire, the commitment."

David started the little 78-seat restaurant with all the right ingredients, and they were not found in the kitchen. Rather, it was the Overtons' leadership, strong work ethic, and desire to do something nice for others that generated the long-standing recipe for success at The Cheesecake Factory. To this day, David is still inspired by the memories of his mother in action. At one point in time, much to David's dismay, Evelyn made a decision to close down her fully functioning bakery and move to another location, which was not immediately ideal for producing huge orders. As David recalled, "When we opened the new bakery, nothing was going right. The machinery wasn't working, but my mother was determined and stayed up for something like 36 hours, just to get an order out. If she hadn't done that, we might have lost the account. She had employees who followed her lead and worked nonstop until the baking was done. We didn't lose the account because of my mother's sheer will. So, I guess I got a lot of that from her." We don't guess, we know.

Dare

What kind of person decides to try out a new restaurant idea without any restaurant experience (David Overton never even worked in one.) under the microscope of Hollywood and doesn't get egg on his face? One who sees risk as "innovation," David told us. "Sure, there was this 5 o'clock moment when we were doing the Beverly Hills deal. I knew that if I did nothing, it would not have gone forward. And I asked myself if I really wanted to do this. Of course, I pushed forward. At that moment, I could understand how some people would feel overcome by failure." But David's excitement and desire to build a distinctive corporate culture laid the groundwork for The Cheesecake Factory's incredible record—from individual stores' generating in excess of $3 million annually to the company's surpassing the $1 billion revenue mark in 2005.

With a solid foundation and a proven model that baffled the restaurant industry, David was ready to expand his horizons. In the mid-1980s, the Marina del Ray and Redondo Beach locations took David in a new direction with the opening of his first full-service bars. David and Linda worked for hours trying out new drink ideas and giving them names such as Typhoon Punch and Flying Gorilla.

Then one day, a friend of David's enticed him to open in Washington, D.C., and bring the "quesadillos and guacamole"—two words that, back then, required explanation for those in and around "the D.C. beltway." David was ready, but he knew this would be a real test. Things would be different in D.C. with a 13,000 square foot, bi-level, glass-enclosed design and a clientele with a reputation for receiving preferential treatment. On opening day in January 1991, a major snowstorm hit the northeastern United States. D.C. was almost totally shut down. Some people called to find out if the restaurant would be open in such inclement weather; others called to find out if The Cheesecake Factory was just a bakery. "I had 33 servers and we needed about 90. I couldn't find any more people who were willing to quit their jobs over the holiday to come and work for this unknown company. Once we opened and people saw how popular we were, we said 'Whew!' and were able to hire more servers. I still think those 33 servers are the best servers I've ever seen in our company," said Peter D'Amelio, now president of restaurant operations.[83]

By day three, the word was out. East Coast residents are very "cheesecake savvy," but now a new West Coast cheesecake had arrived and was out to de-throne New York's favorite. By the end of the night, there were only a few pieces left, and the closest supply of this fabulous new cheesecake was 3,000 miles away. As Max Byfuglin, president of The Cheesecake Factory Bakery told us, "We got the call that said, 'We are out of almost everything. We don't even have any more of the Original (Evelyn's original cheesecake recipe).'" Normally, a truck would deliver the cheesecakes directly from the bakery in California to the display cases in D.C., but faster delivery was needed. "We figured out that we could get eight cakes packed in specially designed boxes with Styrofoam into one Federal Express box with dry ice. That day we sent over 100 boxes via Federal Express to D.C. The cost was about $150 a box to ship them, but we could not *not* have cheesecakes!" Max exclaimed.

The craving for cheesecake was contagious in D.C. and has continuously brought waves of locals and tourists to the growing list of Cheesecake Factory locations from coast to coast. And with the success of the D.C. location, the company went public in 1992: an unbelievable feat for a restaurant chain with no more than a handful of locations.

Despite its unparalleled success, many food critics have expressed their displeasure with the whole "Cheesecake" phenomenon. They have little regard for David's innovative bent for producing untried and eclectic cuisine. But then again, he was never one to buckle under pressure or criticism. When CNN and *USA Today* provided a forum for critics who announced the fat and calorie content of certain Cheesecake Factory items, retired vice president, Linda Candioty, called and told them, "We want our customers to get every calorie they are paying for." After that, according to Max Byfuglin, "Sales went up."

The fact that the menu has evolved from a simple two-sided piece into a 200-menu-item book may be attributed to David's great passion for the exploration of food and finding new things that people just can't seem to get enough of. Fortunately, at Cheesecake Factory, they can't really complain about the portions, which are large enough to share or save for another day or two. According to David, the concept promotes "sharing and tasting different things." And with such a vast array of menu choices, customers could order something different every day for well over half a year! No one else in the industry can claim this level of fare, or stand as an anchor with the likes of Nordstrom's and Macy's in upscale suburban malls of America.

Do

Over the years, David Overton discovered that his likes closely match those of his customers. He never worries that people won't like the food. Anyone who can't find something they like on The Cheesecake Factory menu must be from another planet. Remaining true to its motto, the restaurant offers "something for everyone." Nevertheless, every Cheesecake Factory item must pass the Overton test. Others may have a hand in creating and tasting, but in the end the final approval for menu items is up to its founder and chief perfectionist. As Peter D'Amelio said, "We deal with the two most volatile things in the world, people and food, and they both need constant attention." They get this and more at The Cheesecake Factory.

Yet even if you have the "perfect palate" of David Overton, the restaurant business is still a manufacturing plant. The challenge is to reproduce menu items on the spot each and every time, by hand, not by machine. And David believes that every repeat guest knows what his or her favorite item should taste like. David explains to his employees, "If they tell you it's not the same as the last time, don't tell them you think it is the same. They know better than you." David is the number one role model in the organization for listening to the customers and doing whatever it takes to please them.

It's a toss-up who are more finicky—the diners or their servers. David had a keen sense of the market early on, and was determined to recruit the best people in the industry and hold on to them. Nowadays, The Cheesecake Factory has such prestige that people flock to the doors to get an interview. The company's comprehensive training programs for managers are enticing to job candidates. Managers, general managers, and executive kitchen managers can earn over $100,000 a year, double the industry average, and work for a company that adds icing to the compensation cake almost every year. For example, the CakeStake program rewards salaried employees with stock options amounting to between 8 and 12 percent of their base pay—if the company achieves 95 percent of its profitability goal. This is all part of "cheesecaking" per David Overton. In his most serious tone, David told us, "It's not easy to take a $12 million complex business and hand it over to a 27-year-old. (Some will go on to manage a business that generates about $942 per square foot, more than four times the typical casual-dining field performance.) We need to have a program that is rock solid." But sweetened compensation packages and training programs are not the only reasons people want to work for The Cheesecake Factory. It's the long-standing corporate culture that David and his parents have instilled; it's pride in the company's unique focus on quality and service; and it's the opportunity to be part of a legendary organization that is the envy of industry giants.

David tirelessly works to perfect his culture—his people, his operations, his food—while at the same time he continues to scale new horizons so more throngs of diners can experience the wonder of it all. In his own words, "The minute we ever forget why the guest is standing out there in line, we're in trouble." And the great Walt Disney never forgot this either.

Downtown School
Dream

"Imagine a place where children can curl up in a rocker or stretch out on the floor to read and discover the world . . . a place were children learn in a nurturing and challenging environment . . . a place where each child's uniqueness enriches the learning community . . . a place where talents and abilities are developed and individual personalities shine . . . where children work together and learn from each other . . . where children use the whole downtown as their classroom . . . a school where parents work around the corner and stop in for lunch to share in the day's activities. This is the Downtown School." Here is the original Downtown School "dream" as cited in the *Community Report* of the Des Moines Business/Education [B/E] Alliance. On August 23, 1993, that "dream" became real when a new type of neighborhood school opened its doors: a school located close to where parents work rather than where they live.

The dream at Downtown School is more than just well-crafted words on paper. It's the way the teachers, the parents, and the students live each and every day. For over a decade, retired principal and B/E Alliance executive director, Jan Drees, has been the torchbearer who assembled an entire network of people who have come to believe that Downtown School's approach is clearly the best way of educating children. As retired board member, Mary Lou Daley, said, "It begins at the top. Jan is fabulous. She gets it. Her enthusiasm, her eagerness, and her knowledge of this kind of curriculum spreads to her teachers."[85]

The realization of this dream did not happen overnight. It took three years of research and long hours of hard work to create Downtown School's child-centered educational model. But the research continues. Renee Harmon, Downtown School assistant principal, said, "Our education model is very eclectic. It takes whatever research has proven to be best for children and we implement that. We are constantly looking at what we are doing, looking at what research is discovering, and changing what we do to fit that."[86]

Believe

The Downtown School Mission reads

> The Downtown School, in collaboration with parents and the business community, will provide a research-based learning environment that ensures each child's success.
>
> Our common goal is to enable children to mature into responsible and respectful citizens capable of independent problem solving, teamwork, and leadership. We are committed to a world-class educational opportunity for the benefit of all students of the Downtown School, their parents, and the community.

When asked to evaluate the culture of an organization, we seek to determine if the behaviors are consistent with the mission. Let's test the critical elements of the Downtown School's mission.

"Collaboration with parents and the business community." In Chapter 6, we described the creation of the Downtown School and the critical roles of both the Des Moines Business Alliance and the Des Moines School District. Collaboration with parents has been nothing short of miraculous. Because of the proximity to the workplace, flexible time, and the dedication of both teachers and parents, parent-teacher conference participation is over 99 percent. Downtown School also boasts an extremely active Parent Teacher Association (PTA). Meetings are often held during the lunch hour in a downtown business conference room. We had the good fortune to attend a PTA meeting during our research for this book. The conference room was about 85 percent full, although the president apologized for the low turnout, stating that typically the room is filled to capacity. We also observed some parents entering the school to have lunch with their children, and others who were on site to watch their children give presentations. During the first two

years of operation, the Downtown School logged 3,492 parent visits. This figure does not include visits before or after school. Parent visits continue at an average of three visits per family per month or about 10,000 a year.

"To enable children to mature into responsible and respectful citizens capable of independent problem solving, teamwork, and leadership." To test this aspect of the mission, all one has to do is walk into any Downtown School classroom. Mary Lou Daley explains, "It is very difficult to find the teacher, but she's there. She is so intertwined, perhaps on the floor or bending over a table. There is no teacher's desk. What is happening is that the children are always working on projects in groups together, and there's a wonderful hum in the room. No matter what age group you see, they are all very productive. It is not pin-drop quiet because this is the time the teacher is reading and everyone must not talk. I used to tell my class (Mary Lou spent 14 years as a traditional classroom teacher.) 'You can only interrupt Mrs. Daley during reading group, if the building is on fire, or if you are going to throw up.'" The "hum" of the learning and cooperative environment at the Downtown School compared to the "pin-drop" quiet traditional classroom that Mary Lou described reminded us of what Art Linkletter once said on "Larry King Live." Years ago, Art created and hosted the television show "Kids Say the Darndest Things," on which he would interview young children. When Larry asked Art how he dreamed up the idea for the show, Art said the seed had been planted many years before when his son started school. Art had asked his son how he liked his first day of first grade. The rest of the conversation reportedly went as follows: His son said, "I'm not going back!" Art asked him, "Why not?" His son replied, "Teacher asked me to read, and I can't read. Teacher asked me to write, and I can't write. I can talk, but every time I talked to the boy next to me, teacher told me to be quiet."

Are there any problem solvers at the Downtown School? We met a five-year-old student named Nathan, who was just beginning his second year. In response to our question about the meaning of "logical thinking," Nathan replied, "Logical thinking is like, for instance, if I used a little thin string on this chair to try to lift it up and a pulley, logical thinking is like this string won't work. It'll break under the weight of this chair." These were his exact words! Sure, Nathan is a bright little boy, but he is not the exception at the Downtown School. Every five-year-old is making presentations, solving problems, and can both apply and articulate the meaning of logical thinking.

"Committed to a world-class educational opportunity for the benefit of all students of the Downtown School, their parents, and the community." Does the

Downtown School provide a world-class educational experience? Apparently a lot of people think so. Nearly 900 students are on the waiting list for admission to the Downtown School. During the first two years of its operation, 2,038 educators, school board members, and business people visited the school. The visitor log includes representatives from 22 states and 10 countries. "Only through innovators like you will the rest of us begin to change," commented one visiting elementary school principal. An educator from Kyrgyzstan remarked, "Even without the ability to communicate verbally, because we do not share a common language, we did understand the philosophy and design of the school by actually seeing the classes and children." Sounds pretty world-class to us.

Dare

For most principals, swimming against the vast current of traditional education in American would result in being swallowed up by the undertow. Jan Drees simply changed the tide, a monumental act of courage for which the parents of her students should be eternally grateful. The educational system in the United States has been failing our children for the past quarter century or more. But it's like the elephant in the room—everybody talks about it, but nobody does anything about it. Jan and the Des Moines Business Alliance decided it was high time to remove the elephant. As a team, they decided to "blow up" the traditional model of education and start from scratch at the Downtown School.

Was this a risk? Nearly every principal in America would answer "Yes" to that question. But, if our schools are in such bad shape, shouldn't everyone rally around such a project? On January 13, 2006, ABC news correspondent John Stossel hosted a "20/20" television special entitled, "Stupid in America: How We Cheat Our Kids." As John remarked, "If you're like most American parents, you might think, 'These things don't happen at my kid's school.' A recent Gallup Poll survey showed that 76 percent of Americans were completely or somewhat satisfied with their kids' public school."

Not only were Jan and the Des Moines Business Alliance bucking the conventional wisdom of the majority of U.S. parents, but they also were up against a huge and powerful tidal wave in the form of the teacher's union and school district administrators. In most school districts, the K-12 public educational system is a monopoly; parents have no choice as to the school their children may attend. Add to this problem the contractual headaches induced by the omniscient teacher's union, and you have the perfect formula for non-innovative teaching. In Stossel's "20/20" report, Joel Klein, Chancellor of the New York City public school system reported, "It's just about impossible to fire a bad teacher. The new union contract offers some relief, but it's still about 200 pages of bureaucracy. We tolerate mediocrity because people get paid the same, whether they're outstanding, average, or way below average." Stossel proceeded, "Klein said he employs dozens of teachers who he's afraid to let near the kids, so he has them sit in what are called 'rubber rooms.' This year, he will spend $20 million dollars to 'warehouse' teachers in five 'rubber rooms.' It's an alternative to firing them. In the last four years, only two teachers out of 80,000 were fired for incompetence."

It has been over 10 years since the creation of the Downtown School, and by all accounts, it has been an overwhelming success. Just imagine what would have happened if the Downtown School philosophy had failed. All of the naysayers would have rallied together to dish out the blame, and the name "Jan Drees" would have topped off the list. Was this the same type of career "dare" Walt took when he decided to make *Snow White*? The naysayers in Walt's day said that no one would sit through a 90-minute cartoon. Boy, were they wrong!

We believe that the courage exhibited by Jan Drees in challenging the traditional education system was the same kind of courage that Walt exhibited over half a century ago. It took more than 60 years for other film companies to begin producing animated feature films. Hopefully, it won't be another 60 years before the rest of our nation's school districts dare to follow the Downtown School's example of "blowing up" the old system and creating a world-class educational opportunity for all students. They need only to remember: "If you do what you have always done, you will get what you always have gotten: stupid in America."

Do

As we have previously noted, the three-year research and planning process to identify the best-of-the-best educational processes was vital to the overall success of the Downtown School. To us, the most impressive aspect of the Downtown School was the project approach to discovery learning, one that has made this school the envy of all those who feel constricted by their own antiquated systems. Jan explains, "All students are expected to successfully complete research projects which include selecting a topic, gathering information from books, site visits, and interviews. Each student is expected to plan, organize, and present his or her information to peers and parents."[87] Five-year-old Nathan told us about one of his class's projects: "We went to visit a bank and got a bank loan. Our class got the loan. We made up this little jewelry shop in the mall and sold jewelry." When we asked him what they did with the money, he responded, "We paid part of it back to the bank and still had some extra. We bought books for the new classrooms."

We asked teacher, Renee Harmon, "What do you do with a child that has little, if any, interest in the selected project?" She answered by sharing this riveting story with us: "One of the projects selected was trucks and transportation. One student had absolutely no interest in this project. He was very bright and extremely creative but wasn't real thrilled about the whole topic and didn't see what he could learn from it. Since this student was just starting to get interested in the Internet, he was encouraged to do some online research on truck designs. He was also very interested in the environment, so he researched the gas mileage for different types of trucks. He also conducted a sample to determine the most popular color of truck in downtown Des Moines. He discussed and presented his findings to his fellow classmates." The benefit of this project approach can be summed up by world-renowned educator, William Glasser: "We learn 10 percent of what we read, 20 percent of what we hear, 30 percent of what we see, 50 percent of what we see and hear, 70 percent of what we discuss, 80 percent of what we experience, and 95 percent of what we teach others."

You may be asking, "Why include an elementary school in a business book?" There are several reasons why we chose Downtown School as one of our seven featured organizations. First, Jan Drees and her team provide a prime example of innovation and leadership exhibited by the creation of an environment where students are self-motivated, and where mutual respect and trust abound.

Furthermore, Downtown School is really much more than just a school. Jan and her team are builders of a workforce that will one day be instrumental in upholding our nation's claim as a leader in the global economy. Recently, ABC's "20/20" reported, "At age 10, American students take an international test and score well above the international average. But by age 15, when students from 40 countries are tested, the Americans place 25th. The longer kids stay in American schools, the worse they do in international competition. They do worse than kids from poorer countries that spend much less money on education, ranking behind not only Belgium but also Poland, the Czech , and South Korea." The business community at large can no longer sit back and allow our schools to fail. Business leaders must learn from the Des Moines B/E Alliance and do something about our educational crisis in America.

Unfortunately, not only has the Des Moines School District failed to insist upon spreading the Downtown School philosophy throughout its domain, it may completely destroy this unique learning environment. As this revised edition of *The Disney Way* goes to print, Jan Drees is retiring from her role as principal of Downtown School.

Jack Welch, retired CEO of General Electric, once stated that one of the hallmarks of a good leader is training a replacement who would be ready to take over at a moment's notice. When we asked Jan if her assistant principal would soon be stepping into the role of principal, she lamented that there were five other candidates who the District was considering, none of whom had any experience in the Downtown School teaching practices. In this case, the problem with the District's adherence to their HR hiring guidelines is that although the other candidates may be able to learn and apply a new set of methodologies, they are not likely to have the degree of passion for the school's vision and values that the assistant principal has had for lo these many years.

Wake-up Des Moines: if those five "principals in waiting" are not true believers in the philosophy that made the Downtown School exceptional, please do not allow them to wreak havoc with this incredible learning environment. Art Wittmack, Des Moines Business Alliance president, continues to be an exceptional advocate for educational reform. He told us that he was not aware that "politics" were involved in the decision-making process. However, he did admit, "What Jan has provided us with is a stable platform from which others can work. If what we have created is dependent upon Jan Drees for success, then we have not been successful. It requires a creative leader, one who understands the goals. We need to reproduce what has been successful in the Downtown School in the entire district, and that can't be done by one person. There's no question that Jan Drees is a one of a kind and without Jan's pioneering work, we wouldn't be where we are. It took that pioneering spirit and that genius which Jan has. But when you go through organizational development, it takes different personalities—from the entrepreneur to the place where you can deal with the HR issues of a larger establishment. We are in one of those struggles right now. I am optimistic that this will be a positive outcome."

We applaud Art and the Business Alliance for their passion regarding educational reform. However, it has been over 10 years since the creation of the Downtown School and not one school in the district has adopted its philosophy. If the Business Alliance is to transform the educational system in Des Moines, they must muster up the same type of leadership and courage that they had 10 years ago when they initially challenged the traditional classroom learning environment.

Certainly, in any business you need a "stable platform" to manage the operations of the organization. But as we have learned from all of our featured organizations, a quality leader is one who believes that the real "magic"—creating an environment of mutual respect and trust—transcends policies and procedures. These exceptional leaders are more than administrators—they are communicators of the highest order who can bring the organization's vision to life; listen to the needs, desires, and dreams of their customers; and lead by example. Yes, Jan Drees is a "one of a kind," but if the Downtown School is going to survive and serve as the template for the Des Moines School District at large, an exceptional, unique,and passionate leader must once again step up to plate.

We asked Renee Harmon if the Downtown School learning environment is right for all children. She responded, "I have yet to meet a student it hasn't been right for." However, it is important to remember that Jan and her team took the best-of-the-best and created their own unique learning environment. Those who dare to follow the example of the Downtown School must be fearless innovators, not imitators! Those who choose this course will work harder than they ever knew they could. There is no instant pudding, but the results will be evident in all the Nathans of the world.

Ernst & Young

Dream

Most of our featured organizations started their enterprises with a dream: George "I guarantee it" Zimmer of Men's Wearhouse, Jan Drees of Downtown School, John DiJulius of John Robert's Spa, Isadore Sharp of Four Seasons Hotels & Resorts, and David Overton of The Cheesecake Factory. Only Ernst & Young and Griffin Hospital had well-established cultures before a new leader with a new dream decided that change was in order. Griffin Hospital didn't have an option; it was either change or die.

In the year 2000, Ernst & Young was a well-established, successful global organization with roughly $10 billion in revenues and nearly 90,000 employees. It would be several years before the Enron scandal would be blamed for the seemingly overnight fall of Arthur Andersen LLP, E & Y's largest competitor. So why change?

Professional service firms are known for putting their young recruits and less senior people through "hell." It's just like pledging a fraternity or a sorority; you take the hazing knowing that some day you'll be able to dish it out. David Maister has studied, taught, and written about professional service firms for more than 20 years. When asked why professional service firms don't change, Maister replied, "Let me give you an analogy from my own life. I am a fat smoker. I don't need another speech to tell me that I should stop smoking and lose weight. Clear lungs, longer life—I accept that it's a fabulous strategy. But please, no more speeches." People in professional service firms, as well as other businesses, have heard all the speeches before. They know the importance of providing exceptional customer service, developing people, being a team player, etc., etc. Maister advises that, "Whether it is giving up smoking or giving great customer service, any kind of improvement requires short-term sacrifice and short-term pain in the name of a better long-term future. The problem in professional services is that because the environment is so bountiful, you can get everything wrong and still have a nice income."[88] In reality, very few businesses are willing to endure short-term pain in hopes of achieving long-term gain, especially when profits are solid.

As we stated in Chapter 7, Jim Turley and his team rolled out a "People First" philosophy early in 2001. They were ready to endure pain to change the century-old culture of Ernst & Young. The E & Y "People First" philosophy is "to be the firm that contributes most to the success of its people and its clients by creating value and confidence."

As chairman and CEO, Jim Turley leads the organization's commitment to putting people first. This is accomplished by creating a supportive culture; making people paramount in all decisions; providing development opportunities for all employees; fostering an inclusive work environment; and building strong and enduring relationships with its people. Jim realizes that culture change is a two-way street. To make the change real at Ernst, each and every employee must also set personal goals, take ownership of his or her own careers, and live the firm's values every day.

Of course, the work is still stressful, the hours long, and the clients demanding, but there is good stress and bad stress. Everyday task-related pressure is typically much easier to cope with than stress that comes directly from one's superior. And pressure on young staff is perhaps nowhere more apparent than in the Big Four environment. "We need to make sure that our partners understand how their management styles impact our people," says Jim Freer, vice chair of people in the United States.[89]

Ernst & Young recently created the position "director of partner matters" and placed Mike Ritter, a highly respected senior partner, in the role. "Mike Ritter will wake up every day thinking about partner stress and what we can do to impact it positively," says Freer.

"People First" is no longer a program at E & Y—it has become a way of life that is imbedded into the very DNA of its culture. Every new employee at Ernst & Young knows that the "People First" philosophy is important and will still be important when they become partners. Making people paramount in all decisions is as much a part of life at Ernst & Young as is running a trial balance for an audit.

Believe

At Ernst & Young, shared values guide actions and behaviors. Not only do these shared values influence the way employees interact with their coworkers, they also guide the way employees serve their clients and engage with other stakeholders. The Ernst & Young Global Code of Contact provides a solid ethical framework for business conduct. Employees are expected to base their decisions and their actions, both as individuals and as members of the global team, on the Code. In fact, full compliance and commitment to the Code is mandatory, and employees must sign a declaration to this effect. This credo underscores who they are and what they stand for:

- People who demonstrate integrity, respect, and teaming
- People with energy, enthusiasm, and the courage to lead
- People who build relationships based on doing the right thing

Dare

Changing a culture that had survived for 100 years was quite a risk for Jim Turley, but perhaps not as big a risk as announcing to the world that at E & Y, people come first. According to Jim Freer, "We've always recognized that people are our most important asset. It's their talent and skills that make us who we are." Bill worked for Ernst before the new philosophy was instituted. At that time, there was no such thing as a "bad client." If the engagement was not profitable, teams looked for ways to increase the scope and, hopefully, the profitability. They did not seek out clients who were in illegal or unethical businesses, but clients who could pay their bills were considered "good clients." In 2001, Jim Turley let it be known that the rules of engagement were going to change at E & Y.

Not long after the "People First" philosophy was rolled out, Jim was speaking to a group of managers and senior managers. He asked them, "Please be totally honest. How many of you work for clients you do not like?" Seeing a large number of hands raised in response, he then asked, "Leave your hand up if the client is highly profitable." Most of the hands went down. Jim then asked those who had initially raised their hands to raise them again. Finally, Jim said, "Leave your hand up if this client you dislike is good for your personal growth and development." Once again, to Jim's surprise, most of the hands went down.

Over the years, David Maister (former professor at Harvard Business School, now a consultant to professional services firms) has conducted similar studies with his own clients. David first gives his audience three categories to classify how they feel about their work: Category One is, "I love this stuff." Category Two is, "I can tolerate it, but that's why they call it work." Category Three is, "How the hell did I end up doing this junk?" According to David, the results are consistent all over the world: 20 percent say they love their work; 60 to 70 percent say they can tolerate their work; and 10 to 20 percent say what they do is junk. David then gives his audience three categories to classify how they feel about their clients: Category One is, "I really like these people. I enjoy serving them." Category Two is, "I can tolerate them. I give them good service, but there is no real difference between today's client and tomorrow's client." Category Three is, "These people are idiots that work in a boring industry." David reports that the results of this question are similar to the first. About 20 percent love their clients; 60 to 70 percent can tolerate them; and 10 to 20 percent cannot stand them. When David asks his audience if they think clients can sense these feelings, the answer is always a resounding "Yes!"

After coming to a similar conclusion, Jim Turley wondered, "Why should we keep doing business with clients we don't like, who are not very profitable, and do not provide an opportunity for our people to grow? At the end of the day, we don't want to be thought of as being in the audit, tax, or corporate finance business. We want to be thought of as being in the business of developing résumés, skills, and careers for all the people that come through the firm."[90]

Once again, like the rest of the leaders of our featured organizations, Jim dared to challenge conventional wisdom. He wasn't trying to create the typical professional services firm. Such firms, according to David Maister, reflect an attitude of, "We won't screw up, but we are nothing special." Instead, Jim Turley turned Ernst & Young into a special kind of firm where they really do put people first.

Do

Making the new "People First" culture a reality at Ernst & Young required hard work, dedication, and commitment at all levels. This transformation involved rolling out several high-profile initiatives: the Gallup Q12 process, essentially an attitude survey; PeoplePoint, which provides a way to give upward feedback to partners, principals, and directors; the People Advisory Forum, which provides management with direct, regular contact with nonpartners; and the CNW (Center for the New Workforce), which supports the development of women leaders as well as other workforce issues. These are just some of the elements that continue to grow and nurture the culture.

Ernst & Young's extensive investment in its people is also demonstrated by a vast assortment of formal and informal training programs that allow people to, as Jim Turley stated, "develop their résumés, skills, and careers." In 2006, Ernst & Young was again named to the *Training* Top 100, a ranking by *Training* magazine. E & Y consistently makes the list, but this time took the number three spot among significant competition from a field of over 500 entries.

"We are delighted to be recognized by *Training* magazine as one of the top 10 companies on the *Training* Top 100 list for a fifth straight year," said Mike Hamilton, Ernst & Young's Americas chief learning and development officer. "The global Ernst & Young organization is committed to a culture of putting our people first. Part of this commitment is providing our professionals with continual training and learning opportunities that help them develop and grow, leading to increased fulfillment in their work and the highest quality service to our clients."

"The professional services industry has seen many changes over the past several years. Ernst & Young has developed, refined, and deployed many new learning programs and events on a global scale to help its people meet these new challenges and reach their goals. Additionally, it has employed innovative workplace initiatives, leading development and learning practices, and cutting-edge technology to improve people's performance," Hamilton added.

Much of the groundwork for the new culture began in the late 1990s under the leadership of Phil Laskawy, retired chairman and CEO. In 1997,

Ernst & Young formalized its flexible work arrangement (FWA) program, which empowers employees to decide how, where, and when they get their work done. According to E & Y, approximately 2,300, or nearly 10 percent of its U.S–based workers, take advantage of the program. The Flexible Work Arrangement is especially appreciated by women at E & Y who are serious about furthering their careers. Women professionals currently account for the majority of FWA participants, although men are increasingly taking advantage of the program every year. Today, 20 percent of the participants are men, up from 17 percent last year and 13 percent two years ago. This program allows thousands of professional women and men to balance their career goals with their personal lives.

As Phil Laskawy told us, "When I was in school, all the smartest kids were girls. When I got into business, I wondered what happened to them."[91] Vice chair of client services, John Ferraro, knows that giving women the chance to succeed makes good business sense. "Our commitment to women's development and advancement is integral to Ernst & Young's success. In 1996, E & Y launched a focused effort to grow its women leaders, both personally and professionally. Since then, the promotion rate of women at the partner level has more than doubled to 25 percent and women now comprise 13 percent of all leadership positions at our firm."[92] From offering childcare to concierge services, it's clear that Ernst & Young is dedicated to helping employees manage both their professional and personal lives.

A true testimony to its values, Ernst & Young is concerned about the perceptions of its alumni. "We look at employment as life-long. Not being with the firm anymore does not mean that you are not a part of the family," Phil Laskawy told us. The strong alumni network is evidenced by the fact that 25 percent of its experienced hires are "boomerangs," or those who left the firm and then returned at some point in the future. And, of course, leader behavior is a key factor in those decisions people make to return to the Ernst "family." As is true of Isadore Sharp of Four Seasons, the leaders at Ernst & Young truly understand their role of setting the right tone for the organization: one of trust and respect.

But is it working? In 2000, Ernst & Young had revenues of $9.5 billion and 88,625 employees, ranking fifth among the then Big Five. Today, Ernst & Young ranks second in revenues among the Big Four, with $16.9 billion in revenues and over 106,000 employees; its largest competitor's revenues and staff decreased over 5 percent for the same period. For eight consecutive years, Ernst & Young has been consistently named to *Fortune* magazine's

"100 Best Companies to Work For." Changing an organizational culture is a daunting task requiring much more than strategic leadership, but Ernst & Young set out to do it and succeeded.

Four Seasons Hotels & Resorts

Dream

Doug Ludwig, recently retired CFO of Four Seasons, first met founder and CEO Isadore Sharp more than 20 years ago when young Doug was an accounting intern working on a class project. Doug told us, "Issy's dream back then was as clear, precise, and thoughtful as it is now."[93] Back then, Isadore was just getting started testing the theory that one could build a world-class, five-star hotel empire on a simple ethic, The Golden Rule. Now, of course, that theory is fact.

Doug joined the Four Seasons accounting department in 1984, after seven years at a Big Four public accounting firm. He remembers how nervous he was being called into Isadore's office on his very first day—the experience certainly made a lasting impression on him. "Wondering what I had done wrong already," Doug recounted, "I was amazed to find out that Isadore just wanted to welcome me to Four Seasons and to share his vision with me." When we asked Doug if Isadore remembered the class project, he replied, "At first, I didn't think so because he didn't mention it, but all of a sudden I glanced down and there was that college report of seven years ago. When you are in the university, you think this is really important stuff; but after seven years of experience, I wasn't quite sure. Nothing was said about the report until I was getting up to leave. Isadore said 'Just a second, I want to talk to you about a few things in this report.' I didn't know it at the time, but Isadore makes it a point to spend time with every new corporate employee on their first day."

Communicating the dream to each and every new employee on his or her first day is just as important to Isadore today as it was back in 1984. Isadore's compassion and humility fit perfectly with the globally acknowledged Golden Rule philosophy on which his company is based.

There is an old adage in public relations that the only bad publicity is none at all. According to Elizabeth Pizzinato, director of corporate public relations at Four Seasons, "The main PR objective of most companies is to get their name in print or on the nightly news. More is better. That's not the case at Four Seasons. Here, in everything we do, it is quality over quantity. What we do with journalists is what we do with guests: we build relationships."[94]

Whether it is the front of the house where there is constant contact with the guest or the back of the house for the corporate business side of Four Seasons, the shared vision of management is always the same: Take care of your people, and they will take care of the guest. Kathleen ("Katie") Taylor, president of worldwide business operations, explained, "There is an unending focus on the issues of our people. They are the constant focus of our energy. It is hard work, and it takes real energy and real commitment. Every one of our GMs and their staffs gets up in the morning obsessed with serving their employees and their guests."[95]

Believe

It is no surprise that the goals, beliefs, and principles of Four Seasons are all people-centered:

> Our greatest asset, and the key to our success, is our people. We believe that each of us needs a sense of dignity, pride, and satisfaction in what we do. Because satisfying our guests depends on the united efforts of many, we are most effective when we work together cooperatively, respecting each other's contribution and importance.

Isadore told us that these statements are only words—what counts are behaviors based on heart-felt values.[96] One notable role model at Four Seasons who lives The Golden Rule is president of worldwide hotel operations, Wolf Hengst. Wolf joined the company in 1978 as the opening general manager of Four Seasons Hotel Washington, D.C. As Wolf jokingly told us, "I'm at an age and position in my career that I can say what I want. What's the worst that can happen to me, early retirement? When I interviewed over 25 years ago, there were only seven hotels. I said then, 'If the philosophy and what I had heard in the interviews does not change, this will be a truly unique company.' It has never changed, not in all these years, not even in one year can I say there has been a change in philosophy. The company has changed in its size; the company has changed in its organizational structure; but the basic belief and philosophy at the core of the company and the culture has never changed."[97]

Respect and trust are truly the foundation for delivering five-star service at Four Seasons, but do these virtues also apply to the corporation's business dealings? we wondered. "Once we sign a business contract," Isadore affirmed, "we file it away and never take it out again. If there is an issue, we do what is right." Katie Taylor, former general counsel at Four Seasons, gave us a lawyer's perspective of this practice. "If you have to go back to the contract, there is something wrong with the relationship," Kate told us. "In common law cultures, relationships of a business nature are anchored by contracts. But we operated lots of hotels without contracts. We once waited a full six months for a signed contract, but it didn't stop us from opening. Another hotel management agreement went on for several years without a signed contract. Everyone realized it when we were going to refinance the property and looked for the contract."

A sense of family is apparent not only with the "old guard" like Wolf, but also with trainees and newer employees. "I have been here only a few years, but it seems like a lot longer, and I mean that in a positive way. I really feel like I've been part of this company for a long time. I think from your very first day at Four Seasons, you actually get to know what the company is all about," remarked Elizabeth Pizzinato.

The real test of a people-centered culture comes in bad times, like economic downturns, terrorist attacks, or changes in a local economy. Maintaining business health at such times for most service firms means unavoidable layoffs. That is not the case at Four Seasons. Wolf explained, "We come out of troubled times stronger. We must continue to do all the things to give employees the motivation to stay with us. We create an environment that makes them believe that they will be here with us for the long term. That is not as easy as it sounds because you also have obligations to other business owners and partners who don't always look at things the same way. It's a hard job to stand up and say to those partners 'We cannot change this. You have to understand that in order for us to have long-term success, we can't just drop everything and pick it up in a year or two. It just doesn't work.' Yes, you do less. No, you don't eliminate." In many companies, upper management or the accounting department challenges expenses and seeks ways to cut costs, especially during tough times. That is not the case at Four Seasons. As Doug Ludwig described, "Even after 9/11, we did everything that was smart to do to save, but we were careful about not compromising the guest experience or the employee experience. The two are very closely linked, and the last thing you want to do is cut corners in the employee cafeteria or locker rooms."

Time and time again, we heard enthusiastic examples of the same story, the success of Four Seasons' shared vision and values. Comments such as, "From the first interview, I knew I wanted to work for this company"; "I have great pride in working for the company"; and "Everyone knows how much they have contributed" all speak to the root of Four Seasons' goals, beliefs, and principles. Indeed, they are more than just words; they come straight from the heart.

Dare

We don't think Issy Sharp really believed that running a business based on The Golden Rule was a risk. Sure, he realized the theory needed testing, but we believe that once feedback on his Golden Rule philosophy starting pouring in from his employees, Isadore dared to move forward.

In the last several decades at Four Seasons, there were many times when Isadore could have abandoned his philosophy or compromised his values. At one point in the company's growth, he told his management group that all plans for expansion would be put "on hold." He thought the company was growing too fast and that quality might be compromised. From then on, Isadore and his team built one hotel at a time, making each one the very best it could be. Today, it would be a risk to change the culture at Four Seasons. Doug Ludwig told us, "We have 30,000 people all around the world who tell us this is the only way to work."

Do

As is true in any organization, hiring the best people is vital to long-term success. Certainly at Four Seasons, hiring the best people is a top priority. Every new employee goes through at least five interviews, the last being with the general manager of a particular location. According to Katie Taylor, "It's not so the GM can say 'Yes, I like this person' or 'No, I don't.' All candidates, even dishwashers, are interviewed by the GM. It shows the potential dishwasher that his [or her] job is really important. He may go home and tell his mother or his friends, 'Wow, I met the GM today,' and on his first day at work he knows the GM, and the GM knows him."

This early exposure to the general manager is very important for any Four Seasons employee. Both the general manager and senior management stay very involved in the daily lives and the responsibilities of their employees. For example, the GM frequently checks rooms after a housekeeper cleans, not to see how clean they are, but to let the housekeeper know that he or she has a very important job. Whether it is the housekeeper, the bookkeeper, or the bellman—all Four Seasons employees know they are part of a team that works together to create exceptional guest service. To be sure, nothing happens by accident at Four Seasons. The systems, the procedures, the methods, and "art" of leading people are all in place and continually reinforce a culture of excellence in service.

Another key to the delivery of outstanding service is the long tenure of management at Four Seasons. The average tenure is over 20 years while the average age is less than 50. This low turnover rate translates into a continuity of the culture. Staff members do not have to consciously think about The Golden Rule every day: they just live it! The strength of this cultural foundation fosters employee trust and commitment within and between all levels of the organization. Employees don't spend time worrying about what their coworkers might do. They just *know* and trust in the beliefs, values, and leadership of Four Seasons. In the words of Wolf Hengst: "We all sing together from the same hymn book. I sometimes have to pinch myself when I think about how fortunate I have been. It all boils down to this: you've got to take care of the employee, take care of the guest, love what you're doing, and you have to *want* to serve. The culture won't change as long as we understand this. If anyone ever loses sight of what the Four Seasons is all about, then we will have a problem."

Griffin Hospital

Dream

When you walk through the halls of Griffin Hospital, it's impossible to imagine that not long ago, 30 percent of the residents in Derby, Connecticut, said they would "avoid" their community hospital if at all possible. Now, Griffin is the pride of the entire healthcare industry, living its mission to "provide personalized, humanistic, consumer-driven health care in a healing environment; to empower individuals to be actively involved in decisions affecting their care and well-being through access to information and education; and to provide leadership to improve the health of the community we serve."

While some hospitals have claimed a "Disney transformation," not one of them can boast being named number 4 on *Fortune* magazine's 2006 list of "100 Best Companies to Work For"—the highest ranking ever achieved by a hospital. Griffin can also boast of being the only hospital in America named to this prestigious list for seven consecutive years. In most hospitals, administrators balk at "pixie dust," claiming, "This isn't Disneyland, it's a hospital." These types would never have the guts that Griffin displayed in asking a critical question of its own staff members: "If you or a family member were admitted to a hospital, describe what you would want the hospital experience to be like." Griffin took those responses to heart and under Patrick Charmel's leadership, a transformation began.

One thing Patrick had on his side during the transformation of Griffin was the longevity of his senior leadership team. Over half of them had worked together for more than 27 years and were essentially "born at Griffin." (Vice president Bill Powanda was *actually* born at Griffin, and his executive office was once part of the original maternity ward. Bill says proudly, "I have been right here all my life.")[98] A key factor that fueled the transformation was the fact that four executive staff members had recent, not-so-comforting hospital experiences for serious personal or family medical problems at three different hospitals. Although none of them reported being disappointed with their medical care, all of them had felt a void in the area of personalized attention from hospital staff. Sharing these experiences was more than a catharsis for these leaders: it was the solidifying of a dream to ensure that Griffin patients never have to wonder whether they can ask a question about their care and get a straight answer; whether they have the freedom to view their medical charts; or whether their families will be respected by hospital staff. This determined and empowered executive team was a source of great strength and inspiration for the entire staff during the days of Griffin's transformation. Together they helped facilitate all-day retreats called "Griffin Days," which deepened their passion for creating the dream of making Griffin "the hospital of choice" for every "guest" who enters their sanctum.

Believe

Griffin Hospital's success in delivering on its promise of superior patient-centered holistic care and customer service is chronicled in its annual reports, like the recent "Creating the Exceptional Patient Experience," and "Clinical Excellence: Creating Exceptional Outcomes." Truly one of the hallmarks of Griffin's success is its unique culture of extraordinary service and teamwork.

Like Disney, Griffin Hospital has always been a place where differentiation is achieved by employees who exercise both good judgment and creativity in their interactions with others—all without a script. "When other hospitals visit Griffin, they give us high praise for the lack of "scripting" in our environment, saying Griffin seemed more sincere than other hospitals that employ scripting for their specific departments. What our guests are seeing is evidence that Griffin's genuine customer service approach was always part of its culture," Bill Powanda stated.

The reason scripting isn't necessary for Griffin's nursing staff or Disney's parks staff or Four Seasons Hotels staff is that authenticity comes naturally to these employees and cast members. It's one thing to use a script on an attraction like The Great Movie Ride at Disney-MGM Studios, where the script is really part of the "show"; it's quite another thing to use a script when working with the family of a terminally ill patient who expects truthful answers on topics ranging from pain management to hospice care.

Are Griffin's beliefs being rewarded? You bet. Griffin Hospital has been conducting community perception surveys on a regular basis since 1982. Results of the most recent survey completed in November 2005 show that the quality of care at Griffin is on a par with Yale New Haven Hospital and above the other six competitor hospitals. Griffin's emergency room was rated highest of all hospitals in the region, and, overall, Griffin was rated the most improved hospital by a three to one margin.

Dare

If you think culture change is difficult to achieve in the typical American organization, you'd be right. To create a winning culture, the vision and values of the organization must be brought to life and demonstrated every day. Hospitals, however, are "change allergic," according to David Freeman's 1999 *Inc.* magazine article on Griffin. And the unfortunate truth is that, today, one can readily spot evidence of resistance to becoming "guest friendly" in the vast majority of hospitals across the country. It doesn't take long to find those halls of linoleum, bright fluorescent lights, cluttered hallways, and clusters of nurses whispering—all in the name of "good health care."

In Chapter 4, we described Patrick Charmel's success in transforming Griffin Hospital into a wellness paradise, which began in the hospital's maternity ward. Together, Patrick and long-time fellow associate Marge Deegan, vice president of ambulatory services, set out on what would become one of the most "creative" journeys of their lives. They traveled together as the "pregnant" mom and concerned "husband" for the purpose of experiencing hospital birthing facilities directly through the eyes of the customer. No facility totally matched their dream of a place to serve as the stage for one of almost every family's main events—becoming parents. Most hospitals give families the opposite feeling, to which many of the leadership team, including Patrick himself, could attest.

Without uncovering a model to "imitate," Patrick vowed to "innovate." He would bring his team together and produce a "magical" patient-centered, not physician-centered, environment. "In health care," said Marge Deegan, "we develop mindsets that become the barriers to innovation. We had a credible leader in charge of the process. Patrick was always the one who pushed the envelope. He is so professional, and never let on how difficult it was to bring on the new concepts."[99]

And many new concepts in the area of facilities at Griffin were about to take shape. On Patrick's watch, however, new "attractions" at Griffin needed to pass one critical test: how well they could support the credo of patient-centered care he dared to adopt. He listened intently to the focus groups he had commissioned to identify what was needed to create the "ideal" birth experience. The expectations of focus group participants were like a newlywed's "Christmas Wish List" with hefty price tags attached to every item. Most executives in Patrick's position would have asked for a more realistic proposal. In fact, many company leaders prioritize "customer wishes" annually, choosing only a few of the least expensive items or "low-hanging fruit" that are easy to achieve. And, if you were an executive in an organization like Griffin, which was at one time struggling financially and nearly bankrupt, you might opt for cosmetic changes and forget the rest. But, the emboldened Patrick did something that shocked his team members. Just like Santa Claus, he brought the gifts that everyone wanted: a noninstitutional, home-like setting with garden-fresh flowers, family room-style lounges, soft hallway lighting, skylights, custom-built double beds, and a Jacuzzi—and that was just the beginning.

Since the opening of the Childbirth Center at Griffin Hospital in 1987, Griffin has been renewing its status as an innovator in the healthcare industry. It was now the place to go—at least for expectant parents who didn't need to be convinced to sign up for a dose of Griffin's pampering while living through the various stages of pregnancy and childbirth. But selling this patient-centered approach to Griffin's doctors was a whole different experience for Patrick and his management team. Thankfully, it didn't take long for old-line doctors to move out and for a new crop of altruistic doctors to join the Griffin team.

When the decision was made to take the patient-centered care concept hospital-wide, the rest of the hospital's doctors knew they couldn't pass it off as simply a maternity "thing." Patient empowerment, open medical records, and formal care conferences can be very threatening to physicians who are accustomed to having ultimate control.

Medial director Dr. Kenneth Schwartz told us, "I've yet to see a negative outcome from patients reading charts, and a number of positive things have happened. About a year ago, I had a patient come in, having passed out. He was a little out of it for the first day he was here. He was a very intelligent guy, a local retired minister. A couple of days later, I came in and made rounds on him, and he said, 'I want to thank you for allowing me to look at my chart.' He said, 'I really wanted to talk to you about this. I think the history recorded is a little inaccurate because I was a little woosy when I first came in.' Then he clarified the details, which was actually very helpful. That's a typical positive response that you get out of the system."[100]

Patrick Charmel and his team created a new approach to patient care that shattered the myths and beliefs that have long been hospital tradition in America.

Do

Many hospitals have brought in consulting teams who share the "secrets" of Disney's on-stage and back-stage areas. But, most of them are not practicing the Planetree model: the philosophy based on the belief that if patients have access to information and education regarding their illness and hospitalization, they can become active participants in getting well. But it is much more than just information sharing. The hospital provides a healing and nurturing environment with warm and supportive caregivers. "Lots of hospitals try to sort of steal the Planetree concept," Dr. Schwartz explained. "They might have sculpture, water, a piano playing in the lobby. You can pretty-up any hospital. But, the philosophy is the tough part of it, because that's the part that requires support. That's where the competitive advantage is."

As we previously described, that doctor-driven hierarchy is still very much alive in some of the most prominent and powerful medical centers in the country. The good news, however, is that due to its widely publicized success, Griffin Hospital is now under the microscope. Over 500 U.S. hospitals have paid $3,000 for the privilege of touring and learning from this once modest and obscure facility in a small Connecticut community. They will meet a team of people who are clearly a "family" who strive together, in good times and bad, to achieve their mission of excellence. Peering behind the picture-perfect Griffin "stage" that has become legendary, there are countless untold stories of the Griffin family taking care of one another as they do their patients. As Barbara Stumpo, VP of patient care services, related, "We had a guy who worked in critical care, and he was only here a short period of time. He was diagnosed with metastatic cancer, and he was a young guy who had a little child at home. He was trying to get through chemo, and would come in and work a couple hours probably to get a break from his home setting. The administration here at Griffin really supported him. Every one of them donated vacation time to his paycheck—the docs, the nurses, the entire administration. He had a full paycheck until after he passed away. People are what make this place so special. It's the sincerity, the compassion, the respect."[101]

Hospitals throughout the United States are in desperate need of what Patrick Charmel has modeled for Griffin—the Dream, Believe, Dare, Do credo. Management consultants from Ernst & Young (another one of our featured organizations) describe the changing healthcare paradigm that could serve to force many in the industry to adopt the Planetree approach and reinvent themselves: "The trillion-dollar American healthcare market is on the brink of the biggest transformation yet. The primary force behind this change is not technology or managed care but the growing mass of educated and empowered consumers. 'Healthcare consumerism' will alter how healthcare organizations will operate, how they compete, and, perhaps, why they exist."

After embracing the patient-centered Planetree model, Griffin took ownership of the Planetree organization in 1998. The Planetree national headquarters is on Griffin's campus in Derby, Connecticut, and is a subsidiary of Griffin Health Services Corporation. Today, the Planetree Network has grown to over 100 member hospitals in the United States, Canada, and the Netherlands, whose staffs are trained, coached, and nurtured by Planetree president, Susan Frampton, and her competent team of professionals.

According to Griffin vice president, Bill Powanda, hospitals who adopt the Planetree philosophy do so for one or more of the following reasons:

- *Pure altruism*—a belief that this is the right way to treat patients
- *Strategic initiative*—a way to differentiate themselves, particularly if they are in very competitive markets
- *Brand promise*—assurance of being backed by Planetree, which provides support through its network membership

Those fortunate organizations that have CEO support to bring Planetree into their facilities will live and learn a new vocabulary that reinforces how people behave; they'll be saying, "That's very Planetree," or "That's not very Planetree" as a critique and confirmation of what is patient-focused and what isn't. As Susan Frampton told us, "In each Planetree hospital, there is something different when you walk through the doors . . . the warmth, the whole atmosphere. It's understanding the patient's perspective, knowing that you're creating memories that last a lifetime."[102]

Planetree provides hospital employees with a level of freedom that allows them to "go the extra mile" for their patients. Christine Cooper, director of radiology, cardiology, and neurology at Griffin Hospital, exhibits Planetree behaviors in arenas that most people would say are beyond her control. On one very busy day in the radiology department, she was aware that patients were getting restless with having to wait a long time to be tested. The radiology department at that time was using an outside company for their mobile MRI service and expected them to deliver Planetree-style service. One irate patient decided he could no longer wait for his name to be called and stormed out of the building. Later that day, he called back to report that he was never coming back because the service was so "lousy." Chris took matters into her own hands. Not only did she convince the MRI company to issue $100 gift certificates to four patients for their aggravation, but she also took time out of her busy schedule to send personal letters to each one of these individuals. Chris believes that her partners in delivering patient services must be held to the same high standards as her hospital lives by . . . now, that's very "Planetree."

The Planetree approach has produced dramatic results for Griffin Hospital. Griffin uses an independent, private marketing research company call center to conduct patient satisfaction surveys. The center completes 100 telephone surveys monthly (about 15 percent of discharges) with results reported by the fifteenth day of the succeeding month. The center captures narrative comments from patients that Griffin's leadership team finds extremely valuable in identifying and solving problems. The overall patient satisfaction rating has averaged 97 to 98 percent for the past five years. Griffin Hospital's patient satisfaction ratings are among the highest in the country.

The Agency for Healthcare Research and Quality (AHRQ) recently announced that the results of its CAHPS Hospital Survey (H-CAHPS), a standardized survey of hospital experiences, will soon be available online. This means that the general public may view Griffin's patient experience/satisfaction ratings and compare them to other hospitals and national norms/averages. In a pilot survey conducted for AHRQ, Griffin ranked the highest of all Connecticut hospitals, and Connecticut ranked the highest of the four pilot states. As Griffin's Bill Powanda stated, "Soon there will be a great deal of pressure on hospital management to become patient-focused. The challenge will be even greater for tertiary care university medical centers where the focus has never been on the patient experience or patient satisfaction, but rather on medical research, medical education, and clinical outcomes. Most are not good at 'Creating the Exceptional Patient Experience.'"

With Patrick Charmel's impressive leadership track record, Griffin Hospital is sure to continue to be an industry leader in personalized health care. Last year, Patrick was appointed to a three-year term on the National Advisory Council for Healthcare Research and Quality. Recently, the Yale School of Public Health honored Patrick as the John D. Thompson Distinguished Visiting Fellow of 2006. Those Yale students, many of whom will be the next generation of health care administrators, are the lucky ones who will learn from one great leader how he guided his team through some turbulent waters and ended up building one of the top "100 Best Companies to Work For" in America.

John Robert's Spa
Dream

On their first date, John and Stacy dreamed of owning a hair salon. John DiJulius says, "When I met Stacy, she was already a phenomenal hairdresser. At 19, she had a waiting list."[103] On that very first night, they discussed how Stacy would open a salon and bring to life some of the many great ideas John had for running a business. As John recalls, their first business plan was drawn up on "a bunch of cocktail napkins." Having worked for UPS during college, John quickly discovered that he could make more money as a UPS driver than as a corporate trainee with a marketing degree. As John told us, "I went to work full time as a driver, hoping that I could put enough money away to someday open my own business."

Opening a hair salon, however, was not the sort of business John had in mind when he first met Stacy. Sure, he thought it would be a nice little business for Stacy, but John's plan all along was to save his money for a "real" business. Stacy recalls buying their first salon, "John saw an ad in the paper for a small salon. He was always looking for opportunities. He called them up and before I knew it, he had put an offer in. I was freaking out. I was 22 years old and thought, 'Oh My God! We don't have any money.' We took out a loan using my Nana's GE stocks for collateral. I don't know how John talked her into it, but he did. She must have had her hearing aid turned way down that day."[104]

Their first employees were friends of Stacy's who were also hairdressers. With four employees and a base of over 1,000 clients, John thought the salon was off to a great start. But John and Stacy soon discovered that these employees simply did not deliver the "secret service" (now the credo for John Robert's Spa and others who practice the customer service methods in John's book, *Secret Service*) principles John and Stacy were attempting to instill at the new salon. Stacy told us that one day, one of the hairdressers was running late and told her client she didn't have time to blow-dry her hair. Stacy overheard the comment and announced that she would take care of drying the lady's hair. Once the lady had left, the hairdresser came over to Stacy and shouted, "Don't you ever take one of my clients again!" Stacy lamented, "This is exactly how a lot of people in this industry act. They feel very threatened, but the client unfortunately is the one who suffers. The client did nothing wrong. She came in on time and expected great service." After this incident, the lady switched her allegiance from the self-centered hairdresser (who, by the way, is long gone from John Robert's) to Stacy, to whom she remains loyal to this day.

After the first six weeks of business, John Robert's' original hairdressers quickly disappeared; they were either fired or they left. As John remembers them, "They wanted nothing to do with our dream. They wanted to do things their way." John and Stacy wanted no more stereotypical hairdressers at their shop. Other salons put up with staff who might not show up for work, might come in late, might have a hangover, might leave the shop between clients, and would never think of helping their coworkers. People who treated their careers in such a cavalier fashion would never fit into John and Stacy's dream.

John and Stacy wanted to create a unique environment where they could provide and serve as a model for legendary customer service. To achieve such a feat, they must stay the course. As John told us, "If that meant going out of business, so be it. I'd rather go broke than compromise our standards." Stacy said she thought the world was going to come to an end, "I was young, Nana's stocks were up for collateral, and I thought I would be disowned by my family and have the Italian curse put on me."

But, fears cannot deter those who are passionate about their dreams. Like all of our featured organizations, John and Stacy decided to buck traditional wisdom. Instead of hiring experienced hairdressers from established salons, they would hire cosmetology school graduates and train them to be "mini-Stacys." John says, "Before Stacy was an owner, she was a great employee. She was always concerned about the salon and about the client." Delivering first-class service is never the easy way to run a business, but John and Stacy knew it was the only way to achieve the long-term success they dreamed of.

Has the experiment worked? Since 1993, the business has grown from a simple 900-square-foot salon into a collection of three salons and spas that have been custom designed exclusively for relaxation and restoration of the body, mind, and spirit. Features and services include a spa with four treatment rooms; a vichy shower; a steam shower; a manicure/pedicure sanctuary; a tranquil spa lounge; a men's salon; a sports-themed room complete with a pool table; a color lab for mixing personalized color formulations; 20 styling stations; an experience area where guests are greeted upon entering and encouraged to test products as well as browse through team portfolios; and, finally, a café that serves up tasty, healthy smoothies and a variety of other refreshments. What started with four hairdressers who could barely spell "secret service" is now a team of 140 who bring John and Stacy's credo to life. From the brink of losing Nana's stocks (and the fear of being forever "cursed") to generating over $4 million dollars in annual sales, John Robert's has redefined the salon experience and is truly a model for any industry.

Believe

As is true at Ernst & Young, John Robert's employees get top billing. John explains, "What that means is that if you are going to work at John Robert's, your team members need to be a high priority—as high, if not higher than our guests." This is reflected in the John Robert's mission, *"For every long-term employee to regard their decision to work at John Robert's as one of the best decisions of their life."* Eric Hammond, director of operations, explained, "We have a great team philosophy. When I first came to work here, I tried to figure out how it came to be. It starts with the leaders and just trickles down. We don't do a ton of stuff that encourages team play. It's just the foundation that John Robert's is built on."[105]

John and Stacy believe that it's everyone's job, including their own, to live the John Robert's mission. One day a client witnessed Stacy sweeping the floor and asked her, "Can't you hire someone to do that?" Stacy, John, and their management team lead by example, based on their brand of "secret service." Most new hires at John Robert's seem to quickly adopt the teaming and service standards that are now tightly woven into the very fabric of the company. As Eric explained, "When someone comes in who really isn't a team player, they stick out like a sour thumb. In those rare instances, we make every effort to coach the employee and bring them into the fold." In the early years of John Robert's, Eric was training a new employee who didn't understand the benefits of teaming. After discussing her performance at several management meetings, Eric was on the verge of recommending her termination. But when he realized it was really his responsibility to coach and train new employees, Eric vowed to do everything he could to help her "turn the corner." And as Eric now proudly admits, "She's my 'go to girl.' She's the first one I turn to whenever I need help. She's the one I ask to coach any new employee that may be having problems with teaming. She even jokes about almost getting fired during her first few weeks on the job."

Today, it would be nearly impossible to begin a career at John Robert's without understanding the company's core values. And with a minimum of four interviews over time, each candidate has the opportunity to evaluate if and how those values mesh with his or her own. Only about 1 in 25 who apply will be hired. In John's words, "We want to make sure they are not just running up and down the street looking for the best deal. We don't hire from other salons." During the initial interview, candidates receive a list of the John Robert's nonnegotiables.

Service. Unless candidates are clients of John Robert's, they most likely do not understand what John Robert's service is all about. During their first interview, they'll hear a few powerful stories of exceptional customer service at John Robert's: a spa attendant who did some quick grocery shopping for an elderly client while she was receiving a spa treatment; an employee who picked up her client at home during bad weather; and many other examples of how John Robert's staff go the "extra mile" to make the client experience "magical."

These "magical moment" situations may not happen every day; however, the expected "secret service" for each and every client is "magical" by most salon standards. The client cycle begins with the *Pre Experience*, which occurs before the client enters the salon and involves a polite telephone conversation with an appointment taker who never rushes the conversation and who uses your name at least four times. (This not only makes the client feel good, but the repetition helps the employee memorize the client's name.) The next phase is called the *Start of the Experience*. Walking into John Robert's is like walking into no other salon. You are immediately greeted by a hostess who announces your arrival to the operator. The hostess neatly places your coat on a hanger, brings you a refreshment of your choosing, and addresses you by your name throughout the conversation. While the operator analyzes your needs and expectations, you receive a stress-relieving massage before your hair is meticulously shampooed and conditioned. Male clients also receive a mini-facial. Now you are ready for the *Service* phase. During this phase, your hair is cut and styled, your arms and hands are massaged, your jewelry is cleaned, and you are given an explanation of the products used with no pressure to buy. Woman clients will have their makeup touched up in the *Post Service* phase. Additional services and promotions are also explained to all clients during this phase. In the *Conclusion of Service* phase, clients have the opportunity to purchase products and schedule their next visits. During the *Post Experience*, clients receive a friendly phone call within 24 hours; a thank-you card within 48 hours; quarterly newsletters on a regular basis; and a card on their birthdays.

Education. John told us that the industry average for salon training is three hours per year per employee. John Robert's requires employees to receive over 200 hours of training each year. One morning each week, all John Robert's employees participate in training classes; and two days each year, employees are required to participate in special days of training (with pay).

Attendance. As John tells his employees, "In this industry, hairdressers are notorious for being late. At John Robert's, if you are 14 minutes early, you are a minute late." John does not want his hairdressers running into the shop minutes before their first appointments.

Transportation. All employees are expected to have reliable transportation to work.

Community Service. In John's words, "It's an oxymoron, but volunteering is mandatory at John Robert's. If that does not excite you and get your blood flowing, then maybe you are not the right fit. It doesn't mean you're wrong, but we like to attract people who try to practice world-class behaviors in the four areas of our lives: *Guest Service, Teamwork, Community Service, and Family.*"

Attitude. It's almost impossible to get fired at John Robert's for making an honest mistake. John claims that, "If you spill bleach on a women's fur jacket while coloring her hair, and it costs us $5,000 to replace it, you won't get fired. But, if you make a career out of being grumpy and you bring that attitude to work with you, you'll be out of here fast."

Pay. At the very first interview, the pay structure is explained to each prospective employee.

John told us that about half of those who interview at John Roberts find out the culture is not right for them. Some say, "Hey dude, all I want to do is cut some hair." Others say, "I thought you said this was going to be difficult . . . this is everything I have ever dreamed of."

John and Stacy truly believe that the "magical" client experience begins with a "magical" employee experience. John says it best: "Take my buildings, equipment, all my money, my land, but leave me my people and in one year, I will be back on top again."

Dare

Both John and Stacy came from modest backgrounds. Back in 1993, the financial risk alone was almost enough to deter them from realizing their dream of opening a salon. Stacy was overwhelmed thinking about their lack of funds, the potential of amassing debt, being a new mother and, on top of all this stress, running a salon. But after the initial shock wave had passed, John Robert's began to stabilize. The new employees had a client following, and John still had a dependable paycheck coming in from UPS. For a while, life was good. Six short weeks later, the chairs were all empty and the only employees left were Stacy and Cathy (John's sister). John started coming in after work to help save the company.

At that point, the safe move would have been to hire another group of hairdressers and hope for the best. But John had another plan. He came home one night and announced that he was going to quit his job at UPS and go to beauty school! This one-time college baseball player and well-paid truck driver was going to become a hairdresser. Stacy remembers, "When John first came into the business, I was not real thrilled. I asked him, 'What do you mean you're going to beauty school? You should be going to law school.'" After our original employees walked out, John thought that at the very least, he and Stacy could make a living in their two-chair shop without compromising their service values. Stacy says, "After he got his license (hairdresser's license), I don't think he realized how passionate he was about the industry, not the technical part, but the business part. Believe it or not, John is really good at haircutting and still cuts hair. After he came into the business, we really started cooking."

We do believe that John's energy, work ethic, and service mentality would be enough to catapult him to the top ranks of countless organizations. But John was born to be an entrepreneur. Like Walt Disney, John dared to follow his dream, and I think we can speak for the more than 30,000 John Robert's clients—we're glad he did!

Do

The teaming, the training, the obsession with "secret service," and the community volunteerism are all keys that have made John Robert's Spa so successful. And certainly, attention to detail is apparent throughout the organization. First-time visitors to John Robert's are given a white cape instead of the traditional black cape. Not only do most newcomers feel special with such treatment, but the employees also take care to turn these first-time guests into lifetime guests. The industry average for retaining new clientele is 35 percent; at John Robert's, it's nearly 70 percent.

It's the little things at John Robert's that people remember—from the scalp massage to the mini-facials to the jewelry cleaning to the between-visit bang trimmings—that translate into big returns. To the casual observer or penny-pinching accountant, greeters may seem like a needless extravagance. But John told us that their greeters are carefully trained to cross-sell services and introduce new products. The sale of one or two services a day will cover the salary of the greeter, but more importantly, the first 5 to 10 seconds in a salon sets the stage for the entire client experience. As Eric Hammond tells it, "You can get a haircut down the street for much less. You are coming to John Robert's for an experience."

And that experience is why John Robert's clients are loyal. They could easily book their next salon appointments at one of the other 30 salons within three miles of John Robert's largest facility and spend about half what they spend at John Robert's, but they choose not to. When they can feel pampered like superstars, why would they go anywhere else? And, in times of trials and tribulation, as was definitely the case on the afternoon of September 11, 2001, clients came to their special refuge from the storm. Many clients didn't even have an appointment that day. They just wanted to be where they felt safe and secure and, most of all, to be treated like family. This place is John Robert's.

Men's Wearhouse

Dream

When we first met George Zimmer, who was decked out in a sweater and jeans, sporting the "permanent" grey beard, and spewing out lines like "Mammals have the ability to detect authenticity in other mammals" in a gravelly voice, we could picture him as a distinguished professor of philosophy. But, when you see him with his employees on the dance floor at one of his annual Christmas parties, you might see him as an elder classman trying to resist dancing the night away. Admittedly, says George, "I'm an institution unto myself."[106] He is totally authentic. He's the kind of guy who engages you in his dream, no matter what he's doing. He was even able to engage his own father in his dream.

The story goes that when George Zimmer graduated with a degree in economics from Washington University in St. Louis, he joined his dad's apparel-manufacturing company based in Dallas. His first assignment was as a purchasing agent in Hong Kong. After returning to the United States, he sold clothes out of the back of a Buick Electra. One day, a customer wanted to return some unsold goods and vowed to purchase a large amount of another item as compensation. Zimmer's father, Robert, thought the request was unreasonable, but George felt it was important to their business to grant it. "George always took strong positions on things he felt deeply about," said Robert. Knowing that George's dream of starting the first Men's Wearhouse would require a $300,000 investment, this supportive father dutifully came to the plate with the needed cash. Today, Robert proudly sits on Men's Wearhouse board of directors. Brother Jimmy, a suit buyer and company advisor, as well as Richie Goldman, a good friend, philosopher, and image-maker, also became early partners who bought into the dream.

George was determined to create a shopping experience that was a whole lot of fun, not stuffy and "buttoned-down" as in the typical stores, shopping centers, and malls. George once told a group of executives that most men view suit shopping with the same enthusiasm as getting a root canal. From that first Houston-based store, George reinvented the suit-shopping experience and fashioned the company into North America's leading retailer of tailored men's clothing. And, after 30 years, the store at 6100 Westheimer in Houston, Texas, is still thriving!

When entrepreneurs are still in the dream stage of a new venture, necessity is the "mother of invention." Young Zimmer and his partners couldn't even afford a cash register in the early days, so they made use of a cigar box for several weeks. It came in handy on the very first day when the sales reached $3,000.

What has made George's dream come alive over the years—not only for himself, but for millions of others who hear his basso delivery of the simple but powerful phrase, "I guarantee it"—is the passion for his customers and for his employees. He exudes that personal commitment to "servant-leadership," leaders as servants, as business guru Robert Greenleaf penned in *The Servant as Leader* over three decades ago. Men's Wearhouse employees also become servant leaders, and they hold one another accountable to that end. They know that people enter their doors often with very little knowledge of buying suits, and yet they treat each customer as a unique individual who, like a friend, just stopped by for some good advice from someone who facilitates, not forces, a decision. George Zimmer's special brand of authentic "servant leadership" has always been critical to the success of Men's Wearhouse team, and it is now embedded into the company's total culture. "In business," as George Zimmer told us, "the degree to which you feel your boss and your colleagues are authentic is going to play a great part in how enthusiastically your employees strive to achieve the goals of the business."

Believe

It is one thing to say that believing in human potential is worthy of inclusion in a list of business values; it's quite another to live it. George believes that, "In order to be successful, you have to create an environment in which people are able to reach more of their potential more of the time."

The only way to achieve this is to care about your employees through consistent, and as George told us, "authentic" behaviors. "I wish every employee would have the opportunity to witness the agony that goes into making the decisions that affect their lives, primarily in George's office," says Eric Lane, recently retired president and COO.[107] According to Eric, there is a tremendous effort on the part of the entire senior management team to support the stores, a radical shift from the typical retail establishment. "In most organizations," Eric told us, "if you are a burned-out merchant, they put you 'out to pasture,' and that means in the stores." In contrast, Men's Wearhouse stores are the lifeblood of the company. As Shlomo Maor, associate vice president of training told us, "At one time I was a store manager, the highest position that we hired at that time. Then, I moved from there to district manager, and after that to regional manager. I found that I couldn't impact people every day, that they were too far away. Then I realized that I could do it by developing a training program. So I started 'Suits University' at one of our stores in Atlanta on a Sunday morning. I came in from 9 to 12 in the morning and worked with people who came to learn, all on a volunteer basis. What motivates me isn't money. What motivates me is when people tell me that a piece they learned in 'Suits U' helped them. I teach them all that they must work together and impact the sales of others. That's how you become successful."[108] That's servant leadership in action.

And certainly, the management believes in supporting and nurturing its employees. Management also believes that if employees support and nurture each other, those employees will, in turn, treat their customers accordingly. When it comes to customers, George Zimmer is like a mind reader who seems to be able to comprehend their psyches. As Eric Lane explained, "I can't tell you how many times I've been in George's office when we are walking through, for hours on end, a customer experience; when they come in the store, what should we say, how will they respond. It's all choreographed at the highest level."

Dare

Daring to go down a path untraveled...that was Walt Disney, and that is also George Zimmer. Why does Men's Wearhouse have lower turnover than nearly every other retail establishment? Perhaps it's that they view "having fun" as a definite must for avoiding boredom and stagnation, and they champion employees who create new rules. In the ranks of most other retail chains, either of those things could get you fired in an instant. But, George is legendary for his "Hippie culture" style, as Shlomo Maor puts it.

How many companies have a pool table where employees and vendors are encouraged to unwind from the pressures of their jobs? Even when the company was busting at the seams with growth in early 2000, "George sent out an edict saying 'the pool table stays,'" reports Doug Ewert, executive vice president of merchandizing. And how many retail companies buy Nerf balls, ping-pong paddles, putters, and golf balls for their employees, and yes, their customers, to play with? The expectation is that if employees are filled with positive "energy," that will translate into happy and loyal customers.

The level of trust may be best evidenced by the company's treatment of job applicants. Unlike most retailers, Men's Wearhouse does not require pre-employment drug screening or conduct criminal background checks on candidates. The whole hiring process might seem a bit crazy to some, but at Men's Wearhouse, there is an anticipation of a long-term relationship. This is anything but standard retail practice. Training methods at the company also fall right in line with their approach to nurturing employees. "I think this is one of the best investments a company can make, investing in their people and naturally allowing the way they're treated to trickle down from their people, toward their customers, which ultimately takes care of the bottom line of the business," asserts Shlomo Maor.

When employees feel cherished, they are often more willing to take risks without fear of repercussion. Pushing the limits at every level is expected behavior at Men's Wearhouse. As Eric Lane told us, "If everything in a store is selling, you know people aren't pushing the limits. They have tremendous autonomy to try things out, and they may fail." And when people fail at Men's Wearhouse, there is forgiveness, just as there is in a healthy marriage. They fix it and move on.

When it comes to pushing the limits, George Zimmer is the supreme role model at Men's Wearhouse. Recently, George invited Deepak Chopra to join the company's board of directors. The Chopra philosophy is grounded in holistic medicine that is intended to foster physical, emotional, and spiritual wellness. Zimmer believes that Chopra is a natural fit with his company mantra of people development, team-building, and community service.

Do

Richard Goldman, image maker at Men's Wearhouse once said, "Early on, George and I realized that whether you're a sales associate from Boise, Idaho, or the president of the company, we all come from families. So, we felt that if we could create an atmosphere that sort of felt like family, we'd be successful. For some people, the 'business family' takes the place of their family; for others, it enhances their existing families. We knew that to make sure your customers are treated right, we had to treat the people who work for the company right"—athough with over 500 stores and nearly 8,000 employees, George Zimmer isn't as much of a hands-on leader these days. He makes every effort, however, to see each employee in person once a year, and he continues to provide the resources and experiences for them to grow and strive for "self-actualization" (the final sentiment of Men's Wearhouse mission statement).

For company managers and wardrobe consultants alike, one of the most anticipated experiences of the year is summer training. In every company region, a few people from each store don their shorts and tee shirts and head for a resort where 24 hours of enrichment takes place, Men's Wearhouse–style. The intensive session is a combination of short training sessions, with games and activities such as beach volleyball, dancing, and poker. "It's like Groundhog Day (the movie) for those of us who lead these sessions," comments Doug Ewert. "You start all over again four or five days in a row in a region for six weeks. We will not cut these motivating training sessions . . . that will be the last stuff to go."[109]

It's no wonder that Men's Wearhouse has some of the finest retail sales-people in the world. Entitled "What We Do," the following is written in company-recruiting bulletins: "*We are always looking for great people to fill our openings for Wardrobe Consultants in all of our markets. If you would enjoy working as an integrated member of a team, focused on helping people dress well and feel good about themselves, this position is a good fit for you.*" As George Zimmer has often said, "We are really in the people business, we just happen to have clothing on our racks." And, this is a man who clearly understands his business.

Epilogue

The Magic Continues

*Well, after 40 some odd years in the business, my greatest reward,
I think, is I've been able to build this wonderful organization . . . also
to have the public appreciate and accept what I've done all these
years—that is a great reward.*[110]

Walt Disney

From a young boy's doodling to a worldwide empire with a host of magical characters that are instantly recognizable by both children and adults—this is The Walt Disney Company's legend and legacy.

Would Walt recognize his brainchild as it is today? The physical plant has greatly expanded, of course. Disneyland now offers The California Adventure; and Walt Disney World, which didn't open until after Walt died, is now composed of four separate parks, including the newest and highly celebrated Animal Kingdom. And Disneyland Paris, Walt Disney Studios Park, Tokyo Disneyland, Tokyo DisneySea, and Hong Kong Disneyland illustrate the company's international reach. The Disney Cruise Line, Disney Vacation Club, ABC, and Broadway stage shows exemplify the variety of business activities that make up today's Walt Disney Company.

Yet chances are that Walt would feel right at home. That's because the culture and traditions he established—his dreams, his beliefs, his goals, and his style of managing the business — provided the direction that makes The Walt Disney Company one of the most admired companies in the world. The "good show" mentality, which dictates pulling out all the stops to exceed guest expectations and which demands superior performance from everyone, holds as much sway now as it did when Walt Disney first decreed it.

That The Walt Disney Company manages continually to top itself and delight the world with its magic year after year, decade after decade, is a tribute to its leadership, both past and present. Part of Walt Disney's greatness was that he laid down a solid foundation of beliefs and values, including a standard of performance excellence and a mechanism (Disney University) for inculcating his cast members with these values.

Committed to Beliefs

The spectacle, the excitement, the breadth of product—all of these things contribute to the legend. Yet if there is one thing that keeps people coming back, it is the consistency of the experience. The Walt Disney Company is the master at creating controlled environments that never disappoint. Because the company goes to great lengths to communicate its beliefs and traditions to every cast member, the Disney product offers people a comforting familiarity that is hard to duplicate in today's fast-paced world. That's not to say that there are no surprises, merely that all the surprises are on the upside.

Disney's insistence that customers be treated like guests continues to be of paramount importance in providing that always-positive, expectation-exceeding experience. Thus a visitor to any of the theme parks will find that a question is answered as pleasantly today as it would have been in the Disneyland of the 1950s and 1960s. Cast members are never too busy to stop and chat with guests; crowd control is performed with a smile; and lost children are pampered with small pleasures. The human touch is still very much in evidence.

Yet without a corresponding belief in and commitment to employees, the customer philosophy would soon flounder. The two go together, as the song says, like a horse and carriage, and you can't have one without the other.

Maintaining the company's focus amid enormous growth—the number of employees has more than tripled since 1984—requires that Disney be ever more vigilant about recognizing the significant role that each cast member plays and then emphasizing that all the pieces are needed to ensure the success of the entire team. By making cast members feel that their input makes a difference, Disney inspires further contributions.

Despite a decade of boardroom turmoil, honesty, reliability, loyalty, and respect for the individual are as much a part of the Disney culture today as they were in Walt's day. And the way the company sees it, living those beliefs still means working hard to exceed a guest's expectations and always delivering the "good show." What's more, if customers are the reason for being, it naturally follows that *everyone*—cast members, partners, suppliers, and so on—must be united in their effort to reach the goal. This is the *Believe* principle in action.

Thriving on Challenge

One of the initial decisions that Michael Eisner and Frank Wells made in the 1980s involved approval of the script for the decidedly "un-Disneylike" *Down and Out in Beverly Hills,* an R-rated film far removed from the studio's typical family-oriented offerings. The studio had already begun to move gingerly away from its traditional fare before Eisner and Wells arrived on the scene, but with the exception of *Splash,* no movie produced by the previous management had been a hit. The early successes of *Down and Out in Beverly Hills, Ruthless People,* and a series of other film releases proved that like Walt, the team of Eisner and Wells had uncanny instincts for what audiences wanted.

After Wells's death on Easter Sunday 1994, one of Eisner's most daring moves, and one that left both critics and competitors sputtering, was the 1996 acquisition of Capital Cities/ABC for $18.9 billion. The marriage, which cemented a relationship that began when ABC helped Walt Disney open Disneyland in 1955, silenced critics who had questioned whether Eisner had the nerve to make a really big acquisition.

In another gutsy move, Eisner chose to renovate a seedy theater in New York's bawdy Times Square area and to bring *The Lion King* to Broadway. At the time the commitment was made, no one could say for sure that a neighborhood known for its sex shops and drug trafficking could be successfully transformed. The musical has been sold out since opening and long ago recouped its estimated $20 to $25 million production cost.

Eisner made another bold departure from Disney tradition by sinking $800 million into the construction of Disney's Animal Kingdom at Walt Disney World, which opened in April 1998. "It's basically anti-Disney," Joe Rohde, creative executive with Walt Disney Imagineering and lead designer of Disney's Animal Kingdom in charge of the park, said in an *I.D.* magazine interview.[111] Not only does the 540-acre park feature live animals instead of the much more easily controlled animated ones, but it also strips away illusion in a fashion totally uncharacteristic of Disney.

That's not to say, however, that there is *no* illusion. Disney is still in the business of creating magic, and the artfully crafted African savanna created out of Florida scrub has its quotient of illusion. But the very nature of a venue populated by 1,000 animals means that the experience can't be tightly orchestrated in typical Disney style. If reviews are any measure, however, this daring new mix of reality and entertainment is meeting with typical Disney success.

A willingness to take calculated risks on innovative ideas means nothing if a company doesn't have what it takes to follow through in the execution of those ideas. Disney has maintained its founder's firm belief that execution requires extensive training, planning, communicating, and paying attention to detail.

The renowned Disney training program still turns out cast members who are thoroughly prepared for their roles. So successful is the program, in fact, that Disney now markets its methods to other organizations. And if planning and attention to detail are wanted, one need only look at the eight years of planning and $800 million worth of attention to detail that went into the Animal Kingdom—details so convincing that the South African ambassador to the United States was quoted in *Time* magazine as saying, "This is the bush veldt. This is my home."[112]

The newly anointed "keeper of the keys," Bob Iger, is not shy about accepting a challenge. Within the first six months of his role as CEO, he nego-tiated a deal to purchase Pixar and announced that Disney will partner with Apple to provide downloaded video content for Apple's popular iPods.

But perhaps nothing so thoroughly evidences the strength of Disney's execution as its unrivaled talent for synergy. As an analyst once told Kathryn Harris of the *Los Angeles Times*, "This is a great company in an operating sense . . . they've gotten everything out of the mouse but the squeak."[113]

Thus, a new film begets an absolute deluge of new marketing possibili-ties, from domestic and international home videos and network and foreign television runs to pay-per-view and cable offerings.

And that's just the beginning. Next comes new theme park rides and char-acters, new products for Disney retail partners (toys, clothing, books, games, records, CD-ROMs), new television spinoffs, iPod downloads, and program-ming ideas for Disney's radio networks. Animated features become live-action films—like *101 Dalmatians*—or Broadway stage shows such as *The Lion King, Beauty and the Beast,* and soon, *The Little Mermaid.*

Once the company decides to pursue a new idea, it immediately com-municates that information to every segment of the company that might be able to exploit it in every other potential market or product. This notion of cross-pollination has become a major driver of the company's profitability.

Lessons in Leadership

It has been our pleasure to get to know the leaders and staffs of our featured organizations and discover their own Dream, Believe, Dare, Do magic.

All are industry icons that set a standard by which others in their fields should be judged. For example, the dramatic results of the Downtown School illustrate the need for a dramatic paradigm shift in the American educational system. Why is it that over the past 20 years, with the countless reports citing the failure of our schools, few school districts have made an effort to rectify the situation? It has often been said of education, "If this was a profit and loss business, it would either change or die." As Des Moines Business Alliance board president, Art Wittmack, said, "Businesses have long said, 'Leave education to the educators; we'll just take the product.' Clearly the laissez-faire mentality of 'We'll let the legislature or the school board to address these issues' has not been successful in the past."[114] Then it hit us—the trouble with U.S. education is not unlike the trouble with typical U.S. customer service: both are rooted in apathy and a "that's someone else's problem" mentality.

The University of Michigan business school's National Quality Research Center compiles and analyzes the American Customer Service Index (ASCI). This study began in 1994 when the index for the retail sector was close to 75 percent, then 11 years later at 73.5 percent. Over the past 20 years, many other authors have revealed their disdain for the state of customer service in America. It still amazes us that even though Disney has been the "poster child" for "be our guest" service since the opening of Disneyland in 1955, painfully few companies have been inspired to emulate Disney's culture. Yet, when Dell introduces the latest and greatest new feature on one of its computers, within 60 days, the HP engineers are able to incorporate their version of the feature into their own products. They are able to take apart a Dell computer and discover the secret. Yet, every day, The Walt Disney Company is wide open, and thousands of people around the world can actually see the "secret"—treat customers like guests in their own homes. They do this in front of the whole world, but few get it!

Our featured organizations masterfully apply Walt Disney's definition of leadership to grow and nurture their cultures: "The ability to *establish* and *manage a creative climate* in which individuals and teams are *self-motivated* to the successful achievement of *long-term goals* in an environment of *mutual trust and respect.*" There are many striking leadership similarities between our featured organizations. Let's consider the key elements of Walt's definition beginning with "establish". Like Walt, each of our leaders established or changed their organizations to create "magical moments" for their guests: an upscale casual dining adventure offering 200-plus menu choices; a truly unique five-star hotel experience based on The Golden Rule; a financial services firm where the staff cares for the client and the firm cares for the staff; a hospital that is patient-centered rather than physician-centered; a clothing store where wardrobe consultants live the "I Guarantee It" philosophy; a school where students take accountability for their own learning; a spa with "the Norm factor"—where everybody knows your name. As diverse as these organizations are, they all have a common thread—leaders who "dreamed" of a building something unique that differentiated them from their competition; "believed" in the value of their people; "dared" to take risks along the way; and then just "did it!"

The next key in Walt's definition of leadership is "*manage a creative climate.*" Walt defined managing as "developing your people through their work and at the same time having fun." Walt believed that leaders are responsible for developing and training people and providing them with the tools to succeed. All of our featured organizations are passionate about providing opportunities for their employees to increase their competencies. Ernst & Young has even achieved national recognition for its training, currently ranking as number three on *Training* magazine's Top 100 list. Aside from "hard skills" training, our featured organizations are among the best at placing "soft skills" training at the forefront of their cultural initiatives. They all provide an orientation experience in which employees become immersed in their respective cultures and, upon "graduation," are energized and self-motivated to live the vision and values of their organizations. It is also important to note that in each of these organizations, *fun* is not a dirty word. Sure, everyone has those days when everything seems to go wrong—when deadlines pile up, or when you wish you had called in to report that you were "sick." But as one person told us, "I don't always like my job when I go home at night, but I am always excited to get back at it in the morning." When employees truly embrace the values of the organization, they not only feel a sense of pride but can also experience the freedom to be themselves ... and yes, have fun.

Let's consider the meaning of "self-motivated". All these leaders have realized that when properly trained, their employees can and should be making decisions to create those special moments for their customers. Be it the door-man at Four Seasons, or the hairdresser at John Robert's, or the manager at Ernst & Young—they all know that management has entrusted them with one of the most important elements of any business: the customer experience. An empowered workforce is a self-motivated workforce.

Like Disney, our featured organizations have a working definition of "long-term" that speaks volumes about culture. In the typical company, *long-term* thinking relates to a strategic objective for adding products, services, and perhaps new locations. Companies such as Four Seasons and The Cheesecake Factory define *long-term* thinking in terms of values and beliefs upon which their growth is based. They go to great lengths to ensure that their cultures can support new ventures and still remain true to their credos.

Arguably the most important part of Walt's leadership definition is *"mutual respect and trust."* Without exception, these two values represent a common thread woven through each of these organizations from The Cheesecake Factory's five-year profit-sharing programs that rival many 30-year retirement plans, to the Downtown School's teachers who never raise their voices in anger in their classrooms, to Ernst & Young's "People First" philosophy, to Four Seasons Hotels' Golden Rule strategy, to Griffin Hospital employees' willingness to risk their jobs to retain their cherished leader, to John Robert's relationship with the patients and families of Cleveland's Children's Hospital, to Men's Wearhouse leaders who take responsibility when their employees fail.

Since the dawn of our new century, these seven organizations have cemented their "best practices" success. We believe that Walt Disney would be proud of their many accomplishments and especially for the proof that there is still magic in his original credo: Dream, Believe, Dare, Do.

In Tune with the Nation

Disney thrives on the business of making magic. Success of the magnitude Disney has achieved always brings out the critics and the fear-mongers, those who cry that the company is too powerful and wields too much influence in our society. But investors don't share the angst; for the past 20 years, they have driven the price of the company's stock higher and beat the S&P performance by over threefold. They sense that The Walt Disney Company has its finger firmly on the pulse of the nation, indeed the world.

There may be some disagreement as to whether the public's blood is pumping with longing for a return to the old-fashioned values of family, hard work, and excellence that Disney symbolizes, or whether a public preference for escapism is at the heart of Disney's popularity. (No one, by the way, disputes that the escapes Disney constructs are anything short of magnificent.) In any event, the crowds that flock to virtually every Disney venue would seem to bear out the assessment that Disney surely has the Midas touch, whatever its source.

Walt Disney's legacy, then, flourishes at the astonishing institution called The Walt Disney Company. Like our nation, it is a restless enterprise, always seeking new and better ways to entertain its audiences, to put on the good show.

What's more, every dream continues to be achieved with a management style that remains true to Disney's original vision: a firm belief in core values backed up by hard work from a well-trained and dedicated team that relentlessly strives for perfection. The company today is a vital, living monument to the enduring power of Walt's way.

We have examined the four principles that make up the Disney management style in separate chapters for the sake of our book's organization, but it is their integration and interplay that work to change companies. As you envision their implementation in your company, think in terms of a holistic integration and imagine the benefits to be derived.

For example, giving employees a chance to dream and to express their creativity not only reinforces their value as people, but also inspires them to bring forth innovative ideas from which the company can draw. By the same token, a firm set of organizational beliefs not only ensures consistency in operations, but also encourages all parties—coworkers, partners, suppliers—to work cooperatively to further those beliefs.

Unshakable convictions, in turn, nourish the self-assurance and confidence in one's instincts that are needed to overcome a fear of risk-taking. Daring to take risks encourages still further creativity and maintains the vibrancy of an organization. It creates a sense of fun and adventure that inspires individuals and teams to reach higher and work harder. And in the end, the factors that make it possible to follow through and turn the dreams into reality—that is, training, planning, communicating, and attention to detail—all double back to promote more creativity, more concern for customers, and more commitment to teamwork.

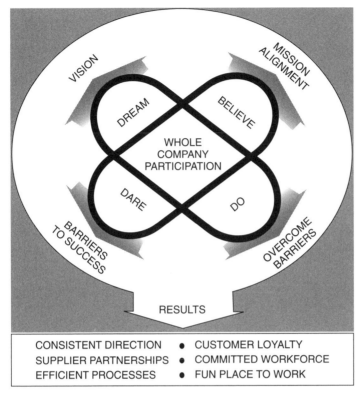

Figure E-1. The Dream, Believe, Dare, Do Process

We see the cycle as one that constantly reinforces itself, and we believe that by incorporating the basic elements of the Disney management technique, every organization can lift itself out of the ranks of the ordinary. Figure E-1 shows it all in simple graphic form. Ask the questions and take the actions as outlined in these chapters. And most of all—make your *Dreams* come true, *Believe* in yourself and your team, *Dare* to make a difference, and then . . . just *Do* it!

Appendix

The Cheesecake Factory
Standing Ovations (Awards)

- 2006—*Hale Aina* magazine: Best Dessert Menu Gold Metal.
- 2005—*Nation's Restaurant News:* Menu Masters Hall of Fame.
- 2005—*Las Vegas Review Journal:* Best Dessert.
- R&I Consumer's Choice in Chains Crystal Award.
- 2003—*Nation's Restaurant News:* Grand Lux Café named for "Hot Concepts."
- 2003—*Restaurants and Institutions* magazine: named founder David Overton as "Executive of the Year."
- 2003—*Restaurants and Institutions* magazine: Choice in Chains— Casual DiningGuest Satisfaction Award for the second consecutive year.
- 2003—*Nation's Restaurant News:* Menu Masters Award—Corporate Chef, Robert Okura honored with the "Chef Innovator Award" for his outstanding contributions to foodservice research and development.
- 2003—*Nation's Restaurant News:* The NRN 50: R&D Culinarians Corporate Chef Robert Okura awarded the title of "one of the top 50 Research and Development Culinarians" in the country.
- 2003—*Cheers Magazine:* "Cheers Award" for Beverage Excellence; "Best Spirits Program"; Russell Greene, vice president of beverage and

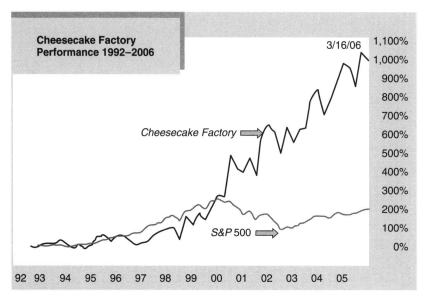

Figure A-1. The Cheesecake Factory financial performance

bakery operations honored with the "Best Spirits Program" award, which recognizes outstanding beverage programs, cutting-edge creativity, and efforts that set the beverage standards for the rest of the industry.

- 2003—14th Annual Elliot "Motivator of the Year" Award: Heidi Martin Gilanfar, vice president of recruitment. This award was developed to recognize those individuals who are pioneering the way and setting new standards of excellence in the area of human resources.

Business Summary

- 105 full-service, casual dining restaurants under The Cheesecake Factory® name in major metropolitan areas in the United States.
- Grand Lux Cafe®, an upscale, casual dining restaurant concept with locations in Las Vegas, Chicago, Los Angeles, Dallas, Houston, Garden City, New York, and Sunrise, Florida.
- One self-service, limited menu "express" foodservice operation under The Cheesecake Factory Express® mark inside the DisneyQuest® family entertainment center in Orlando, Florida.
- Two bakery production facilities. The Company also licenses two bakery cafes under The Cheesecake Factory Bakery Cafe®.

For financial performance see Figure A-1.

Downtown School
Standing Ovations (Awards)

- 1999—*Working Mother* magazine: named one of the "10 Best Schools for Today's Families."
- 1997—National Center for Community Education recognized in their publication Community Schools Across the Nation: 135 Community/School Partnerships that Are Making a Difference.
- 1996—The governor of Iowa presented the school with the statewide F.I.N.E., First in the Nation in Education award.
- 1994—Community Solutions for Education award sponsored by the Coalition on Education Initiatives and *USA Today* for grass roots programs which improve learning opportunities for young people through comprehensive community involvement.

Business Summary

- Began in 1993 with 45 students.
- 2005–2006 school year: 271 students with almost 900 on a waiting list.
- National 2005 average of fourth and fifth grade children reading at or above grade level was 30 percent as reported by the National Assessment of Educational Progress and *Education Week* magazine; Downtown School goal is 90 percent of their students at or above grade level; they have reported 89 percent above grade level and 8 percent at grade level as they enter middle school.
- National 2005 average forth and fifth grade math scores at or above grade level was 35 percent as reported by the National Assessment of Educational Progress and *Education Week* magazine; at Downtown School 75 percent exceed grade level.

Ernst & Young
Standing Ovations (Awards)

- 2006—*Fortune* magazine's "Top 100 Companies to Work for" in the United States for the eighth consecutive year.
- 2006—*Training* magazine's "Top 100," third place out of over 500 entries; the fifth year in a row the firm has been honored for their commitment to a vast array of learning and development initiatives in support of its people.

- 2005—(November) "Most Admired Knowledge Enterprise Award;" The KNOW Network, a community of leading knowledge-based organizations dedicated to networking, benchmarking, and sharing best knowledge practices, named Ernst & Young one of its "20 Most Admired Knowledge Enterprises" award winners for the eighth year in a row. Recipients were chosen by an international panel of Fortune Global 500 senior executives and leading knowledge management experts. Ernst & Young is also a member of the MAKE Hall of Fame.
- 2004—(September) *Working Mother* magazine's "100 Best Companies in the United States" for the seventh consecutive year; and the eighth year overall that Ernst & Young has earned a spot on *Working Mother* magazine's list of "100 Best Companies for Working Mothers."
- 2003—(August) CFO magazine Accounting Services "Firm of the Year" in Australia; the award recognized Ernst & Young's commitment to quality and leadership, particularly their role in influencing the debate on International Accounting Standards and Corporate Governance.

Business Summary

- Ernst & Young provides a broad array of services relating to audit and risk-related services, tax advisory, and tax reporting services.
- 107,000 people in 140 countries.
- $16.9 billion in 2004 revenues as reported by *Forbes* magazine.

Four Seasons Hotels & Resorts

Standing Ovations (Awards)

- 2006—Nineteen Four Seasons properties won the AAA Five Diamond Awards.
- 2006—Nine Four Seasons properties received the Mobil Five-Star award.
- 2006—*Fortune* magazine's "100 Best Companies to Work For" in the United States for the ninth consecutive year; Four Seasons ranked number 28 among leading employers in the United States.
- 2005—Andrew Harper's *Hideaway* reports 24th Annual Survey of The World's Best Hotels, Resorts & Hideaways: Four Seasons Hotel

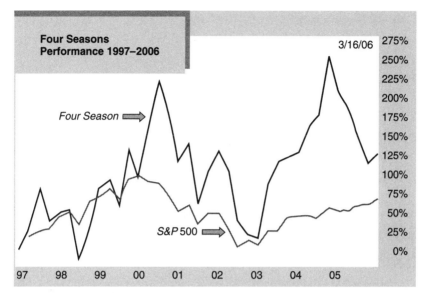

Figure A-2. Four Seasons Hotels & Resorts financial performance

George V Paris named "Top International City Hotel" for five consecutive years.

- 2005—Andrew Harper's *Hideaway* reports Four Seasons properties captured four of the "Top 20 U.S. Hotels"; three of the "Top 20 U.S. Resorts"; three of the "Top 20 International Hotels."
- 2005—*Condé Nast Traveler* reported that of the 20 hotel and resort categories, Four Seasons had 14 properties nominated in the top three positions.
- 2005—Ranked highest in the luxury hotel segment for the second consecutive year in the J.D. Power and Associates North America Hotel Guest Satisfaction Index Study.
- 2005—Awarded the Association of Fundraising Professionals (AFP) Greater Toronto Chapter Outstanding Philanthropist Award.
- 2005—Awarded The Conference Board of Canada Honorary Associate Award.
- 2005—Awarded the American Lodging Investment Summit (ALIS) Lifetime Achievement Award.
- 2005—(February 2) The *Wall Street Journal:* "Four Seasons—The grandfather of global luxury-hotel chains, from New York to Jakarta. Sets the standards the other chains aim for. . . ."
- 2005—(April) Clemmie Hambro, *Tatler:* "If God is in the details, then God is currently residing in Four Seasons."

- 2003—Awarded the Ontario Ernst & Young "Entrepreneur of the Year" Program's Lifetime Achievement Award.

Business Summary

- Portfolio of 70 luxury hotels and resort properties.
- 17,300 guest rooms.
- Located in 31 countries in North America, the Caribbean, Europe, Asia, Australia, the Middle East, and South America.

For financial performance see Figure A-2.

Griffin Hospital

Standing Ovations (Awards)

- 2006—*Fortune* magazine's "Top 100 Companies to Work For" in the United States ranked Griffin Hospital fourth. It is the highest ranking ever achieved by a hospital. Griffin is the only hospital in the country to be named to the prestigious list seven times.
- 2006—Griffin Hospital president Patrick Charmel received the John D. Thompson Distinguished Visiting Fellow Award at Yale University. The fellowship is to bring leaders in health administration to Yale's public health school to share their career experiences.
- 2004—Total Benchmark Solutions awarded Griffin Hospital the "Top 100" Quality Award. The award is based on analysis of data related to Heart Attack Care, Heart Failure Care, and Pneumonia Care provided to the Centers for Medicare and Medicaid Services (CMS) by U.S. hospitals.

Business Summary

- 160-bed not-for-profit hospital.
- 1,240 employees.
- In 2000 Griffin acquired Planetree (known for helping other hospitals "personalize, humanize, and demystify the health-care experience"), which now has 103 members, including New York Presbyterian Medical Center, Hackensack University Medical Center, and hospitals in Canada and the Netherlands.

John Robert's Spa
Standing Ovations (Awards)

- 2006—*Salon Today* magazine selected John Robert's as one of the "Top 20 Salons in America."
- Ernst & Young's "Entrepreneur of the Year Award": John DiJulius.
- Selected as one of the "Top 100 businesses" in Cleveland for six consecutive years.
- Voted the "Best Salon" in Cleveland.
- John Robert's was selected as one of the "Top 99 Best Companies to Work For" in Northeast Ohio for four consecutive years.
- A two-time Pillar Award winner for outstanding community service in Northeast Ohio.
- NEO Success Award for top performing companies in Northeast Ohio for five continuous years.
- Won the prestigious Northeast Ohio's Training and Development Leadership Award for the excellent training programs they have developed.
- 2000—*Crain's* Cleveland magazine named John DiJulius as one of the "Top 40 under 40" (CEOs under 40).

Business Summary

- Innovative health and beauty facilities; three locations in the greater Cleveland metropolitan area.
- 140 employees.
- Over 30,000 clients.
- Approaching $5 million in annual sales.

Men's Wearhouse
Standing Ovations (Awards)

- 2006—*Fortune* magazine's "100 Best Companies to Work For" in the United States for the third time.
- For the past five years, Men's Wearhouse has been donating men's clothing and free alterations and hosting clothing drives and volunteering for two organizations: Working Wardrobes in Orange County

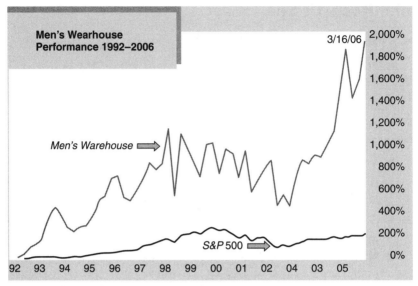

Figure A-3. Men's Wearhouse performance

California and Career Geer in New York. Their missions are to provide a path for men and women in need to achieve self-sufficiency through job-readiness and life skills workshops, personal grooming, and job networking services.

- Men's Wearhouse gives each of its stores a donation budget. This provides its employees the opportunity to support local organizations that they know and trust.

Business Summary

- Specialty retailer of men's suits.
- U.S. operations included 593 retail stores in 44 states under the brand name Men's Wearhouse and K&G.
- Canadian operations included 114 retail stores in 10 provinces under the brand name Moores Clothing for Men.
- 10,757 employees.

For financial performance see Figure A-3.

Notes

1. Bob Thomas. *Walt Disney: An American Original,* New York, Pocket Books, 1976, p. 86.
2. Interview with George Zimmer, founder and CEO, Men's Wearhouse, August 2001.
3. Interview with Scott Stevenson, president, Telecommunications Association of Michigan, February 2006.
4. Interview with Richard Benn, vice president, program development, CMA Canada, February 2006.
5. Interview with Regina Samy, vice president, Windsor Capital Group, February 2006.
6. Joe McGowan, Peter Schneider, and Joyce E. Davis. "How Disney Keeps Ideas Coming," *Fortune,* April 1, 1996.
7. Interview with Patrick Charmel, CEO, Griffin Hospital, July 2001.
8. Interview with Cathy Higgins, nurse, Griffin Hospital, July 2001.
9. *Walt Disney's Famous Quotes,* The Walt Disney Company, 1994, p. 43.
10. Mike Vance. "Managing by Values," *Creative Thinking* (audiotape series), Chicago, Nightingale Conant Corporation.
11. "The Quiet American," *The Economist,* November 8, 1997, p. 76.
12. Van Arsdale France. *Window on Main Street: 35 Years of Creating Happiness at Disneyland Park,* Nashua, NH, Laugher Publications, Inc./Stabur Press, Inc., 1991, p. 83.

13. Van Arsdale France. *Window on Main Street: 35 Years of Creating Happiness at Disneyland Park,* Nashua, NH, Laugher Publications, Inc./ Stabur Press Inc., 1991, p. 83.

14. *People Management,* Walt Disney World Company Seminar Productions, Lake Buena Vista, Florida, 1986.

15. Interview with Gerald Wilhite, general manager, Abbey Press, March 2006.

16. Interview with Isadore Sharp, CEO, Four Seasons Hotels & Resorts, September 2001.

17. *Walt Disney's Famous Quotes,* The Walt Disney Company, 1994, p. 9.

18. Interview with John Young, retired executive vice president, Human Resources, Four Seasons Hotels & Resorts, September 2001.

19. "Stranger within Our Gates," as told to us by John Dunn, chairman and CEO, Dunn Hospitality, March 2006.

20. Interview with Patrick Charmel, CEO, Griffin Hospital, July 2001.

21. Interview with William Powanda, vice president, Griffin Hospital, March 2006.

22. Interview with Susan Frampton, president, Planetree, July 2001.

23. *Walt Disney's Famous Quotes,* The Walt Disney Company, 1994, p. 88.

24. *Walt Disney's Famous Quotes,* The Walt Disney Company, 1994, p. 90.

25. Interview with Doug Ludwig, former CFO and executive vice president, Four Seasons Hotels & Resorts, September 2001.

26. Thomas J. Allen, Jr. *Managing the Flow of Technology,* Cambridge, MA, The MIT Press, 1977, pp. 234–265.

27. "Time Based Competiton" (video with workbook), Harvard Business School Management Programs, 1993, p. 8.

28. Alfie Kohn. *No Contest: The Case Against Competition,* Boston, Houghton Mifflin, 1992, p. 47.

29. Alfie Kohn. *No Contest: The Case Against Competition,* Boston, Houghton Mifflin, 1992, pp. 47–48.

30. Kenneth Shouler. "King of the Garden," *Home Cigar Aficionado,* 1998, p. 5.

31. Dr. William Cross. "Changing Management Styles," WNIN TV appearance, Evansville, Indiana, August 1993.

32. Interview with George Zimmer, founder and CEO, Men's Wearhouse, August 2001.

33. Customer Service Track Team Report, Bristol-Myers Squibb–Mead Johnson Nutritional Division, 1994.

34. Interview with Eric Hammond, director of operations, John Robert's Spa, April 2006.
35. Interview with Ginny Little, patient, Rainbow Babies, Cleveland, OH, September 2001.
36. Interview with Jennifer Kinn, employee, Rainbow Babies, Cleveland, OH, September 2001.
37. Interview with Felisha Makris, employee, John Robert's Spa, September 2001.
38. Interview with Max Byfuglin, president, The Cheesecake Factory Bakery, Inc., August 2001.
39. Interview with Steve Schaaf, president, Des Moines Business/Education Alliance, September 2001.
40. Interview with Jan Drees, executive director, Des Moines Business/ Education Alliance and retired principal, Downtown School, Des Moines, September 2001.
41. Interview with Roger Brooks, CFO, AmerUs, September 2001.
42. Interview with Tracy Donovan, teacher, Downtown School, Des Moines, September 2001.
43. Alex Tayor III and Joyce E. Davis, "Iacocca's Minivan," *Fortune,* May 30, 1994.
44. Interview with George Zimmer, founder and CEO, Men's Wearhouse, August 2001.
45. Interview with Terry Dischinger, Dischinger Orthodontics, February 2006.
46. Michael D. Eisner. "Letter to Shareholders," *The Walt Disney Company Annual Report,* 1997.
47. Interview with Phil Laskawy, retired chairman, Ernst & Young, September 2001.
48. Interview with Jim Turley, chairman and CEO, Ernst & Young, September 2001.
49. Interview with Jim Freer, vice chairman of human resources, Ernst & Young, September 2001.
50. Interview with Deborah Holmes, director, Center for the New Workforce, Ernst & Young, September 2001.
51. Interview with Jim Speros, chief marketing officer, Ernst & Young, September 2001.
52. Walt Disney. *People Management,* Walt Disney World Company Seminar Productions, Lake Buena Vista, Florida, 1986.

53. Interview with Jan Drees, executive director, Des Moines Business/Education Alliance and retired principal, Downtown School, Des Moines, September 2001.

54. Interview with Judi Cunningham, executive director, elementary and early childhood programs, Des Moines Public Schools, September 2001.

55. *People Management,* Walt Disney World Company Seminar Productions, Lake Buena Vista, Florida, 1986.

56. Robert Stallings. Interview with Bill Capodagli, Evansville, Indiana, 1991.

57. Special Conference Report: National Catholic Development Conference, "Offer Donors a Chance for Greatness," *Fund-Raising Management,* November 1992, p. 20.

58. Viktor Frankl. *Man's Search for Meaning,* New York, Simon and Schuster, Touchstone Books, 1984, p. 75.

59. Mary Walton. *The Deming Management Method,* New York, The Putnam Publishing Group, 1986, p. 195.

60. C. S. Hall and G. Lindzey. *Theories of Personality,* 3rd ed., New York, John Wiley and Sons, 1978, p. 64.

61. Valerie Oberle. *The Disney Approach to Quality Service,* Walt Disney World Company Seminar Productions, Lake Buena Vista, Florida, November 1995.

62. Interview with Shlomo Maor, associate vice president, Training, Men's Wearhouse, August 2001.

63. Interview with Eric Anderson, director, Training, Men's Wearhouse, August 2001.

64. *Foundations of Leadership,* Walt Disney World Company Seminar Productions, Lake Buena Vista, Florida, October 13, 1996.

65. Interview with David Overton, chairman and CEO, The Cheesecake Factory, August 2001.

66. Interview with Linda Candioty, retired executive vice president and company secretary, The Cheesecake Factory, August 2001.

67. Interview with Peter D'Amelio, president and COO, The Cheesecake Factory Restaurant Division, August 2001.

68. Disney Imagineers. *Walt Disney Imagineering: A Behind the Dreams Look at Making the Magic Real,* New York, Hyperion, 1996, p. 51.

69. David Hardy. "Think Out of the Box," *Personnel Psychology,* Winter 1996, pp. 1036–1039.

70. Interview with John DiJulius, cofounder, John Robert's Spa, March 2006.

71. National Healthcare Association Retreat, New York, June 2003.

72. Dick Nunis. *The Disney Approach to Quality Service,* Walt Disney World Company Seminar Productions, Lake Buena Vista, Florida, November 1995.

73. E. J. Dionne, Jr. "Chattering Class," *The Washington Post Magazine,* December 29, 1996, p. W2.

74. *Walt Disney's Famous Quotes,* The Walt Disney Company, 1994, p. 33.

75. Joe McGowan, Peter Schneider, and Joyce E. Davis, "How Disney Keeps Ideas Coming," *Fortune,* April 1, 1996.

76. Interview with Jeff Merhige, executive director, YMCA Camp Kern, March 2006

77. Dr. William Cross. "Changing Management Styles," WNIN TV appearance, Evansville, Indiana, August 1993.

78. Interview with David Overton, chairman and CEO, The Cheesecake Factory, August 2001.

79. Interview with Peter D'Amelio, president and COO, The Cheesecake Factory Restaurant Division, August 2001.

80. Interview with Robert O'Kura, vice president, R&D, The Cheesecake Factory, August 2001.

81. Interview with David Overton, chairman and CEO, The Cheesecake Factory, August 2001.

82. Interview with Linda Candioty, retired executive vice president and company secretary, The Cheesecake Factory, August 2001.

83. Interview with Peter D'Amelio, president and COO, The Cheesecake Factory Restaurant Division, August 2001.

84. Interview with Max Byfuglin, president, The Cheesecake Factory Bakery, Inc., August 2001.

85. Interview with Mary Lou Daley, retired school board member, Des Moines Public Schools, September 2001.

86. Interview with Renee Harmon, assistant principal, Downtown School, Des Moines, September 2001.

87. Interview with Jan Drees, executive director, Des Moines Business/ Education Alliance and retired principal, Downtown School, Des Moines, September 2001 and April 2006.

88. Alan M. Webber. *Fast Company,* May 2002, pp. 130-134.

89. Interview with Jim Freer, vice chairman of human resources, Ernst & Young, September 2001.

90. Interview with Jim Turley, chairman and CEO, Ernst & Young, September 2001.

91. Interview with Phil Laskawy, retired chairman, Ernst & Young, September 2001.

92. Interview with John Ferraro, vice chair, client services, Ernst & Young, September 2001.

93. Interview with Doug Ludwig, retired CFO, Four Seasons Hotels & Resorts, September 2001.

94. Interview with Elizabeth Pizzinato, director, corporate public relations, Four Seasons Hotels & Resorts, September 2001.

95. Interview with Kathleen Taylor, president, worldwide operations, Four Seasons Hotels & Resorts, September 2001.

96. Interview with Isadore Sharp, CEO, Four Seasons Hotels & Resorts, September 2001.

97. Interview with Wolf Hengst, president, Worldwide Hotel Operations, Four Seasons Hotels & Resorts, September 2001.

98. Interview with William Powanda, vice president, Griffin Hospital, March 2006.

99. Interview with Marge Deegan, vice president, Ambulatory Services, Griffin Hospital, July 2001.

100. Interview with Dr. Kenneth Schwartz, medical director, Griffin Hospital, July 2001.

101. Interview with Barbara Stumpo, vice president, patient care services, Griffin Hospital, July 2001.

102. Interview with Susan Frampton, president, Planetree, July 2001.

103. Interview with John DiJulius, cofounder, John Robert's Spa, March 2006.

104. Interview with Stacy DiJulius, cofounder, John Robert's Spa, September 2001.

105. Interview with Eric Hammond, director of operations, John Robert's Spa, March 2006.

106. Interview with George Zimmer, founder and CEO, Men's Wearhouse, August 2001.

107. Interview with Eric Lane, retired president and COO, Men's Wearhouse, August 2001.

108. Interview with Shlomo Maor, associate vice president, Training, Men's Wearhouse, August 2001.

109. Interview with Doug Ewert, executive vice president, merchandizing, Men's Wearhouse, August 2001.

110. Russell Schroeder (ed.). *Walt Disney, His Life in Pictures,* New York, Disney Press, 1996, p. 63.

111. John Hockenberry. *I.D. Magazine,* March/April 1998, pp. 59–65, 96.

112. Richard Corliss. "Beauty and the Beast," *Time,* April 20, 1998, pp. 66–70.

113. Kathryn Harris. "The Loneliest Man in the Kingdom," *Los Angeles Times,* March 26, 1995.

114. Interview with Art Wittmack, board president, Business Alliance, Des Moines, April 2006.

Bibliography

Albrecht, Karl, and Ron Zemke. *Service America.* New York: Warner Books, 1985.

Allen, Thomas J. *Managing the Flow of Technology.* Cambridge, MA: The MIT Press, 1977.

Byrman, Alan. *Disney and His Worlds.* London: Routledge, 1995.

Connellan, Tom. *Inside the Magic Kingdom.* Austin, TX: Bard Press, 1996.

Cotter, Bill. *The Wonderful World of Disney Television.* New York: Disney Enterprises, Hyperion, 1997.

Disney, Walt. *Walt Disney: Famous Quotes.* Lake Buena Vista, FL: The Walt Disney Company, 1994.

Dunlop, Beth. *Building a Dream: The Art of Disney Architecture.* New York: Harry N. Abrams, Inc, 1996.

Eliot, Marc. *Walt Disney: Hollywood's Dark Prince.* New York: HarperCollins, 1993.

France, Van Arsdale. *Window on Main Street: 35 Years of Creating Happiness at Disneyland Park.* Nashua, NH: Laugher Publications, Inc./ Stabur Press, Inc., 1991.

Ghoshal, Sumantra, and Christopher A. Bartlett. *The Individualized Corporation: A Fundamentally New Approach to Management.* New York: Harper Business, 1997.

Grant, John. *Encyclopedia of Walt Disney's Animated Characters from Mickey Mouse to Aladdin.* New York: The Walt Disney Company, Hyperion, 1993.

Greene, Katherine, and Richard Greene. *The Man Behind the Magic.* New York: Penguin Books, 1991.

Grover, Ron. *The Disney Touch: How a Daring Management Team Revived an Entertainment Empire.* Homewood, IL: BusinessOne Irwin, 1991.

Hollis, Richard, and Brian Sibley. *Walt Disney's Snow White and the Seven Dwarfs & The Making of the Classic Film.* New York: The Walt Disney Company, Hyperion, 1994.

Imagineers. *Walt Disney Imagineering: A Behind the Dreams Looks at Making the Magic Real.* New York: Disney Enterprises, Inc., Hyperion, 1996.

Kurth, Jeff. *Since the World Began—Walt Disney World: The First 25 Years.* New York: Disney Enterprises, Inc., Hyperion, 1996.

Labovitz, George, and Victor Rosansky. *The Power of Alignment: How Great Companies Stay Centered and Accomplish Extraordinary Things.* New York: John Wiley & Sons, Inc. 1997.

LeBoeuf, Michael. *Imagineering.* New York: Berkley Books, 1980.

Lundin, Stephen C., John Christensen, and Harry Paul. *Fish! A Remarkable Way to Boost Morale and Improve Results.* New York: Hyperion, 2000.

Maltin, Leonard. *The Disney Films,* 3rd ed. New York: JessieFilm Ltd., Hyperion, 1955.

Marling, Karal Ann (ed.). *Designing Disney's Theme Parks: The Architecture of Reassurance.* Montreal: Centre Canadian d' Architecture, Flammarion, Paris, New York, 1997.

Mosley, Leonard. *Disney's World.* Lanham, MD: Scarborough House, 1990.

Naisbitt, John. *Reinventing the Corporation.* New York: Random House Value Publishing, reprint edition, 1988.

Neary, Kevin, and Dave Smith. *The Ultimate Disney Trivia Book.* New York: Hyperion, 1992.

Neary, Kevin, and Dave Smith. *The Ultimate Disney Trivia Book 2.* New York: Hyperion, 1994.

Neary, Kevin, and Dave Smith. *The Ultimate Disney Trivia Books 3.* New York: Hyperion, 1997.

Santoli, Lorraine. *The Official Mickey Mouse Club.* New York: Hyperion, 1995.

Schroeder, Russell, ed. *Walt Disney: His Life in Pictures.* New York: Disney Press, 1996.

Schroeder, Russell. *Walt Disney's Mickey Mouse: My Life in Pictures.* New York: Disney Enterprises, Inc., Hyperion, 1997.

Sheridan, Bruce. *Policy Deployment.* Milwaukee: ASQC Quality Press, 1993.

Smith, Dave. *Disney A to Z.* New York: Disney Enterprises, Inc., Hyperion, 1996.

Solomon, Charles. *The Disney That Never Was.* New York: The Walt Disney Company, Inc., 1995.

Spector, Robert, and Patrick D. McCarthy. *The Nordstrom Way.* New York: John Wiley & Sons, Inc., 1995.

Stewart, James B. *Disney War.* New York: Simon & Schuster Adult Publishing Group, 2005.

Thomas, Bob. *Disney's Art of Animation: From Mickey Mouse to Beauty and the Beast.* New York: Welcome Enterprises, Inc., Hyperion, 1991.

Thomas, Bob. *Walt Disney: An American Original.* New York: Pocket Books, 1976.

Vance, Mike. *A Kitchen for the Mind* (audiotape series). Cleveland, OH: Intellectual Equities, Inc.

Vance, Mike. *Creative Thinking* (audiotape series). Chicago, IL: Nightingale Conant Corporation.

Vance, Mike. *Entrepreneurial Thinking* (audiotape series). Niles, IL: Mike Vance/Intellectual Equities, Inc./Nightingale Conant Corporation.

Vance, Mike, *Motivational Thinking* (audiotape series). Cleveland, OH: Intellectual Equities, Inc.

Vance, Mike, and Diane Deacon. *Think Out of the Box.* Franklin Lakes, NJ: The Career Press, 1995.

Walt Disney World Resort: A Magical Year-by-Year Journey. New York: Disney Enterprises, Inc., Hyperion, 1998.

Walton, Mary. *The Deming Management Method.* New York: The Putnam Publishing Group, 1986.

Zemke, Ron. *The Service Edge.* New York: NAL Books, 1989.

Index

About the Authors

BILL CAPODAGLI, Managing Partner of Capodagli Jackson Consulting, brings managerial experience at several top consulting firms and graduate-level teaching experience to the firm. He is a popular speaker at both national and international conferences where he teaches audiences the *Dream, Believe, Dare, Do* Disney Way model.

LYNN JACKSON, Bill's partner, holds a graduate degree in Organizational Development and she continues to train and consult with organizations that are striving to implement the *Dream, Believe, Dare, Do* principles.

BILL CAPODAGLI and LYNN JACKSON have amassed over 2,700 hours benchmarking the Disney organization; trained thousands of people in *Dream, Believe, Dare, Do* methods; and spent over 10 years compiling information on Disney practices.

Capodagli Jackson Consulting is currently in demand for training and consulting services. It has taught hundreds of businesses, from hospitality to healthcare, how to apply Walt's original success credo. It presents effective, easy-to-learn *Dream, Believe, Dare, Do* tools to assist both executives and front-line employees alike achieve long-term success. Capodagli and Jackson's popular "Creating the Magic with Dream, Believe, Dare, Do" programs have gained national recognition as high quality learning experiences for those striving to bring the real "keys" to achieving excellence—Walt's Way—to their organizations.

BILL CAPODAGLI AND LYNN JACKSON have written two others books: *The Disney Way Fieldbook, How to Implement Walt Disney's Vision of Dream, Believe, Dare, Do in Your Own Company* and *Leading at the Speed of Change: Using New Economy Rules to Invigorate Old Economy Companies.*

For more information on booking a keynote presentation or seminar, contact Capodagli Jackson Consulting at 800-238-9958 or dreamovations@aol.com. Capodagli Jackson Consulting's Web site is capojac.com.